Strategic Foresight

Strategic Foresight

A New Look at Scenarios

Alfred Marcus

palgrave
macmillan

STRATEGIC FORESIGHT

First published in 2009 by
PALGRAVE MACMILLAN®
in the United States—a division of St. Martin's Press LLC,
175 Fifth Avenue, New York, NY 10010.

Where this book is distributed in the UK, Europe and the rest of the
world, this is by Palgrave Macmillan, a division of Macmillan Publishers
Limited, registered in England, company number 785998, of Houndmills,
Basingstoke, Hampshire RG21 6XS.

Palgrave Macmillan is the global academic imprint of the above companies and has companies and representatives throughout the world.

Palgrave® and Macmillan® are registered trademarks in the United States,
the United Kingdom, Europe and other countries.

ISBN: 978–0–230–61172–6
ISBN: 0–230–61172–9

Library of Congress Cataloging-in-Publication Data is available from the
Library of Congress.

A catalogue record of the book is available from the British Library.

This book is printed on paper suitable for recycling and made from fully
managed and sustained forest sources. Logging, pulping and manufacturing
processes are expected to conform to the environmental regulations of the
country of origin.

Design by Newgen Imaging Systems (P) Ltd., Chennai, India.

First edition: July 2009

10 9 8 7 6 5 4 3 2 1

To my wife, my sons, and the next generation and to my friends who survived persecution and dispossession and who made new lives for themselves in new countries.

A lesser sage once proclaimed: "You can't always get what you want, but if you try sometimes you just might find you'll get what you need."

Contents

Figures and Tables

Acknowledgments

Many people assisted me in writing this book, in ways imagined and in ways not imagined. Though I take full responsibility for the ideas, the book was a collective endeavor. I owe a large debt of gratitude to the Carlson School of Management where I have been on the faculty since 1983–1984 in the Strategic Management and Organization (SMO) Department. SMO is a diverse, intellectually vibrant, and congenial department. I want to acknowledge our dean Allison Davis-Blake, the current department chair Myles Shaver, and colleagues like Andy Van de Ven, Ian Maitland, Aks Zaheer, Sri Zaheer, Paul Vaaler, Harry Sapienza, Shaker Zahra, Pri Shah, Mary Zellmer-Bruhn, and Dan Forbes. Bruce Erickson, no longer an active faculty member, is sorely missed. I would have loved to talk to him about this book. The office staff—Kate, Noelle, and Julie—is terrific. I also owe great thanks to the Center for the Development of Technological Leadership (CDTL) at the University of Minnesota where I teach in the Management of Technology Program. The ideas in this book were first introduced in the CDTL classroom. Massoud Amin, the director, is a wonderful person, whom, as everyone knows, is really always "at your service." Massoud is the coauthor of the book's last chapter, which is based on lectures we gave in Cairo as part of a CDTL program. I also want to thank Lockwood Carlson of CDTL and CDTL's helpful staff who make teaching there such a pleasure. The idea for the book's title—strategic foresight—comes from a CDTL ongoing forum on this topic.

Colleagues at the Center for Integrated Leadership (CIL) at the Carlson School as well are deserving of thanks. I was co-academic director of CIL for two years, along with Jay Kiedrowski of the Humphrey School of Public Policy, and had the chance to organize seminars in the winter of 2007. We invited such speakers as Paul Schoemaker (peripheral vision), Phil Longman (population), Catherine Mann (global. debt), and Robert Rotberg (failed states). Peter Rich assisted me in organizing these seminars. Barbara Crosby, current co-academic head of CIL, commented on an early draft of material that found its way into the book. Anna Lloyd, the former executive director of CIL, too, is deserving of thanks.

A good portion of the book was written when I was a visiting professor at the Technion. At the Technion I taught an MBA strategy elective which was based on ideas in this book. I want to thank Technion students and acknowledge the colleagues with whom I interacted during my stays there including Boaz Golany, dean of Industrial Relations and Management, and Eitan Naveh, Mia Erez, Avi Feigenbaum, Dovev Lavie, Uzi Haan, and Avi Shtub. Special thanks go to Arieh Ullman another visitor at the Technion. Arieh teaches full time at SUNY Binghamton. Fellow faculty like Hugh Courtney of the University of Maryland and Anatoly Candel of Caldwell University made invaluable comments. Editors such as Jay Hershey, David Pervin, Art Kleiner, Michael Hopkins, and Tim DeVinney helped me refine and clarify my thinking. About Ralph Jacobson, consultant extraordinaire, I cannot say enough. His "tools for management"—see the Web site and book—are among the best. Ralph spent large amounts of time helping me formulate the ideas found in Chapter 2. My editor at Marsh Press Libby Rubinstein should be thanked as simultaneously with this book, I was working on a revised case book for Libby called *Winning Moves*. Material from the case book has found its way into this book.

My PhD students contributed a great deal, especially Adam Fremeth (see chapter 6) and Mazhar Islam (see chapter 4). Don Geffen, a former coauthor, read and commented on parts of chapter 1. Another coauthor whose work is reflected in this book (see chapter 4) is Zach Scheaffer of Israel's Open University. John Moloney, a Carslon School MBA, did an independent study which taught me a great deal about demographics and security. Zach and John as well as Mazhar contributed to chapter 4. Lorraine Eden of Texas A&M University provided the opportunity to give a talk based on ideas in chapter 4 at a special conference organized by the Academy of International Business in Coral Gables, Florida in the fall of 2007. She provided insightful, useful, and encouraging comments. Sheryl Kaiser, a co-author of a previous book we wrote called *Beyond Compliance*, helped with the ideas in chapter 5 about government. Sumit Majumdar, a former student and colleague, assisted with the ideas about the telecommunications industry in that chapter. Sriram Nadathur, a Carlson School MBA student, helped with the boxed insert about the business cycle. My financial advisor, Hank Wilkinson, sends me interesting newsletters on the state of the economy whose ideas are reflected in the chapter. I want to acknowledge Tim Hargrave for the dissertation he did on the oil industry and the lectures I heard him give on global warming. They are found in chapter 6. I am also indebted for ideas in chapter 6 to colleagues at INCAE in Costa Rica—Sara Cordero, Renee Castro, and Lawrence Pratt. I teach there once a year as part of a Carlson School program. Marc Juare and Nirav Vora, Carlson School MBA students who participated in this program, assisted with ideas about the current energy mix in the United States and how it might be changed. Greg Unruh from Thunderbird University helped with my understanding of peak energy. George Richardson of the SUNY Albany was kind enough to share overheads and ideas about systems thinking (see the afterword).

I gave seminars on ideas found in this book at the Katz School of Business at the University of Pittsburgh and the Tepper School of Management of Carnegie-Mellon University in the fall of 2008 and winter of 2009 and want to acknowledge Katz Faculty Ravi Madhavan and Ph.D. student Jason Park and CMU faculty Linda Argotte and Laurie Weingart and post-doc Ella Miron Spektor.

My wife, Judy, is an invaluable partner in everything I do. She is a professional at loving kindness. My son, David, does a super job as Web editor and associate book editor of *Dissent Magazine. Dissent's* chief editor, Michael Walzer, is the gold standard as scholar and person whose works on political philosophy will be read decades from now. My other son Ariel is keeping up the family tradition as an undergraduate at the University of Chicago. I owe a debt of gratitude to the University of Chicago for educating me, but more importantly for educating Ariel.

Great friends are invaluable. If not members of my actual family, they feel like they are. One of the best of my friends, David Kronfeld, helped with the editing of chapter 3. Other friends with whom I am blessed are: Ed and Anne Monique Rapoport, Ted and Jane Brodie, Nathan Szajnberg, Naomi Vilko and Sid, Michael and Julia Shapiro, Michael Greenberg and the rest of his family, Simon Goldman, Irv Thorne and Beverly, Gerald and Judy Shapiro, Asher and Paula Arbit, Alan Baumgarten, Marcia Gelpe, Mark Freed, Ron Krebs, Max Donath, Lee and Judy Snitzer, Irving Leonard Markovitz, and Myron Dowell. I want to especially thank Myron who keeps me current about what is happening in the world via his regular e-mails.

Finally, I am grateful to my editor at Palgrave Macmillan Laurie Harting for taking on this project. The book's anonymous reviewers did a very good job. I also would like to acknowledge the staff at Palgrave Macmillan who helped put the book together.

Introduction

S trategic foresight is having a view of what can be done by the organization today to positively influence the future. Enlightened foresight has more than just the organization in mind. It involves an examination of the actions the organization can take to benefit itself and society. It requires that people in the organization have a view about what the organization should do to improve its position and prevent the organization and those around it from being harmed.

Whenever someone thinks about the future, he or she creates stories about what can occur next. Scenarios are stories about the future that people in organizations construct.[1] They construct these stories both tacitly and informally and explicitly and formally.[2]

Scenarios are a commonly used technique, but their use in business is often misunderstood. Their purpose is not to predict or forecast the future but rather to *imagine* what *can* happen next. They are created to influence the course of events not to accommodate them. The endeavor should not be judged a success or failure based on the accuracy of the predictions. If the world evolves in a more benign way, then the exercise is worthwhile; and if malignant consequences are avoided, it is also a success.

People in organizations must make commitments today that will only bear fruit in the future, but the future is far from certain. Multiple stories of the future open up people in organizations to the possibility that the future does not necessarily resemble the past. They begin to prepare for a future that may not look like today. Scenarios are representations of different future states that can be used (1) to help businesses generate options about what to do next and (2) to assist them in testing these options. Given different future states, what might businesses do? And to what extent will these actions succeed? These two questions are the ones that scenarios can help a business, or for that matter the people in any organization, answer.

Turbulent Times

In business, surprises have been the norm for a long period of time.[3] Consider the following:

The 1950s. In this period the U.S. economy was dominant in the world, constituting as much as 50 percent of global GDP. The cold war had just started and was heating up. U.S. defense spending constituted more than half of the federal government's expenditures. President Eisenhower made his famous "military-industrial" complex speech. Though there were undercurrents of discontent, the period was one of conformity and the organization "man." In the business community, IBM employees were required to wear white shirts and ties. The most successful and admired U.S. company was General Motors.

Had one been alive then one would have thought these conditions would last forever. Businesses made bets based on their beliefs that these conditions would continue indefinitely.

The 1960s. Few anticipated the uproar and turmoil of the 1960s—the civil rights movement followed by women and gay rights movements, the assassinations of John Kennedy, Robert Kennedy, and Martin Luther King, Black power, pandemonium on campuses, demonstrations against a war in which more than 50,000 Americans died, and violence at the 1968 Democratic national convention. Few also would have anticipated the cultural changes associated with these upheavals, the rise of Rock music, festivals like Woodstock, the drug taking, and the illusive freedoms young people sought.

Business as an institution was in retreat in the 1960s. Who would have thought that this state of affairs would change?

The 1970s. The great upheavals of the 1960s were followed by the equally great turbulence of the 1970s. The Bretton Woods Agreement, established after World War II, had made the U.S. currency the standard by which all other currencies were pegged. However, under the strain of a United States merchandise trade deficit the dollar collapsed and had to be floated. As it lost value, the oil producing nations lost income and formed the Organization of Oil Producing Exporting Countries (OPEC). When Egyptian and Syrian troops invaded Israel in 1973, OPEC imposed an oil embargo that quadrupled the price of U.S. gasoline. The upshot was an economy in disarray. Government officials and the Federal Reserve were without a remedy for the high inflation and unemployment. Then, another sharp turn in the course of events took place—there was the fall of the Shah of Iran, the imposition on that country of a radical religious regime, and a horrible bloody war with Iraq. Oil prices again spiked and interest rates skyrocketed.

At the time, it seemed that the main challenges facing Americans would be how to cope with a continued weak economy and high oil prices. Businesses were uncertain about what to do and were hesitant to make long-term commitments.

The 1980s. Yet things turned around. Who would have imagined that after the severe recession of the early 1980s such a strong economic recovery would take place? The recovery was built on a combination of restrictive monetary policies to curb inflation and stimulatory fiscal policies to arouse growth. The fiscal spur came from new government spending for defense and a supply side tax cut to lower tax rates for the wealthy. Oil prices plummeted partially because of the recession, partially because people were more efficient in their energy use, partially because new government programs saved energy, and partially because of petroleum discoveries in the North Sea, Alaska, and elsewhere. The dollar, meanwhile, gained in value relative to other currencies, which made imports to the United States comparatively cheap. Japan and other Asian nations took advantage of the situation. By the end of the 1980s, the main question on many people's minds was the rise of Japan as a world economic power.

Businesses were obsessed with the question of how to deal with the Japanese challenge. Projections were made that if Japan's GDP continued to grow at the same pace, then Japan would eclipse the United States as the world's dominant economic power.

The 1990s. Who would have imagined that the bubble in the Japanese economy would burst so quickly? Meanwhile, the Soviet Union, the nemesis of the United States for so long, unraveled, perhaps the biggest surprise of all. Its demise opened the world to a whole new round of globalization. People, ideas, money, technology, goods, and services flowed freely. A general rise in living standards took place brought on by technological advances in communications, information technologies, and electronics. While the Japanese economy stalled, other Asian economies picked up steam. The main reason Nixon and Kissinger had gone to China was that with the U.S. defeat in Vietnam, the nation needed an Asian ally to counter the Soviet Union. Neither Nixon nor Kissinger could have anticipated that the Chinese people would so warmly embrace capitalism and trade so vigorously with the West.

The future looked bright at the turn of the millennium. Venture capital money flowed freely and people were optimistic about what was to come next. Most people in business expected a bright future.

The 2000s. Who could have imagined that with the unleashing of the Internet, the deciphering of the human genetic code, and other scientific achievements that the progress of the 1990s would slow? If by history is meant unending conflict between competing ideologies, then commentators were talking about its end.[4] The United States, the only super power left, had proved its overwhelming military might by beating back the Iraqi army in the first Gulf War. However, what took place next was business scandal, the bursting of the tech bubble, the terrorist attacks of 9/11, another U.S. invasion of Iraq, the troubled aftermath of that tragic and indecisive conflict, and the economic meltdown of 2008. The additional jolts late in the decade were a subprime mortgage debacle, a sharp slide in housing prices, and a huge pickup and then decline in oil prices. Unemployment mounted rapidly in the United States and elsewhere.

Did this mean déjà vu and a return to the Great Depression of the 1930s and something as ominous as the spectre of Nazi Germany, this time in the form of an Iranian regime with a poisonous ideology that was threatening the world with its aggressive nuclear weapons' program? Would these challenges continue indefinitely or would they temper off and abate? What new challenges would emerge in their wake?[5]

Whatever happened, it would affect people in business. How should they adjust the strategies of their organizations to what might happen? What investments should they make and which forego? Which investments would pay off and which would not?

That there would be continued changes in the environment of business was certain. That these changes could not be predicted with great precision also was certain.

What Is Foresight?

People in business must recognize that current conditions do not last indefinitely. They must envisage what can take place next. The reason is not necessarily to better adjust to what happens but to influence the future in a positive way and prevent worst case outcomes. By considering the future people in organizations can increase the chances that their companies will do well and avoid harm.

Foresight is the art of anticipating what *might* happen next and attempting to do something about it. This anticipation should not result in passivity. It should not result in submission to what happens, but in efforts to move the future in directions that bring benefits to an organization and society.

Preparation for the future begins when every person in a business is given the chance to contemplate what can happen and the power to do something about it.

- Do the people in an organization have a view of the future?
- Do they have an understanding of what they can do to affect it?

The problem is that in many organizations, the ability to think about the future has been reserved for top leadership. People lower down in the hierarchy are just the operational hands of great minds above them.[6] They have been stripped of their right to think independently and to act based on what they believe will take place.

The scenarios from which organizations work should not be exclusively composed by elites, retreating and removing themselves from ordinary duties, looking at the world from lofty heights, led by experts and consultants to arrive at fixed understandings. To the contrary, scenarios and scenario-like thinking should be the province of everyone in the organization who is affected by change and who regularly acts to influence the organization's direction. The success of the organization depends on the capacity of people within it to continually rethink the future and to flexibly adapt to it.

The Role of Scenarios—Generating and Testing Strategies

This book argues that scenarios can play two critical roles in organizations:

1. Scenarios can play a role in generating strategies. Alternative futures can be imagined and their impact on industry structure—on a firm's customers, suppliers, competitors, entrants, and substitutes—can be analyzed. Distinct opportunities and threats then can be identified and strategies formulated to take advantage of the opportunities and deal with the threats. The strategies that are devised should involve some combination of (1) product or service repositioning;

(2) mergers, acquisitions, divestitures, and alliances; (3) globalizing; and (4) innovating.

2. Scenarios also can play a role in testing these strategies. Once a number of strategies that an organization can pursue have been identified, they can be tested for their relative effectiveness. Considering different future states, how successful would the organization be if it pursued these different options?

Thinking about What Comes Next

These exercises will not resolve all the uncertainty. People in the company still have to decide how to manage the residual risk. The first chapter of this book, therefore, discusses these issues:

- Should people in the organization gamble on what they believe to be the most probable outcome?
- Should they take a robust route and try to have a strategic initiative in place to deal with every contingency?
- Should they delay taking action until further clarity emerges?
- Should they commit to a certain course of action for now but have backups, just in case?
- Or are things so open that they can try to shape the future—can they define what takes place next to their liking?

The overall plan of the book is to provide guidance on how to think systematically about scenarios in six realms: (1) population, (2) security, (3) politics, (4) macroeconomics, (5) energy and the environment, and (6) technology. Classic narrative genres—romances, tragedies, and comedies are discussed in chapter 2. They correspond to the common practice of creating positive, negative, and in-between scenarios of what can take place next. Strategies like repositioning, restructuring globalizing, and innovating are discussed in chapter 3, where many company examples are given. Chapter 4 takes up population and security challenges that businesses face. Creating scenarios means looking for patterns and drivers in trends, attaching vivid names to possible developments, and being aware of weak signals and wildcards. Three demographic scenarios are discussed in chapter 4—"Old and Feeble," "Moving and Seeking," and "Young and Militant." Their implications for a firm like Wal-Mart are examined. The security scenarios discussed in the chapter are titled "Davos," "Pax America," the "New Caliphate," and Cycle of Fear. They come from a study by the National Intelligence Council.[7]

Chapter 5 continues in this vein of attaching vivid names to possible future states. In government, the vivid names given are "Free-to-Choose," "Well-Regulated" and "Special Interests." They are derived from theories on the roles governments play in modern societies. In the macroeconomy the vivid names are "Turmoil and Instability," "Progress and Crisis," and "Stable-but-Slower Growth." They are derived from historical analogies. Amazon, SBC, Monsanto, 3M, Danaher, and Federal Mogul provide examples of the impacts on businesses and how businesses have responded to these challenges.

Chapter 6 completes the model of attaching vivid names to scenarios. Energy and environmental issues are considered. The vivid names given to possible future states are "Fossils," "Renewables," "Mixed," and "Surprises." Fundamental forces driving change in this realm—demand, supply, climate change, and technology—are discussed and applications made to two energy-intensive companies—the electric utility, Xcel Energy, and General Motors.

The afterword (written with Massoud Amin) examines the role of technology. Can technology provide solutions to the issues raised in this book? To what extent is it a key differentiator for companies? To what extent does it enable them to deal with the challenges and provide them with the means to achieve long-term competitive advantage?

CHAPTER 1

Meeting the Challenges of the Future

This book is about the art of foresight—that is the principles, methods, and techniques for looking forward into the future and trying to anticipate and influence what is to come next. It is about developing a view about what an organization should do next. Given uncertain outcomes, what actions should it take? What strategies should it adopt?

Though reflecting on how today's conditions become tomorrow's realities is vital, vision, or the art of anticipating what is to come next, is not easy. Discerning what to do with this knowledge, having a good idea, and figuring out how to realize it, is even harder. In most organizations, operational requirements take precedence over cogitation about the future.

Organizations and the individuals that compose them have different ways of approaching the future. These different methods yield different results. The purpose of this book is to provide people in organizations with the means to create a better understanding of the future and to use it to enact winning business strategies. The aim is to shed new light on scenarios and scenario-like thinking in organizations.

Weaknesses in Scenario Development

A number of well-known weaknesses and limitations exist with how organizations currently create and use scenarios. These weaknesses have inhibited the further development and diffusion of this technique.

- Among the most important critiques of scenarios is that they emphasize preparation for external events rather than actions that participants in organizations can take to shape these events. The reason for engaging in scenario-type thinking and becoming aware of possible futures is not to submit to their inevitability, but to influence them.

- A second common critique is that scenarios are mainly crafted by organizational elites, top level or central organization thinkers and their consultants. The premise of this book is that each person in an organization can benefit from a more disciplined and rigorous way of thinking about the future. Each person has a need for foresight that can help the organization generate and test options about what it can do.

- A third common critique of scenarios is that organizational elites arrive at a premature consensus about how the future will evolve. This consensus stifles dissent. The point of view of this book is that scenarios must be subject to regular criticism and revision from a broad spectrum of people within the organization who engage in dialogue and discussion about the future and generate and test options about what the organization can do to insure its success and survival.

- A fourth common critique of scenarios is that they are fixed at a point in time by the organization's elites. The theme of this book is that each person in the organization should be given the chance to probe into the future by conducting formal and informal thought experiments, trials, and simulations. The feedback and learning from these formal and informal thought experiments, trials, and simulations should influence the organization's ongoing deliberations and calculations about what can happen, what the organization can do, and the steps it should take.

The view people in an organization should have about the future should be dynamic and aligned with changing conditions. Overcoming past limitations in how scenarios have been used should make organizations more able to cope with shifting circumstances.

Involving Every Person

This book is not necessarily aimed at top management or top executive teams but at every person in an organization who must think about the future, anticipate what is to come next, and take action based on what will follow. It is aimed at people at high and low levels in an organization, at dreamers and doers, at executors and administrators as well as at entrepreneurs and innovators, at all of those whose key task is to make decisions about an organization's future in the face of uncertainty. It is intended for people engaged in advanced training who fill executive education classes, and to MBA and undergrads who takes courses in strategic management. This book is meant to provide those who work in organizations now and who will populate the organizations of tomorrow with the means to develop the art of foresight and generate winning strategies for themselves and their companies.

People in organizations make commitments today, often irreversible ones, without full knowledge of what will come next.[1] They have to reflect on what conditions will be when the commitments they make today bear fruit. In generating ideas about what they are going to do and whether the actions they take will yield results, they must think about the future. Their thoughts about the future are formal and conscious as well as unconscious and instinctive. As human beings, we are hardwired to think about what is to happen next.

Today, more than ever, people in organizations must deal with contingencies that they cannot fully anticipate. The uncertainties include currency fluctuations, swings in raw material prices, threats of inflation and drop-offs in economic growth, persistent instability and unrest in various parts of the world, and technological surprises that can disrupt the equilibrium in industries. For examples of how the future affects the commitments that people in organizations make today, see the following boxed insert. Recognize that these examples are just a small subset of those that exist and that a thoughtful person can generate many more.

How the Future Affects Commitments Businesses Make Today?

- Will lending crises grow, closing off the development of new credit instruments, impoverishing many more people and preventing them from improving their standard of living?
- Will consumption of material goods in advanced industrial societies decline substantially, without a pick up in developing nations, because of a prolonged worldwide recession?
- Will hyperinflation then set-in because of rising commodity prices, making long-term investments in capital goods and infrastructure extremely risky?
- Will energy prices be relatively high or low when new technologies such as hydrogen fuel cells are commercially viable and capable of being introduced on a broad-scale level?
- Will protest movements stop the building of additional electrical power generating plants, whether these plants will be coal or nuclear, thus causing electrical power shortages in the world?

- Will technologies that convert plant material to energy flourish, substantially driving down energy prices and disrupting existing energy markets?
- Where will the world's best scientific and technical workers be located?
- Will shortages in specialized engineering expertise limit technological innovation and the growth of new business ventures? Will these shortages be greater in developed countries such as the United States and Japan or in developing nations such as Brazil and China?
- Will more people be temporary workers, enhancing the status, importance, and centrality of temporary employment agencies for coordinating labor?
- Will demand grow rapidly from immigrants for products and services similar to those from their countries of origin, thus altering consumption patterns in developed nations?
- Will there be insufficient water in the world to grow food for an expanding population? Will this mean that mass starvation is more common?
- Will biogenetically engineered seeds overcome the problem of drought? Will such seeds be able to add nutrients to the foods consumed making humans healthier and heartier? Which companies will benefit from this type of revolution?
- Will the healthy living and preventive medicine movement really take off? Which companies will be able to capitalize from it?
- Will life-enhancing drugs greatly expand life span and quality of life? What business opportunities will this create?
- Will the pressure on global food supplies continue, dramatically raising the price of food for the poor and creating hunger riots?
- Will the elderly be financially secure and healthy enough to appreciate new leisure time opportunities? How will the opportunities be provided?
- Will terror seriously jeopardize shipping lanes, stimulating new markets for manufacturing in the United States? Will U.S. manufacturing be able to pick up the slack?
- Will fall-offs in global security increase demand for personal protection devices and high-tech surveillance equipment? Who will provide these devices and what kind will they be?
- Will the trend toward democracy come to an end in Latin America? Will it grow in the Middle East? What are the implications?
- Will the effects of global climate change be slow and gradual or fast, dramatic, and devastating? How will people, companies,

> governments, and societies cope? What is business' role? Will it suffer, decline, or unleash the enabling technologies that will help societies adapt?

Questions of this nature have impacts on whether the commitments businesses make today will prove worthwhile in the future. Because an investment made today depends on future uncertainties, the art of foresight is essential. Given the uncertainties, what strategies should businesses pursue? And what is the likelihood that these moves will be successful?

Imagining Sequences of Events

Consciously and formally and unconsciously and informally people in businesses must consider what is to come next. They create alternative visions about what is likely to happen. Sometimes they do so in a very detailed way. Their projected sequences of what is likely to happen are not necessarily predictions or forecasts; rather they are simply their ideas about what can take place, what might the outcomes be, and how present conditions can move from here to there.

Typically, large fortunes are made because someone has the foresight to effectively confront conditions of great uncertainty. They can see into the future and recognize opportunities and threats that are unclear to others. They generate moves to capitalize on these conditions and test them against alternative visions, or scenarios, of what might happen. In exercising foresight, the risks are great but so too are the rewards.

People look into the future to consider their options. They reflect on what they can do to influence the course of events, and will the actions they take be positive or negative. Their perceptions of how the present will evolve into the future are the scenarios they construct. Any business person who makes future commitments must engage in this type of exercise, even if the exercise is not formal and is just a mental exercise or experiment.

It makes sense for business people to imagine sequences of events that lead into the future. Scenarios are plausible stories, usually more than one, about what can happen. Since the future is, in fact, indeterminate and subject to forces beyond an individual's control, prudence dictates that people ask "what if" questions and construct stories about how the future may evolve. The "what if" questions should strip them of their illusions. They should eliminate both their unbounded optimism and excessive caution.

Net present value calculations do not have this power. Typically, business students are trained to do these calculations. They are the means taught in finance classes to cope with future uncertainties, but these calculations are based on a host of untested assumptions. Even when sensitivity analysis is employed, the key assumptions underlying net present value calculations are not brought to the surface. Sensitivity analysis is a technical exercise, not a discussion about what can go right or might go wrong in the future. As the capacity to predict well and with accuracy only applies to a small subset of business problems, where parameters are well known and the past is a good guide to the future, the foundation for doing net present value calculations is weak.

Net present value calculations are only as good as the assumptions they make about what happens next. When these assumptions are overtaken by the actual course of events, they can lead to businesses to go in the wrong direction. A person in business who puts money at risk for gain to be achieved later faces great uncertainties. He or she must consider what conditions will be like when investments they propose to make today bear fruit in the future. The upfront money spent often is substantial and even small changes in future conditions can delay a payoff or eliminate it entirely.

Scenario-management is more nuanced and hedged than net present value analysis. Rather than having a single most likely outcome, it entertains the possibility of different outcomes. The outcomes do not necessarily resemble the present. Rather than aligning organizational resources to achieve specific goals, using scenarios to make decisions creates a space within the organization for discovery. The goal is not to implement a predetermined plan but to respond effectively to unfolding conditions.

Hedging against Uncertainties

Different hedging strategies are appropriate given different types of uncertainty depending on whether an outcome can be well-described and/or quantitative odds assigned (see table 1.1).[2] With each level of uncertainty, an associated hedging strategy is relevant. A discussion of these hedging strategies follows. Their strengths and weaknesses are highlighted.

Gamble on the "Most Probable" Outcome

Companies often act based on what they perceive to be the most likely outcome. They make bets with confidence, only to be surprised later if the world does not evolve as they assumed. A prime example of a company

Table 1.1 Levels of uncertainty and hedging strategies

Hedging strategy	Certainty *A single best forecast can be made*	Risk *Quantitative odds can be confidently ascribed to outcomes*	Ambiguity *Qualitative outcomes can be described*	Unknown
Gamble on the "most probable"	*	*		
Take the robust route		*	*	
Delay until further clarity emerges			*	*
Commit with fallbacks			*	*
Shape the future			*	*

* Stands for preferred hedging strategy.

that made a large bet based on what it believed to be the most probable future was Iridium's $5 billion investment in its satellite network. When it made this bet it was reasonable to assume that demand would be large, but events did not turn out as Iridium expected.

Another example is Sony. Based on what the company believed to be the most probable future, it bet wrong in 1975 when it introduced the Betamax video cassette recorder (VCR). It thought it was offering the most innovative product and format, yet years later it had to withdraw from the market because Matsushita's VHS was lower priced and better adapted to the movie rentals.

Sony repeated this mistake in 1993, again betting wrong when it introduced the MiniDisc music player. Despite heavy investment in the technology and in content from its record label, the MiniDisc did not gain traction and lost out to digital portable MP3 players like the iPod that better saw the cost viability of flash memory. In both instances, Sony adhered to what it believed to be the most likely scenario but circumstances did not evolve in this direction. If a company makes a large bet on the future, there has to be little doubt that this state of affairs will come into being.

There are instances when making bets of this kind, however, is reasonable. Investments by established companies like a McDonald's or a Home Depot in new stores are good examples of extending the scope of proven business models and wining by virtue of superior execution without being concerned about the risk of serious upheaval.

Take the "Robust" Route

Rather than bet on a single future, companies can choose the most robust strategy, or one that is viable regardless of what takes place. This kind of strategy may be referred to as "no regrets." People in the company use scenarios to bound the range of futures their organizations face without having to guess right. Often-regulated utilities have taken this route. They hedge their bets against a number of possibilities. For instance, the key future question may be about the relative cost of different fuel sources. Utilities create scenarios in which natural gas or wind is the low cost fuel and invest in *both*.

The diverse opinions that different people in the organization have about the future can be drawn upon to create divergent scenarios. A company then can make a variety of robust moves that assure that it does well in each instance. Still, this approach remains difficult to carry out. The number of directions in which a company can move is huge. Only if a company has substantial slack can it invest in ways that will protect it and make it less pervious to harm regardless of what takes place. Perhaps a pharmaceutical company as diverse as a Pfizer is able to cover the waterfront, but a biotech startup is not likely to have the resources to do so. It cannot do gene therapy R&D in many different therapeutic areas, for instance. It must focus.

The challenge with taking the robust route is that it is difficult to identify strategies that work well under all scenarios. It is also likely to be expensive to implement these strategies. Once they are chosen, they are not likely to give the boost in performance that is wanted. Robust strategies reduce risks and lower rewards, while making a bet on a likely scenario, though it involves great risk can yield a very large payoff.

Delay until Further Clarity Emerges

In the face of uncertainty, a firm may decide to stay the course for now. It delays taking action until the situation becomes clearer. It does not take action currently but it follows developments carefully and waits for a better moment to act. If there is high uncertainty over expected cash flows from full-scale investments, the commitments the company is considering are of long duration, and there is little threat of a competitor becoming dominant in the meantime, a firm may decide not to invest now but to wait and see. It postpones its investments until more information becomes available, and it is more certain that it has the knowledge and skills to pursue opportunities that may be emerging.

While waiting the firm makes flexible commitments that minimize downside losses should worst case scenarios come into being. It can divide its investments into small increments, not fully committing at once but gradually over time in accord with additional clarity it gains and confidence it acquires from moving forward slowly in trial-and-error fashion. Scenarios become benchmarks. They indicate which future state seems more likely and what the company would do then.

Flexible commitments can provide confidence that if full-scale ones are made later the firm has the capacity to achieve high payoffs. A firm buys information and time to deal with the uncertainty. It puts off its decision, postponing full-scale investment and keeping its options open, but while it waits for the situation to become clearer, it may lose market opportunities to more aggressive competitors.

The risk is that when the firm decides to fully put its stake in the ground it will be too late. Its competitors already will be there, and it will not be able to dislodge them. Such was the case with both Xerox and Kodak in their slow adjustments to a digital world. Sears, Digital, and other former market leaders also were displaced because they waited too long to respond to disruptive changes. The same pattern holds true with regard to U.S. auto companies and their investments in small vehicles in the 1970s and in hybrid cars more recently. The price of oil rose 400 percent in matter of weeks in the early 1970s and North American automakers found their mainstay full-sized product lines hard to sell, yet they decided to wait and see. It took them years to design, manufacture, and market more fuel-efficient models. Meanwhile, they lost valuable market share to better positioned foreign competitors. This pattern again was repeated. Major U.S. manufacturers face possible bankruptcy.

It is not clear that there is good way to postpone, stage, and make flexible commitments without being shut out of substantial gains. If a company only commits to slow change and incremental adjustment it may miss fundamental transformations.

Delay, on the other hand, may work in the case of Boeing's decision not to pursue the super jumbo jet option. Whether it will go in this direction hinges on whether the Airbus A380 succeeds and demand grows. Once the situation becomes clearer, Boeing believes that it can stop hedging and give up the flexibility that until now it has preserved.

Boeing can afford to let Airbus take the early risks because Airbus is so heavily subsidized by various European governments to defray development costs. Meanwhile, Boeing has its own scenario of the future, that it is point-to-point and not point-to-hub-to-point. Consequently smaller aircraft will be favored and not super jumbo aircraft. Boeing believes that it can churn out the super jumbo jets very quickly if market demand picks up. The super jumbos it can churn out will be technically superior because they can incorporate more current information; for instance, the need for fuel efficiency, which today has attained greater importance than when Airbus designed its plane.

Though later commitments are almost always less costly than earlier ones, the payoffs also tend to be less. Holding back tends to be a low risk, but potentially low-gain strategy. In the worst case, waiting invites total failure.

Commit with Fallbacks

An alternative is to fully commit to a single scenario, but with fallbacks in case this scenario is not realistic. This path is not a refusal to commit. It is not avoidance of going full thrust. By aggressively moving forward, a company treads in areas that others fear to go.

To fully commit is not done with the illusion that the company knows with certainty what to expect. Instead, the company can justify the risk it is taking because it is convinced that its *initial position* and *capabilities* provide it with a long run competitive advantage. It thoroughly analyzes the risk on this basis. Does its initial position and capabilities justify the action?

But since the company recognizes that the future may be different than it hopes, it protects itself with a fall back plan. Sports teams, for instance, take out long-term contracts with players, betting on a future of continued superior performance. But they hedge their bets with escape clauses that insure against worst case scenarios such as player injury or inappropriate conduct.

Even in the capital intensive oil industry, fallbacks exist. Early exploration does not necessarily have to be followed by additional exploration. Late exploration does not necessarily mean marketing the oil—a production site can be sold before a company reaches this stage. Major petroleum companies have created fallback positions in renewable energy in the event that fossil fuel supply is severely constrained. BP's "beyond petroleum" initiative is not just public relations gimmick but a fallback position that preserves the company's flexibility.

Another example is Microsoft that often takes a dominant position in a platform or technology but also protects itself with fallbacks. For instance, in the late 1980s Microsoft maintained options not only in MS-DOS and Windows based systems but in IBM's OS/2 and in applications that ran on Apple. Today, the firm continues to have an extensive portfolio of options in consumer electronics, mobile phones, and telecom infrastructure as well as PCs. Similarly, Johnson and Johnson (J&J) shies away from irreversible commitments in a single direction without having fallbacks. The company retains options in combining drugs and devices, in prevention over treatment or the opposite, and in ongoing opportunities that exploit the synergies between these possibilities. Companies like J&J carefully monitor the environment for signals as to when to exercise or abandon these options. They have the flexibility to preserve, nurture, or terminate them. This flexibility comes from limited commitments that are maintained via such means as acquisitions, alliances, joint ventures, and partial equity stakes that allow them to gradually build skills, lower costs, and learn more before they act.

In the face of uncertainty, firms also experiment to see what works. For instance, Capital One Financial Corporation conducted thousands of different product/price/features tests in the credit card market in the late 1990s. Another example would be Intel (see chapters 2 and 3). Starting out as a producer of computer chips for the memory market, it had a fallback position in microprocessors. In the late 1990s, it experimented with options that would take it beyond microprocessors, but ran into trouble and ultimately it had to abandon many of them. With toehold investments in many different technologies, a company must retain the right to sell them off if necessary. If the company chooses to go forward, it must identify how it will combine the options it has chosen with the assets it already has. The fallbacks a company creates must not be prohibitively costly to give up. If they are too expensive to give up, long term, or far afield, they are not likely to be a good hedge against risk. The fallbacks also should not be isolated initiatives. They have to fit into a broader scheme or pattern.

Committing with fallbacks is a good way to deal with the uncertainties of not knowing how the future will unfold. Yet there are problems in choosing the main commitment, the fallbacks, and how many fallbacks are needed. Answering these questions is not trivial.

Committing to fallbacks works best if there is a payoff structure such that investments that fail entail tiny losses, while those that succeed yield very high returns. For instance, a company can choose to restrict the scenarios to which it responds to extreme cases. Goldman Sachs' subprime hedge, for instance, was to bet *both* that a lending boom would continue unabated and abruptly end, putting Goldman Sachs in a position where it would not be harmed regardless of what took place. This was in contrast to other investment banks that bet on a single outcome.

Shape the Future

Another alternative is not to be passive in the face of diverse futures, but to try to actively drive and influence what takes place.[3] A firm uses the resources it commands to increase the odds that the most desirable outcome, the one it wants the most, prevails. To achieve its goals, it must be in the position to form coalitions and partnerships with other companies and institutions in society including governments, civic organizations, and nonprofits. A host of joint ventures, partnerships, and complicated arrangements with other entities is called for. Political deals may be needed if the future is not to be passively received but rather molded in accord with the firm's wishes. An example would be Monsanto's life sciences strategy of the mid-1990s that involved the shedding of the firm's chemical assets, the acquisition of seed and gene technologies, and partnerships with firms such as Cargill to increase the rate of farmer's adoption of genetically modified product. Monsanto was in a race to make the future before other firms got there (see chapter 5).

SBC (now AT&T) also has been a shaper, mainly using its political clout to build a very strong position in long distance, consumer voice, and data services as well as local service. It is the epitome of a former regional Bell operating company that has used regulation to allow it to compete in new markets (also see chapter 5).

Enron is an example of an unsuccessful shaper too enamored of pushing the limits. It tried to shape deregulated energy markets with complex, financial instruments which were not fundamentally sound. Enron shows that a company cannot force a market to go in a direction that is not based in reality.

A shaping strategy must revolve around a point of view of where an industry should evolve—where does the company wants to see it in 5 or 10 years. There are many examples that can be cited: AutoNation's consolidation and national branding, which changed the face of the retail auto sector; Fedex's overnight delivery methods; Southwest Airlines' no-frills model for domestic air travel; Dells' removing the middle person in PC sales; and the pioneering efforts of Amazon (see chapter 5) and eBay in Internet commerce.

When does it make most sense to try to shape the future? When there is rapid discontinuous change and the future is very hard to forecast. Under these conditions, outcomes are hard to describe, let alone to give odds to them. If industry structure, conduct, and performance are up for grabs, a firm may be able to displace entrenched business models. With no dominant scenario, there is an opportunity to be a leader and to make order out of the chaos by taking a high-stake bet.

Shapers stay a step ahead of adapters, who have trouble catching up. They move into the void caused by such factors as deregulation, globalization, and patent expiration. By forging boldly ahead, they build brand loyalty, lock up access to best supply and distribution sources, create advantages based on experience, and establish close ties with profitable customers. For incumbents, this route is hard to take. They are not likely to blaze new trails. They tend to stick to what they know best, a safe and secure position in an established industry. Xerox, for instance, failed to press ahead with what became the PC revolution, despite having developed many of the industry's innovations in its own labs. Xerox stumbled because it was averse to taking on too much risk.[4]

Often shapers are companies with few other options. They are outsiders or those in difficult straits willing to take a bet on nonmainstream goals. But their shaping strategies cannot be carried out alone. Shapers only succeed when they influence key players such as regulators, third party associations, and other gatekeepers. They typically need an active set of alliances to get where they want to go. This strategy is high risk and also high return.

Shapers enter situations that are in flux. The future is open. It can develop in many directions and the directions it takes are hard to specify with precision. Opportunities abound but so do the risks. Shapers may have a clear vision of where they are headed, but they also need strong internal capabilities to demonstrate that the new business models they propose are feasible. They must develop or acquire the assets and capabilities to make these models work. Shapers also need backers with deep pockets and an appetite for risk who are willing to recognize value in the endeavors they propose and mobilize support for them.

Shapers often do not succeed. Often, they push too hard and fail to accomplish what they set out to do. The space in which they are operating is Darwinian in nature. This strategy is very high risk, and the rewards that justify it are not always attainable.

Risk and Uncertainty

Some hedging strategies are more akin to risk, according to the scheme created by the late economist Frank Knight.[5] Knight distinguished risk from uncertainty based on the capacity to place objective odds on conditions such as flipping a coin or rolling dice. Net present value calculations work best under conditions of risk. Under conditions of risk, odds can be known with certainty or they can be established based on empirical evidence from the past. The past empirical evidence, though, may be merely probabilistic; there are no guarantees that the future will replicate the past.[6] These conditions are opposed to conditions where the odds are subjectively assigned, where they essentially are made up based on judgment.

According to Knight, competitive advantage and superior economic performance emanate mainly from bets placed under conditions of uncertainty. When the risk is known, the competition is too intense to earn anything but the most mundane returns. Under these conditions, high levels of economic gain soon evaporate, competed away because all the economic players have similar good information. An economy in such conditions is at nearly perfect equilibrium. When the economy is in this state, there is little strategic advantage to be won. Execution is likely to win out over strategy.

Scenarios enable people in companies to test strategies they might adopt when the uncertainty is great. In constructing scenarios, people in companies must decide what type of uncertainty they confront. If it is small and they can forecast what is likely to happen next, then it makes sense to gamble on the most probable outcome. If they can limit the uncertainty to a range of futures that they can specify in some detail, then a robust strategy where they will be better off regardless of what happens makes sense. However, if there is high uncertainty over likely returns, the commitments are long term in nature, and the threat of competitive displacement is low, people in companies may decide to postpone a decision till further clarity emerges. While they wait for greater clarity, they may lose market opportunities to more forceful competitors. So an alternative is to fully commit to a single future, but to have fallbacks in place in case this future does not come to pass. Finally, with huge ambiguity about what is to take place next, people in companies may try to shape the future. In this case, they need many allies to help them. Shaping the future is not a go-it-alone strategy.

Of course, these methods of hedging are not mutually exclusive. They may be combined, hybridized, and sequenced. For instance, delay first, commit with a fallback, and then decide to shape the future. Or exert influence first and then gamble on the most probable outcome, but only partially, increasing commitment after waiting for more knowledge and clarity. This is where the judgment of people in companies has to be exercised, in devising hybrid strategies that work.

Looking at Scenarios in a New Way

Whatever people in companies do they should test their strategies against uncertainty. Creating scenarios can free people in companies from a sense of complacency. It can mobilize them to discard comfortable notions that they have that the future inevitably will replicate the past.

This book therefore aims to take a new look at the scenario-making process. It rests on these premises.

1. *Scenarios should be more central to the decision-making process.* In too few organizations are scenarios and scenario-like thinking having a

critical effect on decision making. In many, seat-of-the-pants decision making prevails, with scenarios and scenario-like thinking having little impact. Top executives make the excuse that because the future is so hard to pin down with certainty that they can act based on their gut feelings, instinct, and business judgment or experience. They need not ponder carefully what can take place. They do not have to explicitly lay forward their assumptions about what is likely to happen and subject them to critical analysis. In many organizations, scenarios get short shrift when it comes to actually making decisions. Different analytical frameworks or models are used to the exclusion of, or to supplement, any reliance on scenarios and scenario-like thinking.

Some organizations celebrate the official scenarios they create but ignore them when responding to bona fide business problems and challenges. Scenarios play an insufficient role in their important investment decisions. Options that can be pursued early and at relatively low cost are not undertaken and their organizations do not reap the benefits of being in a better position to cope with future contingencies. Relatively small investments made in an anticipatory fashion are deferred or not considered because these organizations do not have good narratives about the future or the people in organizations do not have confidence in or familiarity with the narratives that members of their organizations have generated.

2. *All members of the organization should be involved in thinking and acting about the future.* Scenarios cannot be reserved for an intellectual elite. The entire range of players and viewpoints in an organization should be enlisted. Only then will such cognitive biases as overconfidence, narrowness, and anchoring be avoided.[7] Scenario planning should be decentralized. People lower in the organization should be encouraged to take on responsibility. Scenarios should be close to the point of action to reduce planning-learning gaps. If close to the point of action, they provide for more agility, a trait sorely needed in organizations in rapidly changing environments. Each person in an organization should be involved in thinking about the future, and each can benefit from a more disciplined and rigorous way of doing so.

3. *Scenarios have to rest on a culture of pluralism and dissent.* Reliance on status quo actors and knowledge can create a bias in favor of known unknowns at the expense of completely unanticipated "black swan" events.[8] Marginal ideas brought from the periphery require a tolerance for openness, the possibility of conflict, and the likelihood of risk.

4. *Scenarios have to be regularly updated in accord with the actions that participants take.* Scenarios are not statistical predictions. Rather they are narratives to which people in an organization can relate. They provide a

foundation for additional inquiry and the integration of new evidence. They are not end points, but rather the start of reasoned speculation and continued systematic thinking. The goal is not a final plan or roadmap, but a change in thinking toward continuous learning. As in sailing, participants in organizations need alertness and heightened sensitivity to small perturbations and adjustments to steer a successful course. In constructing scenarios, they must begin to look at the underlying logic of the systems in which they operate and come to understand that these systems are not perfectly deterministic; the initial conditions can branch out in many unexpected directions. Organizations can better plan for and try to influence the course of events based on different projections, rather than become incapacitated by a deterministic result.

Each person in the organization should be empowered by scenarios to deal with the challenges they face. Their choices are not just to accommodate what happens but to work for a better tomorrow, advancing trends they want to see come into being, opposing ones that are not in their interests and the interests of their organizations, and adjusting to those over which they have the least control.

A Tool for Meeting Challenges

The generation of scenarios should be a tool people use to meet the challenges of what happens next, how they will be affected, and what they can do to shape the future, but this is often not the case. Yet, there are examples of successful business strategies that have taken advantage of scenario-like thinking. For instance, Whole Foods took advantage of U.S. consumers' desire for healthier foods, Omnicare built its business around providing for the needs of senior citizens, and Fortune Brands benefited from an increase in the number of the super-wealthy by acquiring firms that cater to them. But to what extent are scenarios actually being used by corporations? If the results of the scenario process only results in reflection, the costs may not justify the benefit.

Since September 11, 2001, the use of scenarios has increased in businesses. Bain & Company's *Management Tools and Trends Survey* shows that in the post 9/11 period approximately 70 percent of 8,500 global executives reported that their firms used scenarios, in contrast to a usage rate of less than 50 percent in most of the 1990s.[9] Satisfaction too was up. In 1993, scenarios ranked fifteenth in satisfaction levels among the 25 management tools that Bain examined, while in 2006 it ranked eighth.

Typically, as uncertainty in the world grows the use of scenarios increases. But are companies obtaining maximum value from their use of scenarios? Some people in organizations still complain that scenarios are not realistic, and they do not add much value. This criticism often comes from people in operational capacities who find the exercise abstract and hard to apply. Senior management tends to have a more positive view. They see scenarios as freeing up corporate thinking and building in flexibility to deal with uncertain events in the future. Often the process of creating scenarios is fairly loose. People are asked to identify key uncertainties. They brainstorm, sit in a room, talk, and come up with action points. Despite this looseness, many people in organizations still consider the process worthwhile.

In offering guidelines for analyzing the sources, patterns, and causes of change and stability in an organization and its environment, this book is meant to enable people in organizations to better use scenarios for thinking critically and flexibly and creating winning business strategies. Step-by-step, this book takes the reader through the process of creating better scenarios to exercise foresight and make improved decisions.

CHAPTER 2

Thinking about the Future

Scenarios are a tool to meet the challenges of future, how an organization will be affected, and what it should do.[1] The purpose of creating scenarios is to prevent negative turning points, encourage positive ones, and make adjustments to the extent that they are possible. For example, in 1985 Intel faced a situation when its main product, dynamic random access memory (DRAMs), had become a commodity. As a result, it made a monumental shift to microprocessors, which since then has defined its destiny.

Under such circumstances, scenarios can help companies assess options like repositioning their products and services, divesting failed business units, pushing forward with global sales, and innovating. Under these conditions people in organizations must think about the future. They must ponder what the situation will be like when the commitments they make today bear fruit. There are many examples of how the future affects the commitments they make today. The impacts on the commitments they make today on future performance are large. The payoffs can be great or they can come to nothing.

Scenarios describe different future states in a narrative fashion.[2] The narratives are not predictions or forecasts; rather they are plausible estimates of how events can unfold and things happen. To support, or not support, a myriad of endeavors people in organizations create such stories about how the future may evolve. This chapter provides guidance for creating scenarios and advice on how to craft good narratives in organizations. How can stories of the future be better fashioned within organizations?

Rules for Creating Scenarios

In creating stories about the future, the following rules should be applied.

- The entire range of players and viewpoints in an organization should be enlisted. An example is Monsanto which involved more than 150 "critical" thinkers from the company in a "contagious bottom-up movement" in the early 1990s that helped transform the firm into a biotechnology leader.[3]
- Opposing points of view should be entertained. Good scenario-writing rests on a culture in which alternative views are recognized and encouraged. This kind of culture, Andy Grove maintains, prevailed at Intel when the company made its monumental shift from DRAMs to microprocessors in the mid-1980s.[4]
- Scenarios should be updated in accord with the actions that organization takes. They require regular criticism and revision. After the stories are developed, they should be reassessed. It is not only essential to evaluate what took place but to consider why alternatives that were considered did not arise. Counterfactual questions should be posed—why did stories considered possible not come into being? Why did events not move in these directions?

Start with the Past

How can employees be motivated to participate in the exercise of creating stories of the future? One good method is to start with the past.

Most organizations and individuals have stories of the past. Ask anyone in the organization what has happened. How have things changed? And undoubtedly you will get a story. Here is how things were. Here are the challenges we faced. Here is how we responded. Here are how things are now. These stories may differ from person to person in detail and in interpretation. They may differ based on how long the person has been in the organization and what role they have played. Nevertheless, there will be a story.

At the top of the organization, there is likely to be an official story, one found in publications like annual reports and on the organization's Web site. This story is the one typically told by top management. Here is how the organization started. Here is how it progressed over the years. Here are the main challenges it faced and here is how it overcame these challenges to become the organization it is today. Here are some of the heroes and the villains who have played key roles in the organization's collective and mythic past.

The scope of the stories that different people in organizations tell also is likely to differ. The stories of some people may encompass the organization as a whole, while the story of others may just involve just a single unit, division, or group. Not only do time, emotion, and scope affect the choice of stories, but the same stories are told differently based on the lessons the tellers wish to deliver.

Stories of the past are told to guide the future; they command audiences to do something. The same events from an organization's past, viewed differently by different members of the organization, are conveyed for different ends. Since the future is an offshoot of the past, these diverse perspectives are important.

Before concentrating on what is coming next, people in the organizations must come to terms with the past. Since stories of an organization's past evolve into stories of the future and influence the decisions people make, the capacity to retrieve and organize past experience and then imagine future possibilities is important. These narratives tell people in the organization who they were and where they are now going.

Move to the Future

An organization and its members not only have stories about where the organization was, what challenges it faced, how it dealt with those challenges, and what the outcomes were; but they have stories about where the organization is now, what are the difficulties that lie ahead, how they can respond to those difficulties, and what the outcomes are likely to be. Narratives of the past typically translate into narratives of the future. People create stories about where they are likely to go next based on where they believe they were previously.

By their nature, the stories organizations and their members have about the future are less clear than stories they have about the past.[5] Because of uncertainty about the future, people have a hard time grappling with it. Their stories about the future tend to be buried in the unconscious, implicit as opposed to explicit. Nonetheless, people in organizations do have stories about the future and these stories play a large role in shaping what they do next. Though stories about the future are more tacit than stories about the past, they are consequential in shaping the decisions that organizations and their members make. The stories people construct play a role in bringing desired future states into being. They provide people with a capacity to shape the future.

People's collective visions become realities. Indeed, descriptions of ideal future states are commonplace in organizations, found in many documents from annual reports to plans that describe how activities will unfold, how they are linked, and what their timing, cost, and outcomes will be. To what extent do these descriptions of ideal states actually represent people's deeper feelings? To what extent do they reflect their real hopes, desires, and fears? Official documents often provide a comforting illusion that organizations have more control than they actually do. People are told that they will be able to manage the future, while they remain emotionally anxious and concerned that events will not turn out as expected.

The meanings people give to the past and the future thus are fluid and open to interpretation and reinterpretation especially when the process involves a broad range of organizational participants. Understanding what has occurred provides an impetus for what to do next. It supplies reasoning for affirming or rejecting old patterns of behavior and starting new projects that put organizations on novel trajectories. The past is a critical and essential springboard for thinking about the future. Figuring out where an organization has been, where it is currently, what challenges lie ahead, and how it can respond is central to how organizations shape their destiny.

All stories have beginnings, middles, and ends and how organizations arrive at their starting points is important. The past provides the starting point for thinking about the future. How organizations arrive at that starting point should be a collective endeavor, not one that is reserved for organizational elites alone.

Rely on Master Narratives

Master narratives help to structure people's understanding of the past and the future. They are the deep structures that arrange what they think, that model and make sense of what they believe has taken place. These master narratives give coherence to otherwise disparate events. Without them, events would not be understood; they would not have coherence or be connected in the storyteller's or audience's mind.

Three main genres are the master narratives on which most people rely, though there are infinite variations (see table 2.1). In a *romance*, organizations make dramatic progress toward a goal. In a *tragedy* they experience extreme reversals and fail to achieve this goal, while in a *comedy* they are confused, puzzled about how far or close they are to the goal or even if the goal was worth pursuing.

Romances

Romances demonstrate the bravery of organization members. They are a way that organizations celebrate the successes and triumphs of heroes

Table 2.1 Master narratives

Classic story telling genres	Outcome
Romance	Heroes and heroines overcome deep troubles and achieve happy endings that provide organizations with greater insight about their identity and permit them to face future challenges with greater confidence.
Tragedy	Heroes and heroines take on vast challenges, face insurmountable obstacles, and make monumental mistakes that lead to organizational failures, downfalls, and diminished prospects for the future.
Comedy	Surprises, incongruities, and confusion reign as an unforeseen chain of events unfolds in which things appearing ridiculous and/or absurd takes place; this leads to perplexing ends, some providing release or comfort but some much more painful and not so positive.

and heroines who may be top managers, various groups within the organization, or the organization as-a-whole. An important subgenre of the romance is the tale of rags to riches. Consider the romantic stories constructed about the rise of many companies—Intel, Dell, and Amazon—to name but a few. Serious obstacles are confronted one after another by heroic figures who ultimately triumph.

Another subgenre of the romance is rebirth and regeneration. Heroes and heroines confront tragedy and revive and renew organizations after decline. Consider the comeback of organizations like IBM or Apple. Once viewed as moribund, they reestablished their past glory. They were lifted up by heroes and heroines who reduced or removed prior anguish, grief, and misery. The important point is that after undergoing the ordeal, the organization is better off. It has a higher sense of purpose, more confidence, and also insights about its identity, which should serve it well going forward. The happy ending toward which prior incidents lead satisfies the expectations of the storyteller and the audience. It justifies the organization's hardships and makes the difficulties seem worthwhile.

Tragedies

Tragedies, on the other hand, occur when organizations take on vast challenges perhaps similar to those they face in romances. They face insurmountable obstacles and make monumental, sad mistakes that lead to calamity and diminished future prospects. These challenges that organizations take on may be thrust on them against their will because of unexpected turns in the economy or government regulation or because of shifts in consumer preferences or surprise moves by competitors. The challenges also can be undertaken voluntarily as big or audacious stretch goals. They can be taken on as legitimate efforts to take advantage of real opportunities and may involve such corporate actions as new product introductions, major acquisitions, global expansion, and becoming involved in disruptive technological innovation.

Whatever the motivation for taking on the challenges, they lead organization members to refocus their energies and seriously commit to courses of action. However valiantly organization members struggle to master the challenges, they prove to be their undoing. The efforts to meet the challenges turn to bitter frustration. Once events start to spin out of control, members of the organization can find no escape. They are locked into the choices they have made. They have no relief or exit.

As events slip further out of control, the threats mount and culminate in catastrophe where people suffer, some may even die, and the organizations themselves disappear. Consider here the instance of Union Carbide after the disaster in Bhopal, India or the cases of the accounting firm, Andersen and of such companies as Enron and WorldCom, beset by terrible scandals that led to their undoing. After the fact, it became clear that major players in tragedies had fatal flaws. They overreached and brought down not only themselves but many of the people around them.

Tragedies reveal the blemishes and imperfections of organization members, defects that may be the result of moral weakness, psychological misjudgment, or social pressures, but flaws, nonetheless, from which lessons can and should be drawn. The causes of the tragedies can be debated again and again for what they reveal about what to do and not to do next. Tragedies cannot be avoided, but lessons can be learned.

Comedies

Romances and tragedies are exceptional cases. Most organizational stories are not this extreme. More typical cases are comedies. Surprises, incongruities, and confusion reign as an unforeseen chain of events unfolds in which things appearing ridiculous and/or absurd takes place. This leads to perplexing ends, some providing release or comfort but some painful and not at all positive.

Clearly, comedies are lighter in tone than romances or tragedies; in those hearing them, they arouse laughter and amusement. The main players in a comedy are depicted in a humorous light. They are seen as foolish. Acting on the basis of false or misleading information, they jump to false conclusions. Though the evidence exists to strip them of their illusions, they fail to be aware of it. They fail to take advantage of it. They suffer from silly biases that cloud their vision and distort their judgment. They may be well-intentioned, but this does not make up for their incapacity to make better choices.

Comedies reveal the honest confusion and misunderstanding that is such a large part of organizational life. In the comic tale, implausible events build on implausible events. What the major characters are doing is neither clear to them nor those around them. Bewilderment and consternation rule and teller of the tale and the audience are puzzled as characters randomly come and go, put on disguises, swap identities, and create chaos, a sense that things are upside down and out of order which to a better informed audience is quite funny.

In a *romantic comedy*, to everyone's relief, the misunderstandings more or less get sorted out in the end. The uncertainties and delusions that set the comic path in motion fall away and some type of clarity finally arises, even if it is not quite what has been expected at the start. Romantic comedies deliver odd, funny, and quirky endings. A firm like General Mills, for instance, acquires another firm like Pillsbury, and members of the organization as well as the analysts that surround the organization believe that the integration will be smooth and simple. It will happen quickly and easily and without much fuss, but instead it lasts much longer, held up by anti-trust authorities who were not anticipated to oppose it. The integration process then is beset by numerous unexpected difficulties. Yet, in the end, after all the unexpected difficulties, the two firms do merge. The combined company does function in relatively happy unison.

The story of Monsanto also might be considered comic. The company aims to solve world problems like hunger with new technology that yields less environmental damage. Yet many in the world view the company as a conniving devil trying to inflict a sinister technology on unsuspecting victims. The company gets bought and sold, is not incorporated by a larger firm that acquires it, since the larger firm believes that it is not a good fit and the future of Monsanto is murky. Monsanto ends up on its own again and proves to be a huge business success. Its technology becomes widely adopted by farmers in the United States, if not the rest of the world, where opposition still exists. All these twists and turns in the story are unexpected. Whether a further romance or tragedy is lurking in Monsanto's future is unknown.

But another type of comedy also exists, a genre that literary theorists refer to as a *tragic-comedy*, and it has a more sinister aspect. Though the premise is the same, a series of misunderstandings built on false premises, disorientation, and chaos, the humor is blacker and the endings more grim, and depressing. The benign burlesque and slapstick of romantic comedies moves in the direction of something uglier and more gruesome. People who slip and fall actually do get hurt. They don't walk away unscathed. The blood on the floor is real. As in tragedies, the vices, follies, stupidities, and abuses of humans are held up to ridicule and contempt. The ending, even if gloomy for a period, is not quite catastrophic.

A farcical quality is essential to what unfolds. An example would be Boston Scientific's purchase of Guidant or AOL's purchase of Time Warner, two acquisitions that have proven to have been among the worst in corporate history. No matter how bad these moves were, however, the firms are still standing. The bad moves they made have not meant their entire undoing. The firms remain on their feet. Time Warner experienced severe setbacks but stayed alive and is starting to show new signs of life and the same fate seems to be in store for Boston Scientific.

In tragic comedies, things turn out not as badly as in real tragedy— some hope still exists that the affected organizations will come back. That they have been dealt serious blows is clear, but their errors may not be fatal. Rather, the whole situation to the hearer of the tale seems a bit pathetic, and in the pathos, the hearer may find much that is funny.

Both romantic comedies and tragic comedies share a strong degree of irony in which what actually takes place is in sharp contrast to what is anticipated. As Wayne Booth, the literary theorist, says, "Isn't it ironic that things are really like this when we wished they were or thought they were like this."[6]

Understand the Journey

These main types of genres, then, structure people's stories in fundamental ways. Most literary theorists agree that these are the classic ones that assist storytellers to bring together random occurrences in an emotionally appealing manner. They take stories in a certain direction by revealing where they are headed. By providing goals for a journey, they allow storytellers to connect incidents in accord with end points that make intuitive sense. Telling stories about the future can be usefully approached by having end points in mind and working backward from them. People in the organization then have a sense for where they are in relation to these end points. They relate well to the story and have a good feel for how to construct it because they intuit the types of transformations they must experience before the organization reaches the end points.

People in organizations need multiple stories of the past and future that reflect different genres so that their organizations can better prepare for any contingency (see table 2.2). People in organizations should avoid having

Table 2.2 Diverse pasts and futures

Elapsed time	Key characters	Motivations	Actions they take	Episodes in their interactions	Culminations of their struggles	Unresolved tensions
ROMANTIC PAST						
Beginning						
Tension						
Working out the tension						
Closure						
TRAGIC PAST						
Beginning						
Tension						
Working out the tension						
Closure						
COMIC PAST						
Beginning						
Tension						
Working out the tension						
Closure						
ROMANTIC FUTURE						
Beginning						
Tension						
Working out the tension						
Closure						
TRAGIC FUTURE						
Beginning						
Tension						
Working out the tension						
Closure						
COMIC FUTURE						
Beginning						
Tension						
Working out the tension						
Closure						

single, dominant story. They should celebrate diverse pasts and diverse futures to better cope with the inherent uncertainty they will confront.

For people in organizations trying to grapple with their past, comedies are useful genres to apply, since they provide after-the-fact relief for the absurdity. After a comedy takes place, the people in the organization can go back and examine what went wrong. They can analyze the twists and turns in the plot that they were not able to anticipate. But in struggling to come to grips with the future, the comic genre is hard to employ. Romances and tragedies have linear story lines in which the logic building to an end is clearer. Comedies zig and zag in unpredictable ways based on surprises that are difficult for people in an organization to foresee. People in organizations are likely to consider either the current equilibrium to persist ad infinitum or perhaps believe that radical but clear breaks will occur, either Shangri-la or melt-down.

People in organizations need a strong vision toward which the organization should move and an equally strong mental picture of what the organization should at all costs avoid. It is much harder for people in organizations to create or convey an evocative comedy with complex shifts back and forth after several rounds of action and reaction. Despite the difficulties of creating comic stories of the future, they are as essential as romances and tragedies, because they illuminate a key aspect of reality, the regular slippage in reaching an organization's goals.

People in organizations should create romances, tragedies, and comedies to eliminate the tendency to believe that the future is going to be much like the past. People are anchored to the familiar. Their bias is to expect things to remain pretty much as they are. Therefore, some people in the organizations should devise stories of a radically better tomorrow. To inspire and give hope, they should work backward from a preferred state of how things can be to how things are now. To awaken others from lethargy, they should try instilling a belief that things can be markedly improved. Think of Martin Luther King and his "I have a dream" speech.

Other people in organizations should imagine the worst possible worlds that can come into existence. Their aim is similar to those who create romances—to jar people from their complacency, grab attention, and force people to reconsider the alternatives. The example here might be Al Gore's "inconvenient truth." His picture of a future tragedy is meant to prevent the anticipated dire results of global climate change.

Still other people in organizations should concoct comedies that challenge both the rosy romances and ugly tragedies. They too should point out in as striking a way as possible that the future is not likely to resemble the past. They should take into account all kinds of complications— actions and reactions by opposing forces that blunt straight-line movement toward either the positive ends of romances or negative ends of tragedies. These people should imagine the many possibilities between "utopia" and "apocalypse" and stress the need and potential for adjustment, accommodation, and feedback. They are more likely to be the tactical thinkers in organizations, not visionaries of perfection or alarmists of doom.

The logic of storytelling should become more widely understood by people with diverse perspectives and orientations if organizations are going to better cope with conditions they confront next. Regardless of what genre is used to portray the past and future, certain storytelling devices are needed. They can be referred to as the 3 C's of storytelling, that is (1) *creating* tension, (2) understanding *causation*, and (3) moving toward some type of *closure*.

Good stories require tension. People are drawn to the story by the tension, or contradiction, which the story illuminates. They sit on the edge of their seat waiting for the tension to be resolved or for some progress to be made toward a contradiction's resolution. All genres of storytelling start with an initial condition of equilibrium, followed by strain or discord, and then resolution or closure, however short-lived or indecisive. These are Aristotle's classic notions of the beginning, middle, and end of a story. They are the essential structure around which any story is built.

The sense of romance, tragedy, and comedy, however, may depend on the position the person holds in the organization. Postmodern literary theory suggests that the classic genres with their fixed endings—positive, negative, and hard-to-tell—neither are universal nor do they encompass all the possibilities. Definitive closure may be an exception rather than a rule. Even the greatest tragedies may have within them a silver lining. When a tragedy strikes, there is an admixture of romance; there will be survivors who continue the struggle. In the same vein, when romance takes place, there is a residue of tragedy; not everyone lives happily ever after.

Complications arise. Some people in organizations may understand what has happened as romance, some as tragedy, and some as comedy. Some people in the organization may prefer to see the past in terms of romance. Others may wish to see it in terms of tragedy or comedy. They have different views of the past and future.

Every organization is likely to contain periods of romance, tragedy, and comedy. For instance, up to 2006, the way Alan Greenspan managed the economy of the United States seemed to be a great romance, with Greenspan the hero, but with the economy's collapse, what seemed to be a romance, with greater insight, turned into a tragedy. Romance evolves into tragedy and comedy. Over time, stories change. Genres shift. People triumph over tragedy but slip again to slapstick. It all depends on how deep a slice of the past people in organizations consider and how far into the future they go.

The perspective people have is important. It is not neutral. People are biased because of their positions in the organization and the needs and interests of the moment. Diversity is to be expected. People in organizations should have the freedom to choose their pasts and futures.

Genres or master narratives mold separate events into coherent wholes. They provide causal structures or maps for disparate events. Accidental happenings after the fact are understood as being consistent, even if they are not experienced as wholes when they take place. When did most people in the 1930s give up the illusion that prosperity was just around the corner? When did they recognize that they were in a calamity, that the Great Depression had taken place? When telling stories, people in organizations use genres, recasting them over and over again as events unfold. The genres connect with peoples' deepest values, wishes, fears, and experiences.

Most people seek a coherent structure to explain what otherwise appears arbitrary and haphazard. A story with a coherent structure tells them not only about the past. It suggests to them what might happen next. The future is a logical progression of what has happened so far. This understanding has enormous emotional appeal. Provided there is more than a single dominant story, it is a healthy process. Diverse stories should be encouraged providing guidance for a variety of interpretations.

Variations on basic story forms should be pursued. Engage the natural tendencies of different people in the organization to understand the past and the future differently. Then people in the organization are less likely to be taken aback if they are asked to improvise and change. The future, fundamentally, is unknown and each genre a person uses brings to light different possibilities.

The diversity of storytelling orientations in organizations should be recognized and used to better grasp and deal with the unknown. The desire to understand the past and future is a strength upon which organizations should draw to make them more resilient in the face of unpredictable events. Multiple stories build in resilience and flexibility. Just as the past should be imagined in a variety of ways, so too the future should be imagined in a variety of ways.

But there are people predisposed because of their character or basic worldview to see all stories in terms of just one genre. Everything always turns out for the best. Everything always turns out for the worst. Everything is always ridiculous—it is a stupid comedy. These people are stuck. All the stories they tell—all the stories they hear—remain the same. A fundamental reason for telling stories of an organization's past and its future is to get these people unstuck, to draw on the differences within an organization to better understand what might take place from more than one perspectives. In doing so, an organization becomes better prepared for the contingencies with which it must deal.

Clarify the Uncertainties

In making long-term investments and commitments, there are great uncertainties that the stories people create about the future can help to clarify. Businesses are under intense pressure to grow and to maintain their profitability. They may be aiming to double the industry growth rate, for instance, while their profitability does not suffer or it also increases, and at the same time they want to make sense of whether a technological domain has promise. Whether it has promise, though, is not simply a technical matter. It depends on whether a system can be built that will be supportive of the technology. Is there a group of accommodating industries? Are other companies on board with the technology and its platform? Are laws in place or government programs that will assist in the advancement of the technology? Will the economy support it? When the technology comes to fruition, will consumers have sufficient disposable income to find it attractive? What need will the technology actually fulfill and for which age groups? What segment of the population will be the early adopters? What kind of pricing mechanism will be needed for the early adopters? What will substitute technologies do? Will competitors quickly arise? All of these questions beg for answers that can be constructed in story form.

The purpose in creating stories of the future is to anticipate changes that can take place. Responsibility for creating these stories about the future should be widely shared in the organization. The stories not only help to clarify, structure, and analyze what people know but what they do not know. They provoke puzzlement. Why did things not turn out like we thought they would? Why did they turn out like they did? What can be learned from what happened? Do the same uncertainties we previously experienced pertain to current and ongoing projects? Stories assist in framing questions about what is both known and unknown, what seems well-founded and what still has to be discovered. In this way, stories provoke learning. They stimulate a search for what has to be better grasped if the organization is going to succeed in its future endeavors. Structuring and analyzing what is recognized and mysterious via story making kindles curiosity about whether an organization is on the right path, if not how it can find the right direction, and if so how can it better travel on this road.

The key advantage in creating stories about the future is to focus on patterns of events, how they are related and might influence each other (see chapter 4). People in organizations should keep away from shining their spotlights on singular events; rather they should try to capture the interrelationships between and among events. They should be searching for insights into systems of relationships and causal interdependencies. They should be trying to make out how events combine to form broader trends, or branch and split off into separate spheres and domains. They seek to know what the fundamental connections within separate spheres or domains are. They also should try to decipher how these separate spheres or domains may fit into a broader and more cohesive pattern.

Constructing stories about the future is a method for explicating the possible patterns of events over a given time frame, why these events arise, how they are related to each other, where they can lead, and where an organization and its members can intervene to deflect a pattern, move it in some other direction, or amplify a particular trend and bring it to fruition earlier than might otherwise be the case. For instance, scenarios may allow people in organizations to highlight the emergence of new technologies or the convergence of technologies in given industries, sub-industries, or specialized markets. They may permit people to identify changes in markets and users demands. They may provide perspective on how standards will arise that will affect users' choices and an organization's opportunities.

Based on the stories that people in an organization create, they may reach conclusions that there are three or four broad overall patterns of events that can arise. Typically, this is where the scenario-making process leads. These patterns may be separate, or there may be strong relationships between them, so that one pattern may lead to another over time, and ultimately all the patterns will be realized, as opposed to one being dominant and realized at the expense of another. Each pattern has its own causal direction but there may be overlap and the causal directions may intersect over time.

The transmission chains for the activation and realization of different patterns should become distinct to the people in the organization who construct stories. For the organization, this type of knowledge that provides tacit understanding of a particularly valuable kind is like a trade secret. It constitutes a unique and hard-to-reproduce competence that can yield high levels of long-term competitive advantage. When people in an organization begin to better understand the chain of events and the triggers for change the organization will be better off, provided that people in the organization can imagine how the organization can best intervene and influence events for the organization's benefit.

The stories people create do not provide specific predictions but shed light on the pattern of events that can occur, how these patterns are interrelated, how they might evolve over time, and what the organization can do about them. The latter is the most important. What actions can the organization take to influence the course of events? What strategies should it put in place? Which should it eliminate? The stories shed light on how the organization can intervene, what approaches it might employ, and whether these approaches have some chance of success. If people in an organization have discrete choices between investing in two or more technological options, the stories they create about the future can provide them with an understanding of the obstacles they may confront, the challenges they may face, and the actions they can take. The stories provide perspective on how they should prepare themselves for overcoming these obstacles. The obstacles themselves can be listed in order of difficulty and a plan of action to act now or learn more can be formulated (see the afterword). Full-scale action does not have to be taken right away. Probes can be made to obtain additional information about the obstacles and to evaluate how hard they will be to overcome. People in the organization often need better information about whether they can enlist and mobilize the support of the key allies they need to make the investments they plan to make work.

Only after creating stories that illuminate how patterns of events are related to each other can people in organizations create and assess how reasonable are the set of opportunities they have in front of them. In short, the exercise of constructing stories about an organization's past and future is not only a good way to map an organization's ongoing reality. It is not only a good way for giving coherence and meaning to that reality, and for understanding more clearly the setting in which the organization finds itself, and how this setting is related to other circumstances that surrounds the organization. The exercise of constructing stories about an organization's past and future is also intimately related to the actions that the organization can take. These actions have long-term implications. Once taken, the organization cannot go back and undo all of them. Once taken, the organization is committed for the long run whether it subsequently wants such commitments or not.

Whether as a mental exercise or formal process, stories about an organization's past and future should unlock the organization's capacity to consider what comes next and assist the organization in preparing for the challenges that lie ahead. A more rigorous and systematic way of thinking about the future based on storytelling should stimulate reasoned speculation and continued systematic reflection about what can happen and what should be done.

Use Diverse Stories for Decision Making

The purpose is not to create a single story within an organization but to recognize differences and use them as a springboard to continue to create diverse stories about the future. The entire range of players and viewpoints in an organization should be enlisted for creating varied stories and thinking flexibly about the future. Each person in the organization benefits from having stories about where the organization has been and where it is going.

These stories, of course, must be subject to regular criticism and revision. Good story making in an organization rests on opposing points of view, on a culture in which alternative views of the past and the future are recognized and encouraged. The strength in creating multiples stories of the past and the future lies not in the understanding of the chances that a particular event or set of events will happen with more or less certainty but in understanding the causal patterns between and among events. The past is a flexible tool for members of the organization to use to better understand where things are headed next. Diverse perspectives about the past that unfold into diverse views of the future should not be suppressed but rather encouraged. These diverse understandings need to be surfaced and brought to light if useful comprehension of the future is to evolve. As long as the world is complicated, unpredictable, and uncertain, multiple stories about the past and the future are needed.

Creating multiple stories builds in resiliency. An organization is not just subject to the external forces that affect its destiny but it has greater influence over them, provided that it has coherent narratives of what has happened and what may occur next and how it may be impacted, cope, and direct the course of events. With good stories about its place in the stream of events, its choices are not just to capitulate to what takes place but to work for a better tomorrow for itself and its stakeholders. It can improve how the future turns out, and the stories the people in organizations create about the past and the future can assist in this effort by laying out the implications of the best (romances) and worst (tragedies) cases and the many in-between (comedies) instances that an organization may confront.

For story writing to positively influence decision making, the following recommendations are in order:

- Vigorous insights about both the past and the future are needed from all parts of an organization—the bottom of the organization as well as the top.
- Probes should be made to assure that conventional thinking is not relied upon in the creation of stories of the past and future and that stories that are constructed question and not justify actions that the organization is proposing to pursue.
- It is not only essential to bring some order to what has taken place in the past and what can take place in the future, but also to probe and

question why things turn out as they do and if they could have been different. Why were stories once thought to be distinctly possible now considered unlikely and irrelevant?

- The stories that people in an organization create should be kept fresh. They need to be regularly updated. They have to be frequently reassessed and reevaluated whether informally as a mental exercise or formally at the highest levels in the organization.

In times as uncertain as ours the future is not guaranteed. The stories that people in an organization create about what has happened and what is to come next can be usefully shaped for positive ends if the people in an organization are enlisted for storytelling.

This method of thinking about the future starts with the challenges a business faces, how attractive the options are, and if the organization has the capabilities to pursue these options (see the next chapter). People in an organization should then be encouraged to craft stories about what has happened till now and what could happen next. They should reflect on the past and on possible outcomes that may come next, on what might happen if under different scenarios the company makes different choices and makes different decisions. This exercise will help prepare the organizations for the eventualities it may confront. Whatever the future brings, its capacity to cope will be greater.

In the end, a more logical and rigorous process of creating stories will not bring anything approaching certainty, for that is not their purpose, but by thoroughly exploring the many tendencies at work, the diverse paths that brought about what has happened previously and the diverse routes to what may come next, an organization will obtain added flexibility. Thereby, the organization increases the chances that its future strategies will be more successful. An organization should encourage its employees to deeply investigate the past and the future and thereby enhance its capacity to adapt to changes in a resourceful way. The stories people in organizations create do not end doubt but open them up to opportunities and threats that they might not otherwise have entertained.

Engage Employees

Consciously and formally and unconsciously and informally people in organizations imagine what is to come next, sometimes in a very detailed way. The future commitments an organization makes will be improved by the use of stories that detail where the organization is at present and where it is headed. Even if the organization drafts better tales of its past and their future, there is no guarantee that decision makers will have a complete understanding of what to do. They just will be better informed and their decisions are more likely to be nuanced. The way they exercise judgment under conditions of uncertainty will be enhanced. Therefore, it is useful for organizations to enlist the people within them to construct stories that may help them in making such important strategic decisions as product/service positioning, mergers, acquisitions, divestitures, alliances, innovation, and globalization (see chapter 3). The stories that people in organizations construct about the past and future provide them with a capacity to identify and exploit opportunities that otherwise might not be recognized.

The problem for some in an organization is the different stories that people in the organization create will only breed confusion. There will be too many arguments about the past and too many competing notions of what the future will bring. All the separate stories in an organization will not necessarily aggregate into a collective one. But those in an organization who are temperamentally or otherwise opposed to the diversity should avoid the temptation to cut it off. They must grant each person in the organization the right to ponder the past and consider what can come next.

The important thing is not to limit the story making to central decision makers, top management teams, boards, and external consultants, but to engage each person in the company. The past and future of an organization belongs to those who work for it. They must bear the consequences of the decisions that the company makes. Their diverse stories of what has happened and what evolves next will shape what the company does and determine whether the company succeeds. Their voices should be genuinely included, not in a token way, but meaningfully and in an ongoing fashion.

Everyone in an organization has key information that can affect the decisions that are made. Top management should not seclude itself in an "ivory tower" removed from the day-to-day contacts with people in the organization who have ongoing struggles and preoccupations that are affecting the organization's destiny. What better way is there for top managers to show that they are curious and care about the concerns of people in the organization than to invite them create stories about what has been and what may be? What better way is there for top managers to show that they are curious and care about the concerns of people in the organization than to invite them into a discussion that is meant to shape the company's future?

Will this invitation be a burden that saps the time and attention of people in the organization from the tasks at hand for which they are responsible and held accountable? Employee engagement does not necessarily have to be achieved via endless face-to-face meetings. Top management can use the Web to create discussion groups. A webmaster job should be created. The job can be held by more than one person. The people holding it can rotate in and out. Their task would be to summarize and consolidate discussion and make sure it is communicated throughout the company. Meetings may be relevant to solicit additional opinions when particular strategies are considered and decisions made. For the process to be effective, the contributions of people in the organization should be rewarded. These contributions should be noted and taken into account when bonuses are awarded and raises allocated.

An organization will be better off if it provides all of its employees with the chance to engage in the process of creating stories about the organization's past and future. Each person should be invited to contemplate what has taken place and will occur next. Each person should be asked to help determine what has worked and what has not. Their views of what should be continued and what should be discarded should be taken very seriously. People in the organization have to feel that their input is valuable, and they have a say in influencing the directions the company is taking. If they are given this feeling, they will be committed to the decisions the organization makes, will understand the purpose of policies pursued, and will carry out these policies in a more methodical, comprehensive, and expeditious way. The benefits of creating stories about a company's past and future are great, while the costs are small.

CHAPTER 3

The Challenges Businesses Face

The stories that people in organizations relate are useful for analyzing and understanding the sources, patterns, and causes of change and stability in an organization and its environment. To create stories of an organization's past and future and use them in enacting winning business strategies, people in businesses must identify the challenges they face. This chapter is about these challenges and how to identify them.

The questions to ask should encompass more than just the challenges. The challenges should engage and stimulate people in organizations to take up the following:

- How attractive are the options for dealing with the challenges?
- Does the organization have the capabilities to carry out these options?
- Does it have plausible stories about how the options will evolve?
- Can it identify and prepare for surprises, should they occur?

Clearly, the challenges an organization faces must be identified, but coping strategies to deal with the challenges also are needed.

Knowing the challenges is not enough. Passivity in the face of them is a route to failure. Options for dealing with the challenges must be generated, and the adequacy of the options evaluated. This chapter not only shows how foresight can be shown with respect to the challenges an organization faces, but also with regard to the coping strategies that people in the organization can devise to deal with the challenges.

What Are the Challenges?

The challenges businesses face are moving targets that change constantly in response to forces outside the organization's control and the strategies organizations use. Stories help businesses sort out the challenges. The stories give them an answer to where they have been and where they might go. In 1985 when Intel's main product, dynamic random access memory (DRAMs), had become a commodity, people in the company had stories about where the company had been—what it had done and accomplished and what it might do next. These stories about what it might do next encapsulated the challenges that lay ahead.[1] Based on stories of its past and future, Intel made a decision about what to do next. The company made a colossal shift in direction, moving from DRAMs as its main product to microprocessors. From then on, this has been a market that Intel has thoroughly dominated. The company has commanded greater than 80 percent market share.

This decision had to be followed up with continuous readjustments. Intel then was tested by the introduction of a flawed Pentium chip that performed wrong calculations, and by AMD. AMD first entered the low end of the market. It then contested with Intel in the area of speed and in the area of power consumption. Each of these challenges forced Intel to reconsider where it had been, where it was going, and how to respond. People in the company crafted new stories.

Whenever a firm confronts the basic problem of what business to be in and how to conduct itself in that business, it must create stories. Today, Intel has new challenges that it confronts:

- What will the role of wireless be in what it does next?
- To what extent will it move to applications and platforms in areas like telecom?
- Will its businesses primarily aim at large commercial computer users or will they tilt more toward professional users and advanced gamers?
- How will Intel cope with the severe economic downturn?

Within the company different stories exist about what these challenges mean. How should the company respond to them? What should it do?

It is not only Intel that confronts such issues. All organizations must generate stories when confronting new challenges. Here are some examples.[2]

- Consider Wal-Mart that has gone from a discount merchandiser to the superstore concept. Should a firm like Wal-Mart now increase its commitment to smaller-sized neighborhood stores? Or should Wal-Mart think more in terms of global expansion? If it thinks more in terms of global expansion, how will it deal with the French giant, Carrefour which has been so successful globally?

- Another example is ESPN. Once known almost exclusively for the broadcasts of sports games, it now originates talk programs. How can ESPN successfully stave off the pressure from professional sports leagues to continually increase the price that ESPN pays for the rights to broadcast their games? Should it create more of its own programming? Should it now move toward the production of movies about sports figures like a fabulously successful one it did about Bobby Knight?

- Or what about AOL? How does it turn its situation around? It has had to move from being an Internet Service Provider (ISP) to being a portal, a shift that it has not been successfully completed. What should a firm like AOL do when its business model is no longer viable? How can it transition to a new business model? Is it best positioned to do this as a division of Time Warner from which it would be divested, or would it be better off if it was acquired by a company like Microsoft?

- Still another example is DuPont. DuPont competes with highly focused Monsanto in the areas of biogenetically engineered seeds. With agriculture being used as a fuel and agriculture demand high, the seed business has become extremely lucrative. To what extent should DuPont therefore shift out of its less-profitable businesses? Should it exit plastics and paints, for instance? The major customer of DuPont's plastics and paints divisions is the automobile industry, not one that is doing well. To what extent should this influence DuPont's choices? In DuPont's competition with Monsanto is the firm's overall diversity a net asset or a weakness?

Firms such as these get a better handle on the challenges they confront by having stories of their past and future.

A good framework to identify the challenges is a "five-force plus" model (see figure 3.1).[3] Five forces define the industry in which a company competes. They are the firm's suppliers, customers, existing competitors, new entrants, and substitutes. The "plus" part is elements in the macroenvironment such as society, technology, international security, law and regulation, and the global economy that affect the five forces. Depending on the company, its industry, and the circumstances with which it must deal, elements in the macroenvironment will differ.

By means of using this model, people in an organization are better able to understand the dynamic interaction between a firm and its industry

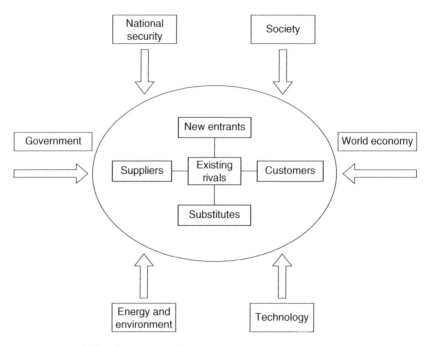

Figure 3.1   The five-force plus model

(the five forces). An industry environment is not stable. It is in continuous flux because of the macroenvironment. As a result of the interactions between the macroenvironment and the five forces, an unfavorable industry (low growth and poor profits) can become a sweet one (e.g., the steel industry at the start of the twenty-first century), and a favorable industry (e.g., pharmaceuticals) can turn sour. A five-force plus model provides people in an organization with insight into the opportunities, the threats, and the inflections that lie ahead.

The purpose of the model is to detect and monitor inflection points. As Andy Grove maintains in his book *Only the Paranoid Survive,* inflections are critical junctures when trends rapidly and radically change direction, speeding up or slowing down in ways that alter a firm's viability.[4] Elements in an industry suddenly can become different than they were in the past. The inflections a firm faces are akin to tipping points that Gladwell describes.[5]

A five-force plus analysis brings awareness to such swings in direction. The model can be incorporated into the stories people tell.

- What are critical junctures that drive a story?
- What are disturbances that create tension and force players to look for ways to resolve it? How hard will it be to resolve the tension?

- What actions can be taken to affect the five forces? Is the industry destined to suffer from stalemate because there is little that can be done? Is there a realistic way around the stalemate to achieve success?

The reason to introduce a five-force plus analysis is not to be passive, but to prevent negative turning points, encourage positive ones, and adjust if the turning points cannot be influenced.

The stories that ensue from a five-force plus analysis should influence the choice and testing of options. Look for the inflections in society, technology, international security, law and regulation, and the global economy that alter an organization's prospects. Then mull over what kind of response is possible. To what extent will the response succeed?

To monitor inflections, indicators are needed.[6] Indicators critical to an organization's success must be followed. A distinction must be made between where the indicators have been moving and where they will go next. Past trajectories can be plotted with greater precision than future movement. Trends can accelerate, peak, or fall off. They can decline much more rapidly than anticipated. Their future direction is not clear. They can cycle up or down in erratic ways without clear signals where they are headed.

Trends are not necessarily good predictors of the future (see figure 3.2). So people in an organization must ask,

- What are the patterns that are behind the trends (see chapter 4)?
- And what are the driving forces (see chapter 6), the critical factors that move trends in different directions?

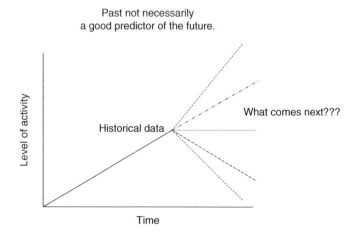

Figure 3.2 The difference between past trends and future developments

The five-force plus model leads to stories that might go in a number of directions. Outcomes may be romantic, tragic, or comic. Each direction calls for a different strategy such as betting on a single outcome, taking a robust approach, delaying, committing with fallbacks, or trying to shape the future (see chapter 1). Strategies involving some combination of product or service repositioning, corporate restructuring, globalization, and innovation will be discussed next.

How Attractive Are the Options?

If the desire is to transition to a new way of doing business, then people in the organization must consider (1) repositioning a company's products and services, (2) restructuring, (3) pushing forward with, or holding back from, global expansion, and/or (4) innovating radically or incrementally. These choices are not exclusive ones. They may be combined and sequenced in various ways to deal with perceived challenges.

Repositioning

This means raising or lowering prices, adding or subtracting from existing product or service features, or entering adjacent or closely related markets. It signifies discovering innovative means to distinguish products and services from competitors by finding original ways to contribute value to customers. For instance (see boxed insert in chapter 4), to differentiate from "always" low-priced Wal-Mart, Best Buy adapted its stores to serve one or more customer segments (professionals, young males, family men, suburban moms, or owners of small businesses). Implementing this approach was expensive, so Best Buy remained uncertain how fully committed it should be to it. Its commitments had to be tested against a number of different stories about the future.

Restructuring

This option means rethinking what business to be in and why. Why has the company assembled the assortment of businesses in which it competes?

- How do these businesses fit together? Do they add value to each other?
- Does it need to own these businesses, or would it be just as well off if it had alliances with them?
- Would the company be better off divesting some units and acquiring others?

For instance, the reason that AOL and Time Warner gave for why they merged was that the Internet would be the ultimate distribution outlet for the combined company's content (articles, recorded music, movies, TV shows, etc.). This model did not work. Should Time Warner therefore try to sell all or part of AOL? When, and at what price? Should it rather divest AOL? What Time Warner decides to do with AOL must be tested against various stories about the future.

Globalization

This option can consist of taking a successful domestic model and diffusing it to fast growing markets in other parts of the world. When a domestic market is saturated and mature, there really are only two choices: (1) innovate heavily domestically with new products and/or services that expand the customer base or (2) reproduce a successful model abroad. While there may be little the company can do domestically, choosing global expansion is not necessarily a panacea. It might not go smoothly. For instance, the commitment Coke and Pepsi have to quenching the thirst of a rapidly expanding worldwide population has been met by controversy after controversy from tainted water in India to opposition from conservative religious groups in Muslim countries like Pakistan. How should these companies pursue global expansion? In what ways should it be carried out? What Coke and Pepsi decide to do next will be tested against stories of the future.

Innovation

The final option is to innovate—either radically or incrementally change the business model with a new strategy.[7] The more radical the change, the more uncertain the results—a company can gain first-mover advantage in whole new business fields that it then dominates, however, radical innovation also is very risky. It is subject to slight perturbations in the external environment that might knock it off course. Consider Monsanto's switch to biotechnology, in which it stripped itself or it was stripped of its other holdings—commodity chemicals, Nutrasweet, and a pharmaceutical blockbuster such as Celebrex—and it bought gene expression and seed distribution companies to replace them (see chapter 5). Monsanto introduced a new business model. It was highly successful, but this transition was not without its stresses that continue to this day. The opposition of the European Union and the bulk of the environmental movement slowed down market development. Nonetheless, the firm's radical approach to change worked better than DuPont's more moderate approach. Should

DuPont now follow Monsanto and move quicker in selling major holdings in products such as paints, refrigerants, blowing agents, aerosols, and polymers? What DuPont decides to do must be tested against different stories of the future.

Not every element in the macroenvironment has the same relevance for these companies. Businesses must choose the elements in the macroenvironment on which they will focus. For example,

- For Best Buy, the most important element in the macroenvironment may be changes in *society*. Before it chooses how to adapt its stores to serve different customer segments, it must examine in great detail this component of the macroenvironment. Its stories of the future must highlight social change.
- For Time Warner, on the other hand, the most important element in the macroenvironment may be *technology*. Before it decides what it is going to do with its ailing AOL unit, it must examine this component of the macroenvironment in great detail. Its stories about the future must highlight technology.
- For Coke, the most important element in the macroenvironment may be *global security*. Before it commits to additional global expansion, it must examine in great detail this component of the macroenvironment. Its stories about the future must emphasize world stability.
- For DuPont, the most important element in the macroenvironment is *law and regulation*. Before it raises its commitment to biotech, it must examine this component in detail. Its stories about the future have to focus on various legal and regulatory issues.

This is not to say that these companies can afford to ignore other realms. Each realm is related to the other. Society, technology, global security, and law and regulation are connected and each of them separately and together will affect the economy. All firms must be concerned about shifts in the global economy. When the economy stumbles, all these firms suffer.

Under different possible futures, will the strategies people in these companies adopt work to their benefit? What risks do they face, and do the risks outweigh the benefits? Will striking out in a new direction, help or harm these firms?

To anticipate how events might evolve, people in the companies should attach vivid names to developments. In each realm—society, technology, international security, law and regulation, the global economy—they should construct separate stories. After attaching vivid names to stories in each realm, they can order stories by preference: Which stories do they prefer? Which do they want to come into existence (romances)? Which do they most fear? Which should they prevent from coming into existence (tragedies)? And which might they have to manage regardless of their desires and apprehensions (comedies)?

- *Romances* can be ranked number one (1).
- *Comedies* can be ranked number two (2).
- *Tragedies* can be scored as a three (3).

Colorful names should be used to telegraph the logic of the romances, comedies, and tragedies. The stories need vibrant titles (see table 3.1).

After vivid names are given, people in companies can return to the five-force plus model. In doing so, they should hone in on what is of particular

Table 3.1   Macroenvironmental impacts

	Impact on customers	Impact on competitors	Impact on new entrants	Impact on substitutes	Impact on suppliers
Society					
1. Moving and Seeking					
2. Old and Feeble					
3. Young and Militant					
Technology					
1. Broadband World					
2. Mixed Access					
3. Internet Slowdown					
Global Security					
1. Goodwill					
2. Pax America					
3. Cycle of Fear					
Domestic Laws and Regulation					
1. Free to Choose					
2. Well-Regulated					
3. Special Interests					
World Economy					
1. Stable Growth					
2. Crisis and Progress					
3. Turmoil and Instability					

importance to them. If table 3.1 is filled out completely, there are nearly 100 possibilities. This is too much for people in any company to ponder. Testing options against so many outcomes is frustrating so people in companies must be selective, picking only critical interactions between the macroenvironment and industry. It is not possible to be exhaustive and examine every interaction in depth. It is necessary to select critical instances for further elaboration and build these without losing sight of the larger whole. What are the likely effects of the critical interactions on the options the company is considering? How will they affect the company's strategies? Though selectivity is called for, people in companies must be ready to come back to table 3.1 and analyze the missing cases, if needed.

A way to reduce the clutter is to cluster desirable and undesirable outcomes together. People in companies can separate out all the romances, tragedies, and comedies, for instance. If this is done, then

- All the desirable outcomes (the number one preferences in table 3.1) yield a fairy tale of "All is Well" (see table 3.2).
- All the undesirable outcomes (the number three preference in table 3.1) yield a horror story of "Woe and Misfortune."

It would be a pity, however, if the mixed cased (the number two preference in table 3.1) are interpreted as status quo and more of the same. How can people in the organization reflect on other possibilities? Not everything clusters. Desirable, undesirable, and middle end results can be combined in many different ways.

Because there are so many possibilities, only some of them can be fully explored.[8] People in companies must be selective. This exercise requires judgment. The purpose must be kept in mind. Do not create scenarios for the sake of speculating about what can happen. The objective is foresight—to identify actions a company can pursue and test them against possible futures. How will the company fare under different circumstances? Thus, it makes sense to divide the middle cases into clusters that are of strategic relevance. For instance (see table 3.2),

- "Success Tech" envisions a robust world economy of stable growth despite a cycle of fear. The strength of the Internet stimulates overall prosperity notwithstanding a high-level anxiety about terror. People are prosperous, connected, and frightened—all at the same time.
- "Market Failure" foresees free economies burdened by military obligations that damage the world economy. Military spending gets in the way of investments in infrastructure, education, and health

Table 3.2   Six Potential Futures

	Desirable	In-between	In-between	In-between	In-between	Undesirable
Macroenvironment 1. Best outcome (romance) 2. Middle (comedy) 3. Worst outcome (tragedy)	"All is Well"	"Success Tech"	"Market Failure"	"Lobby Jam"	"Eco-Tech Demand"	"Woe and Misfortune"
Society 1. Moving and Seeking 2. Old and Feeble 3. Young and Militant	Moving and Seeking	Old and Feeble	Young and Militant	Moving and Seeking	Young and Militant	Young and Militant
Technology 1. Broadband World 2. Mixed Access 3. Internet Slowdown	Broadband World	Broadband World	Mixed Access	Internet Slowdown	Mixed Access	Internet Slowdown
Global Security 1. Goodwill 2. Pax America 3. Cycle of Fear	Goodwill	Cycle of Fear	Pax America	Goodwill	Goodwill	Cycle of Fear
Domestic Laws and Regulation 1. Free to Choose 2. Well-Regulated 3. Special Interests	Free to Choose	Well-Regulated	Free to Choose	Special Interests	Well-Regulated	Special Interests
World Economy 1. Stable Growth 2. Crisis and Progress 3. Turmoil and Instability	Stable Growth	Stable Growth	Turmoil and Instability	Crisis and Progress	Turmoil and Instability	Turmoil and Instability

which keeps the economy from reaching its full potential. The burden of high military spending does not stand alone. There also are high medical costs. Together these lead to large business cycle swings. Government debt consumes a high proportion of GDP and results in bouts of soaring inflation followed by stagnation and high unemployment. Though there is no overall collapse, the U.S. economy and the global economy are on the edge.

- "Lobby Jam" envisages technological momentum slowing because vested interests are not able to resolve property right disputes. However, the world is secure and young people are well-integrated in their respective societies. Nagging property right disputes are what keep back progress. Technology is the main source of wealth and without sufficiently rapid technical progress, prosperity is muted.
- "Eco-Tech Demand" foresees resources problems shackling economic growth (see chapter 6) and provoking governments and youth to strive for solutions. Young people and governments are motivated to solve pressing ecological and energy problems that prove very resistant. The world's spirit is lifted by this surge of idealism but real conditions for many people are not good at all. Many are resigned to just making do. Their protest is blunted because they are willing to make sacrifices for a better tomorrow, though they realize that the better tomorrow is very far-off.

These mixed positions would have managerial implications for companies. Under "Success Tech," for example, Best Buy might decide to invest in new electronics markets that assist old people in monitoring and managing health care. Under "Market Failure" Pepsi and Coke might choose to exit nations where U.S. interests are in serious jeopardy. Under "Lobby Jam," Time Warner might decide to quickly unload AOL. Under "Eco-Tech Demand," Monsanto and DuPont might go full thrust ahead in their pursuit of biotech. But, of course, there have to be backups to these actions, hedges. Undo certainty can lead in a wrong direction.

In creating scenarios, people must be cognizant that the progression of events may not be linear and that surprises can happen. To manage under these circumstances, people should establish contingency plans to accommodate different possibilities and look for convergent, no-regret actions they can take regardless of what takes place. As discussed in chapter 1, they have these five basic choices: Gamble on the "Most Probable" Outcome, Take the "Robust" Route, Delay until Further Clarity Emerges, Commit with Fallbacks, and Try to Shape the Future. These choices, of course, are not mutually exclusive; they can be combined, hybridized, and sequenced.

Because the uncertainty is great, the more stories created the better. With just three stories—for instance, a romance, tragedy, and comedy—the temptation is to identify the middle path as the most likely and the only path to be taken seriously. Since multiple stories intersect over time, there are very many possibilities (e.g., see appendix A). The number of combinations is high. The surprises must be analyzed in terms of impact on customers, suppliers, competitors, substitutes, and new entrants. Surprises affect the commitments the organization is considering. The organization must test its commitments against these surprises. People in firms must look beyond the obvious disasters and utopias for surprising and paradoxical states where unexpected things can happen, but only some organizations will go down this complicated and time-consuming route.

Does the Organization Have Needed Capabilities?

Realizing that an option may be attractive does not mean it should be pursued. Many good options exist, but firms do not have the capabilities to pursue all of them.

Imagine a pharmaceutical or a medical device company with the desire to transition from its current focus on products to managing patient solutions. The drug or device niche it now occupies is highly competitive, patents are in their last legs, R&D is very expensive, and price pressures are intense. The firm therefore determines that managing patient solutions may be a more attractive route to take. It examines the opportunities and threats and the payoffs from pursuing this option under different possible conditions in the future. Making the transition to this option is not going to be easy because the drug or medical device firm lacks capabilities in a number of key technical disciplines. It has neither the marketing nor distribution expertise to excel in patient solutions. It does not seem to have the capabilities to pursue the option.[9]

People in the organization must determine whether they have the capabilities to pursue an option. But if the organization does not have these capabilities currently, it might be able to acquire them. People in the organization should evaluate the capabilities that their firms have today in light of those it can obtain in the future. They should consider the additional capabilities their companies will need, how to obtain them, and whether the costs would be worth the benefit.

- What is the upside potential to the acquisition of such capabilities?
- What is the downside risk?
- What are the possible surprises? and
- What can be done?

An example of this nature is Dell. Its model of avoiding the person in the middle and delivering direct to customers has been enormously successful in selling PCs to U.S. businesses and other institutions, but PCs now are a commodity and Dell has a number of options that under different conditions in future could succeed in varying degrees. These options include selling through retail outlets, going aggressively after the Asian market, and looking at servers and high-end devices for its growth. In each instance, Dell may not have the requisite capabilities to pursue these options.

- If Dell is going to pursue the option of selling through retail outlets, then it will have to acquire new capabilities in logistics, inventory management, and relationship management.
- If it is going to aggressively go after the Asian market, then it will need capabilities in understanding the buying habits of those consumers.
- If it is going to look to servers and other high-end devices for its growth, it will need new capabilities in consulting to compete with IBM and HP.

The people at Dell have to assess how plausible these developments may be. Given the challenge that Dell faces and the options it is weighing, the people at Dell have to create stories of how these events might unfold.

Does the Organization Have Stories about What Might Happen?

Plot lines depict how things can evolve (see chapter 2, tables 2.1 and 2.2).[10] They show how things can get from here to there. The plot lines that people at a company like Dell create must be both plausible and surprising. As discussed in the last chapter, they should be understood in terms of actors or players who have interests and act to realize their ambitions but must confront other actors or players with equally urgent and compelling interests and ambitions. There are key episodes in their interaction, culminations of their struggles and tensions that remain unresolved.

For instance, Dell can try to buy a consulting firm such as Accenture to obtain the consulting capabilities it needs to compete with IBM and HP. This is akin to HP's bid to purchase EDS. Dell's takeover of Accenture, however, may not be friendly, and the bid for Accenture may be thwarted by the Accenture board. The action does not stop here, if Dell ups its bid for Accenture and this time it succeeds in making the acquisition. Still considerable tension remains, as Accenture's employees do not want to become a part of Dell. They are concerned about conditions of their employment—bonuses, incentives, seniority, and the like. Many of Accenture's senior employees threaten to leave.

The people at Dell now have to figure out what they are going to do next. How are they going to deal with this problem? How might they manage the Accenture acquisition? How much autonomy would they give Accenture, and to what extent would Dell change the way Accenture does business? Characters (such as the people at Dell) take action and become locked in struggles with other characters (such as the people at Accenture). The plot is driven forward by tension—a tension that is not easily resolved. With each new episode, characters enter and exit and the tension changes nature but persists.

In generating stories of this nature, a warning is in order. Typical story genres with fixed outcomes may be invoked, but only with caution, for episode may follow episode without resolution (see chapter 4). The central narrative thread in these stories relies on tensions that might persist for long periods of time without a definitive or final resolution. A whole host of characters—a group of protagonists who represent social movements, technologies, and ideas—may be pitted against each other, facilitating or impeding each other in achieving their ends. The logic of the interactions among them is determined by how they give meaning to their goals and intentions, how they structure what they do, and how they thereby come into conflict or harmony with each other. How the tension among actors plays itself out may take a very long time indeed.

Before Dell acquires consulting expertise through an acquisition of Accenture, all of this would have to be examined. For the people at Dell, the implications are not obvious. They would have to anticipate serious disaffection on the part of at least some Accenture employees and decide what to do. The people at Dell then would have to choose whether to actually go through with the acquisition. The costs and benefits would have to be weighed against the costs and benefits of other moves that Dell could make. Would the company be better off if it extended its reach into retail outlets such as Wal-Mart and Best Buy? Would it be better off if it competed against Acer and Lenovo in Asia?

How should the people in a company create the narratives they need to make decisions about their future? They might imagine that they are makers of a film or play for which the script is not in final form and their assignment is to test different plot lines. One strategist at a company has found it useful to ask his employees to act out different plots.[11] He asks them to write the plot lines and to act them out in skits or small plays, an exercise he believes produces richer results than just a discussion. Some employees create positive outcomes (romances). They work backward from a preferred state of how things can be. Other employees imagine the worst (they create tragedies). Still others consider complications (comedies)—actions and reactions by opposing forces that blunt straight-line movement in best-case or worst-case directions.

Can the Organization Identify and Prepare for Surprises?

To identify and prepare for surprises, people in the organization need to think in terms of the time frames in which outcomes might unfold. An example would be a public utility with the challenge of increasing earnings 5–6 percent per year while meeting a state mandate for 30 percent power from renewables by 2020 (see chapter 6). Progress depends on the capacity of renewable suppliers to obtain requisite approvals and the utility to shut down nonrenewable generation and add transmission to accommodate new power sources. Steps toward these goals are not likely to be smooth. The outcomes depend on hard-to-predict technologies fulfilling their promise (e.g., wind-generated electricity storage), economic conditions, and prices.

To anticipate what might take place, it makes sense to divide the future into phases—perhaps the short (2008–2012), medium (2013–2016), and long (2017–2020) term. Envisage each stage having somewhat different outcomes. For instance, romance may follow romance ("Smooth Sailing") or tragedy may follow tragedy ("Sad Tidings"), but there are other possibilities. Romance can be followed by comedy and tragedy ("Descent to Failure"), tragedy can be followed by comedy and romance ("Triumph over Adversity"), romance can be followed by tragedy and comedy ("Revival of Hope"), and comedy can be followed by tragedy and comedy ("Unexpected Turns"). For each of the possibilities, the company should have a backup plan to which it can resort in case things do not go as anticipated.

Looking Systematically at the Future

Thus, a systematic way to think about the future consists of these steps:

1. In creating stories of the organization's past and what is to come next, start by doing a "five-force" analysis. Determine what options exist.
2. Then, ask if the organization has the capabilities to carry out these options? People in the organization need to create plausible stories about how these options might evolve. In doing so, they can identify and prepare for the surprises that might take place.

The goal must be to actively manage the environment and influence it to create a future where people in the organization and those outside of it benefit.

The way to influence the future is to have a plan of action.

- How will the organization get from where it is now to where it would like to be next?

People in the organization need a narrative of how the organization moves from one point to another. They need a summary of the impacts their industry faces from the macroenvironment and a concrete series of actions that they can carry out to take advantage of relevant opportunities and counter threats (see table 3.3).

This plan of action should be specific. Stories of the future should not be matters of idle speculation. They should be channeled into consideration of important business issues.

- How much money should be invested in exploitation of a current model versus how much to transition to a new one?
- Why is the company better off if it follows one course of action versus another?
- What are the risks and the "Plan b" if the company does not succeed?
- What would the options achieve—increased revenue and profits over an expected time frame such as four, eight, or twelve years?

The reason for engaging in scenario-type thinking and becoming aware of possible futures is not to submit to their inevitability but to influence them. Often, this is where companies fail—in translating scenarios they create into action.

Table 3.3 Acting on the opportunities and threats

	Critical macroenvironmental considerations	Main opportunities	Main threats	Managerial implications (actions to take advantage of the opportunities and counter the threats)
Customers				
Suppliers				
Competitors				
New entrants				
Substitutes				

Day and Schoemaker detail the consequences of the failure to use scenario-type thinking—lost markets at Mattel, systematic myopia about low-end competitors at DuPont, Coor's late entry into the low-carb beer market, and so on.[12] The goal must be to actively manage the environment and influence it to create a future to managers' liking. If the results of scenario creation are just reflection, then the costs are not likely to justify the benefit.

European-based companies such as BASF, Nokia, Siemens, and Daimler are noted for their use of scenarios.[13] They may be compared to such U.S. multinationals as GE and DuPont which also have used scenarios to prepare for and shape the future. For example, GE is revamping its portfolio of businesses around an "eco-imagination" theme; and DuPont supports a carbon emissions cap because its materials are used in solar cells, wind turbines, fuel cells, and light-weight automobiles. The question remains how successful these U.S. companies will be. Will they permit their employees to actively participate in the process of creating stories of these companies' pasts and futures that they will use to forge, test, and implement strategies that will successfully guide them?

A good framework for preparing for the challenges that these businesses face is for them to use a "five-force plus" model in which managers seek to understand the dynamic interaction between a firm, its industry (the five forces), and the macroenvironment. They should start with this framework, consider the options, and if the organization has the capabilities to pursue them. Then, they should create stories about what might happen, a task that might be compared to that of a filmmaker or playwright trying to figure out how a script will end. They should reflect on possible endings—romance, tragedy, or comedy. This exercise should help prepare them for the surprises so whatever the future brings the capacity of their organization to cope will be greater.

CHAPTER 4

Population and Security Challenges

To deal with uncertainties businesses confront people construct sto-ries about the future. The stories are not deterministic in that the events they suggest have to occur. Rather, these events *might* hap-pen. Creating stories is a way to develop possible patterns of events that may take place, how the events could arise, how they might be connected to each other, where they could lead, and where an organization and its members might influence them.

Creating good and plausible stories depends on more than idle specula-tion. Why do businesses create these stories? They are looking for "sweet spots" or market niches where they can achieve sustained competitive advantage.[1] How can they best create these stories? This chapter reviews a number of tools for creating them—finding patterns, finding drivers, attaching vivid names, being sensitive to weak signals and wildcards, dealing with the problems of irresolution, and understanding motors of change. The young and educated are an important driving force in the scenarios of the National Intelligence Council (NIC). Its scenarios are discussed in the context of this chapter and compared with those of the oil company Shell.

This chapter then examines the use of a "no regrets" strategy by a com-pany like Wal-Mart. A "no regrets" strategy is a hedge against uncertainty (see chapter 1). Rather than bet on a single future, Wal-Mart can cover all the bases. It has a strategy that is viable regardless of how the future evolves. In carrying out a "no regrets" strategy, Wal-Mart must find seg-ments of the population or niches to which it can bring a unique set of products and services. The chapter ends with a summary of tools that can be used to create scenarios—historical analogies, current indicators, empirical evidence, and theory.

Looking for "Sweet Spots"

Business enterprises are looking for "sweet spots," that is market niches where they have competitive advantage they can sustain for long periods of time against the onslaughts of competitors, new entrants, and customers. Based on information they possess today, they want to move to, protect, and extend these "sweet spots." In these market niches or segments they provide product/service offerings to customers who have few other real choices but to obtain them from these businesses. The customers cannot switch easily to a competitor. To identify and enter a "sweet spot" requires long-term commitments from a business. The investments it makes today may not come to fruition for a long time. However, conditions in the future when these investments bear fruit may be vastly different than today.

Because there are a range of possible outcomes in the future, a business cannot without taking on great risk bet that the future will evolve in a single direction. The investments it makes today will not payoff if the future evolves in a way that is different than anticipated. People in business, therefore, need a range of possibilities in order to appropriately plan for their future investments. They need multiple stories of the future, but what is the right number of stories for people in a business to create? No right answer to this question can be given. The point of creating different scenarios is to show that different possible futures can emerge. Therefore, people in business should create more than one story; however, are just two stories, one "good" and one "bad" sufficient. A third story will be needed, however if it is just about how the status quo continues indefinitely, it may not be helpful since it will be automatically considered the most likely result and will be the only story taken seriously. The whole purpose of building scenarios is to imagine that the future will be different than the present. So to increase the number of alternatives should more than three stories be created? This might be unwieldy. Then, what is the right number of stories to create? There is no correct answer to this question. The problem of the number of stories to create is difficult. How can people in businesses best approach it? The approach that will be discussed is to look for patterns and drivers and attach vivid names to them. Examples will be given of scenarios that are built on this approach.

Finding Patterns

Constructing future stories is a way to describe an emerging reality. It is a means to understand how the setting in which an organization finds itself now can evolve into the setting in which it will find itself in the future when the investments it makes today must payoff. Based on the stories organization members construct, they must asses the degree to which these investments have promise. They must open their minds both to a continuous future and to discontinuous developments they otherwise might miss. The key is not to focus on singular events, but on patterns of multiple events that might be related. How are events in one realm affected by events in another? To what extent does this interdependence mean that there is a potential for breaks from the past? What is the possibility for fundamental shifts and transformations among the variables that affect the organization's performance? People in the organization should consider nonlinear developments as well as linear ones. They should consider patterns not easy to anticipate, patterns that depart from previous trajectories, as well as those which can be expected and do not depart radically from current trajectories. Their investigation into the future should provide insights into systems of relationships and causal dependencies. These should sensitize them to a range of contingencies. People in organizations should ask,

- How are events related to each other?
- How do events combine to form broader patterns?
- How do they coalesce into cohesive wholes? Under what conditions do they branch off and split into separate configurations?
- How can interventions in the course of events make a difference?

The reason for examining the future is to create a more beneficial one for an organization and its stakeholders. These preoccupations must bear connection to the concrete business problems that affect it.

For instance, how is the pattern of events with respect to global security going to affect a firm like Wal-Mart or 3M? A decline in world security substantially raises the cost of doing global business. Consider Wal-Mart. Its aim is to become a trillion-dollar enterprise by about 2012, with less than 60 percent of its growth coming from domestic markets and more than 40 percent from foreign markets. If violence grows in the world, the flow of goods, money, and people are likely to be seriously impaired. Another example is 3M, which to exceed Wall Street's historically conservative expectations and increase shareholder returns, must ramp up its revenue growth rates to consistent levels of greater than 10 percent. Already, more than two-thirds of 3M's sales come from abroad, but if global security deteriorates, 3M's capacity to meet this challenge will be greatly diminished.

Finding Drivers

Both companies need to have a sense for when discontinuous transformation is likely. The patterns that exist in the world may be stable for long periods of time, but they may not be. For example, as opposed to the 1970s, oil prices did not move much in the 1980s and the 1990s (see chapter 6). Oil prices again began to rise steeply in about the middle of the twenty-first century's first decade. Then they rapidly declined again. Few were really prepared for these developments. So where might oil prices move in the future? What are the drivers of change?

People in companies must consider various possibilities. For instance, regime change in Saudi Arabia—clearly, this would be a key driver for change. But regime change in Saudi Arabia cannot be isolated from a host of other factors that affect the regime's future such as the growth of militants in that country and neighboring states.

A classic tool in scenario construction is cross impact analysis (see table 4.1). Start with regime change in Saudi Arabia as the key driver and imagine what its impact would be on oil supply and demand, but do not stop there and consider as well the effects on other drivers of change such as social forces, politics, the world economy, the environment, and technology. Ultimately, this exercise should yield insights into how these realms are related and how together they impact oil prices. For instance, regime change in Saudi Arabia may hasten the commercialization of alternative technology that over time will negate a short-time price hike. Or another example might be that high oil prices may depress the world economy, and a depressed economy will have less need for oil and that will cause oil prices to go down. A firm can speculate about the levels of oil prices at different points of time in the future and create contingencies plans that will permit it to avoid losses and reap benefits if they

Table 4.1 Cross-impact analysis of a key driver

Key driver	*1. Same old Saudis*	*2. Saudis radicalize*	*3. al Qaeda or Iran-like revolution*	*4. Saudis modernize*	*$/bbl crude in 2010, 2015, and 2020*
Oil supply and demand					
World economy					
Technology					
Social forces					
Environment					
Impact on firm $					

are available. Oil prices have a ubiquitous impact and certainly people in firms, such as Wal-Mart and 3M, will find this type of analysis very useful.

The details of such an analysis are important. For instance, if the precipitating factor is changes in the Saudi regime, then there are a number of possibilities of how this change might play itself out.

1. The status quo might prevail and the current regime will stay the same.
2. It may radicalize because of growing Islamic militancy in its own population and in the population of adjacent countries.
3. It may be overthrown. If overthrown, then there are a number of possibilities. These developments can be referred to as stories within the broader story of Saudi regime change:
    a. There may be an al Qaeda revolution carried out in the name of the Sunni majority.
    b. There may be an Iranian-style revolution carried out in the name of the Shiite minority. This minority mostly inhabits oil-producing regions. It is growing more rapidly than the Sunni majority, and it has ties with Iran.
    c. In either case, Sunni or Shiite, the revolution brings extreme radicalization and antagonism to the rest of the world. The new regime that rules Saudi Arabia isolates itself and uses its oil resources as a political weapon. Perhaps it allies with China that needs oil and a new power bloc emerges based on Middle East oil and China's manufacturing might.
4. But another outcome might take place. The current regime might modernize and move toward Western moderation and liberalism.

Drivers do not deliver either/or results. It is not as if the Saudi regime will stay the same, radicalize, be overthrown, or liberalize, but all these results are possible if the time span under consideration is long enough. Indeed, there is a logic by which one outcome may lead to another. Here again, scenario writers should look for patterns and relationship among events and not just focus on isolated incidents.

The pattern that might emerge may be as follows. The Saudi regime is overthrown and there is a revolution that tries to remake Saudi society, but this revolution fails, rejected by the Saudi people because the new rulers cannot govern effectively. Then the monarchy might be restored. The ruling family rather than returning to prior methods of governance institutes reforms. After the shock of its downfall and its return to power, it decides to modernize. However, this effort as well may run into obstacles, so the ruling regime then moves in another direction. It pulls back on its modernization program and goes in a radical direction. Events swing back and forth. They do not necessarily stabilize quickly or easily. Other outcomes are equally possible. For example, the monarchy may attempt to modernize but it will fail like the Shah of Iran did in the 1970s. Then it will be subject to an al Qaeda or Iran-like revolution because of its failed efforts. Whatever ensues, this driver—changes in the Saudi regime—has effects on patterns of events in other spheres. In the world economy oil is pervasive. Although some firms will be more affected, for example those in the airline industry or tourism, all firms will feel the impact of related patterns of events affected by key drivers.

Attaching Vivid Names

By attaching vivid names to key developments, stories come to life (see chapter 3). The vivid names may be headline like in character. For instance,

- To reflect fundamental trends, developments in society can be labeled "old and feeble" to represent aging, "young and militant" to represent violence and belligerency, and "moving and seeking" to represent the migration of people from one part of the world to another (see chapter 3).
- Similarly developments to reflect fundamental trends in global security can be labeled "goodwill" to represent peace on earth, "Pax America" to represent the need for U.S. military intervention, and "cycle of fear" to represent what would take place if weapons of mass destruction got in terrorists' hands.

These representations of the future are examples of the kinds of stories people in businesses may create. They should create their own stories and attach vivid names to them based on the key challenges they confront. As examples, these representations undergo additional scrutiny in this chapter, starting with the role youth play in society and moving to security. Chapter 5 takes up representations of the future that focus on politics and the economy, and chapter 6 will return to energy and environmental issues.

Young and Educated

Young and educated are key drivers of future trends in any society as each new generation puts its stamp on an historic epoch. Young and educated were the starting point for scenarios that the U.S. intelligence community created after 9/11. In the period immediately following the incident, the security establishment brought together experts internal to the Central Intelligence Agency and outside of it, some of the world's most celebrated scenario thinkers. Their work, the epoch-making National Intelligence Council's *2020 Project*, set the tone for the U.S. government's post–9/11 security policy.[2] In their thinking young people were divided into two categories. What one group of educated young people aspires to may be called "Gracious Living." This group is optimistic and entrepreneurial. It favors the opening up of societies and the introduction of cosmopolitan ideas. It believes in freedom of choice and competition. It seeks affluence, though it may be concerned that this affluence cannot or will not be widely shared.

More so than their parents, people in this group are willing to live for the moment and to take on added debt. They are affected by advertising and the media and popular entertainment and cultural symbols like Disney and Coke that are known the world over. Their dominant orientation is materialistic, though they may be aware of materialism's costs, such as increased pollution. This group of young people can be found in the rising sectors of such Asian countries as India and China and such Latin American countries as Brazil, Chile, and Mexico, but they are located throughout the world wherever there is hope that individual efforts can lead somewhere, that self-improvement is possible, and societies can advance based on individual initiative.

Indicative of the rise of "Gracious Living" is the rapid economic growth rates of China and India and their catching up to the wealth and lifestyles found in the United States and Europe. By the year 2050, people in these countries may be living at levels closer to those found in the United States. If current trends continue, China will be closing the gap with the United States. India too will have standards of living that are closer to those found in the United States. Though India is not projected to do as well as China, it in fact may overtake China. India has many advantages over its neighbor. It is a democracy, is less heavily dependent on manufacturing, is developing a large base of sophisticated knowledge workers, and will have a younger population than either China or the United States. China like the United States will age because of its one child per family policy. China, too, because of its dependence on heavy manufacturing is more likely than India to face ecological and natural resource limits to growth. There are no guarantees that the catch-up of either China or India with the United States will be smooth. This assumption is simplistic. Many deviations are possible. U.S. growth rates may be slower or faster than anticipated. China's and India's growth rates may be slower. The future of relative GDP growth rates in these nations and elsewhere in the world are hard to predict.

What was apparent to analysts who created U.S. intelligence scenarios was that another group of young people had a far different orientation. Those in this group also tend to be educated, compared to others in their society, relatively advantaged, and well-off. They are serious, intent, and motivated, perhaps even more so than the young people who aspire to "Gracious Living," but they also are resentful, hopeless, and disillusioned. They tend to believe that their future is constrained and there is little hope that things will get better. Their strong collective identities therefore focus on their ties to religion and to ethnic groups. Many live in countries that were once occupied by colonial powers and their disappointment is with having lost past national and/or religious power and glory. These young people have a tendency to regularly revisit group memories of injustice. Many reach the conclusion that armed struggle and violence are acceptable, if not something that they themselves will carry out. Some believe that armed struggle and violence are a sacred duty—there is no other way to redress wrongs they believe have been inflicted on their religion or national group.

Young people of this type more often are found in the Middle East and in Africa but they exist throughout the world including nations of Asia like Sri Lanka, the Philippines, and Indonesia, and in Latin American countries such as Columbia, Bolivia, and Venezuela. Some have migrated to developed nations. They can be found throughout Europe and the United States. Some have little but contempt for Western values even after they migrate. They are repulsed by the individualism, materialism, free-thinking, loose sexual morals, and self-indulgence they witness. The excesses in Western countries disgust them.

Many in this group are Muslim, but not all. Thus, growth in this group may be hard to stop as growth in the number of Muslims in the world is projected to outdistance that of any religion from 2002–2050. Other religious groups will fall behind. So-called new-age religionists, atheists, Protestants, Jews, and Buddhists, indeed, will lag far behind. Already, Muslims are concentrated in areas of the world subject to high levels of violence where resentment toward the West and Western lifestyles is high. But will continued growth rates in Muslim population necessarily mean there will be an increase in violence? Projections that the number of disaffected young people with a tendency toward violence will grow cannot be made with perfect confidence. This growth in both the number of young people and their tendency toward violence may level off or start to decline depending on a variety of factors from economic opportunity to education; or this tendency may grow at an even more rapid pace than anticipated and may be hard to slow down. To slow it down would require building stable states out of failed ones, creating law and order, and bringing hope to this population.

Later in this chapter the question of youth violence will be taken up in more detail. A number of analytical tools will be applied to the issue— historical analogies (which is often referred to as "backsighting" among scenario writers), trends in key indicators, empirical analysis, and theory. These analytical tools add depth to scenarios.

Relative Certainties and Uncertainties

Scenarios are built off relative certainties and uncertainties among trends. After 9/11 the U.S. NIC created four scenarios. The certainties and uncertainties that are incorporated into their scenarios are listed in table 4.2. For instance, a relative certainty was that globalization is largely irreversible (see table 4.2), or so it seemed. A relative uncertainty is whether it will be less Western. Another relative uncertainty is how quickly lagging economies will catch-up. Also, who will set the standards for future economic growth? Will it be Asian countries or those in North America?

Based on this analysis NIC created four scenarios. They are (Davos), a romance, (Pax America), which can be labeled a romantic comedy, (the New Caliphate), a tragic comedy, and (Cycle of Fear), an outright tragedy. The key element in these scenarios is the degree to which capital, goods, people, technology, ideas, and money flow freely in the world. With the freer movement of capital, goods, people, technology, ideas, and money, there is greater potential for a long boom (Davos) than if there is not. Pax America stands on the United States being the world's policeman. The United States must keep global order to preserve prosperity. The burden on the United States is great. Military spending grows and regard for the United States in the rest of the world diminishes. The New Caliphate suggests what would take place if the United States was not successful as a global peacekeeper. The Middle East collapses and essentially is removed from participation in the global economy. As it falls into chaos, the most advanced and ambitious elements in its population vacate the area, leaving a huge void. A Cycle of Fear adds epidemics and weapons of mass destruction to this mix. Insecurity and fear grip nearly everyone and freedom is curtailed throughout the world.

Shell's Three Scenarios

The four scenarios of NIC have a somewhat similar structure to the three scenarios of the oil company Shell.[3] Many of the same experts

Table 4.2 Relative certainties and uncertainties

Relative certainties	Key uncertainties
Globalization largely irreversible, but less Western	Lagging economies??? Asian countries set "rules"???
World economy substantially larger	Gaps "haves" and "have-nots"??? Back sliding of fragile democracies??? Managing, containing financial crises???
Global firms spread new technologies	Challenge governments???
New economic middle-weights	Whether smooth???
Aging populations	Adapt work forces, welfare, integrate migrants??? EU an ex-superpower???
Energy "in ground" not enough to meet demand	Political instability producer countries??? Supply disruptions???
Growing power nonstate actors	Willingness and ability to accommodate???
Political Islam potent force	Growth in jihadist ideology??? Conflict??? State unity???
Weapons of mass destruction capabilities	More nuclear powers??? Terrorists have biological, chemical, radiological, nuclear weapons???
Instability Middle East, Asia, Africa	Precipitating events??? Overthrow of regimes???
Total war unlikely	But ability to manage many flashpoints???
Environment and ethics	New technologies: Exacerbate or resolve???
U.S. power	Other countries challenge??? United States loses scientific and technology edge???

participated in the creation of both sets of scenarios. Shell's scenarios have been prominently displayed on its web page. They point to the type of world the company hopes will come into existence and to the dangers in the kinds of worlds that actually may appear. The company had two scenarios in 2001—*Business Class* driven by "efficiency" and *Prism* dominated by "social cohesion." Its scenarios took their structure from the conflict between "markets" represented by the value of "efficiency," "community" represented by the value of "social cohesion," and the state. In 2005, Shell added a third scenario and envisioned a world in which the state had greater influence. This is because of 9/11, which Shell viewed as a crisis of security, and the spate of corporate scandals, which the company saw as a crisis of trust. The "state" stands for "security" and "trust" in Shell's 2005 scenarios.

Shell's 2005 scenarios were

- *Open Doors*—a pragmatic world with a strong emphasis on efficiency. It is a secure world of mutual recognition, voluntary best-practice, close links between business and civil society, and cross-border integration.
- *Low Trust Globalization*—a legalistic world of guaranteed state security. It is a risky world, absent market solutions and subject to intrusive checks and controls from overlapping jurisdictions.
- *Flags*—a dogmatic world where social cohesion and security trump efficiency. It is an even riskier world where dogmatism, zero-sum games, and basic conflicts over values stifle continuing globalization.

Clearly, Shell is a leader in the corporate world in the creation and use of scenarios. This goes back to the 1970s when the company skillfully used the scenarios it created to deal with higher priced oil (see chapter 5). But despite its long-standing reliance on scenarios Shell has had notable failures in recent years. Of course, these failures cannot be attributed to the firm's use of scenarios, but its use of scenarios has been subject to criticism for not making the firm more flexible and open to outside forces.[4]

Shell's process of scenario building largely has been generated by elites (see chapter 1). It is top down. Only recently has Shell let up a bit and obtained more employee involvement. The scenarios it creates also are fixed at one time. Their influence on ongoing decision making therefore is not great. Once the company commits to long-term capital investment, it discards its scenarios and has a single point of view about how the future will evolve.

NIC's scenarios, while more complex than Shell's, share many features with Shell's. These scenarios have been generated by elites. They are static and it is unclear if they influence decision making. If the reason for the construction of scenarios is to open organizations to innovation and allow members of organizations to see new opportunities in contexts where surprise is costly, the scenarios of the NIC and Shell have not proven to be good instruments for achieving this goal. They may enshrine conventional thinking more than open up people to innovative thought. Might not a different approach to creating scenarios, one that relies on a more complex, realistic path for analysis, lead to a more nuanced, diverse, and realistic understanding of the many paths the world can take?

Weak Signals and Wildcards

A better approach would make more use of weak signals and wildcards. Weak signals are noisy indicators on the periphery of normal activity that may be ignored, while wildcards are low-probability/high-impact events that can constitute important turning points or inflections where trends begin to move in different directions. Too often top executives in organizations fail to detect weak signals that are on the periphery and are ill-prepared for the wildcards. People on the front lines in organizations often have better information about the weak signals and the wildcards. They can provide early warnings that can alert organizations to the kinds of changes that they must make.

With regard to NIC's scenarios, a number of wildcards deserve further scrutiny. First, what impact will the European Union (EU) have? NIC mentions the EU and recognizes it as a major force. The EU has more people than the United States and GDP per capita that is very close. The EU could tilt the balance among possible future worlds.

Scenario writers should be searching for balance-tipping forces like the EU. A balance-tipping wildcard would be if Turkey became a part of EU. But will it be accepted? How open is the EU to a nation like Turkey? Scenario writers should look for stories within the stories. With regard to Turkey, there are a number of possibilities:

1. From the perspective of Turkey's entrance into the EU, an Ataturk future would be the *romance*. For Turkey, the Ataturk future is one that stands for secularism and populism. It represents republicanism, nationalism, statism, and reformism.
2. In contrast, the *tragedy* would be a republic that was religiously based—one which would be represented by Shariah law, religious politics, and forced intolerance in education and elsewhere in society.

Within stories lie further stories. Urbanization is an important one in how the Turkish story will unfold. What is the capacity for Turkish cities to absorb young people from the countryside? The young in Turkey are a linchpin—the education they receive, the opportunities they have, and the messages they get from the media and other influential figures in societies. Scenario writers should be looking for linchpins.

Another linchpin, a global issue, one not restricted to Turkey, is developments in public health. That is, what will happen in the many parts of the world where populations are rapidly aging—developed nations such as Japan, Italy, Spain, Scandinavia, the United States, the United Kingdom, as well as developing nations such as China? Will people see advances in public health that vastly extend life expectancy and improve the quality of life? Will the vitality and productivity of people be maintained for longer than has been the case in the past? What happens will depend on many factors. Again, it is necessary to create stories within stories. Within this realm a number of stories within stories are possible:

1. The *romance* would be if there was integration of therapeutics, diagnostics, and genetics resulting in better prediction and prevention, lower costs, and growth in wellness. There would have to be more partnering between consumers and health care providers and innovative solutions to insurance problems. Health care companies, in this scenario, would thrive by providing not just services and products but solutions to people's needs.

2. The *tragedy* would be decline based on economic setbacks that slow medical advances resulting in less R&D, more side-effects, and recalls. The public would start to lose faith in conventional medicine if the genetic revolution failed to deliver on its promise. Industry would have to consolidate to cut costs. Overall, there would be less innovation and fewer breakthroughs. People would receive less care and be more left to their own devices.

3. The *comedy* is more than a simple unbroken line—familiar advances coming from select therapeutic advances in drugs, devices, diagnostics, and/or genetics. Physicians still would be at the pinnacle of the health care system and costs would continue to escalate rapidly. But the growth in consumer information on the Internet would accelerate, and there would be growing demand for this information because people's trust in conventional medical care would decline. Severe cost pressures would force people to rely more and more on information that they gathered themselves. The downside would be if they turned more to unfounded and unproven nontraditional medical techniques out of desperation and frustration.

Within broader scenarios, scenario writers should look for these stories within stories, the wildcards, linchpins, and balance-tipping forces. On the periphery and not part of a main story's thrust, they can upset existing patterns and drive trends in unexpected directions.

Irresolution

Most scenarios assume some type of resolution—a culmination to what has been put into motion, but what if this culmination does not come into existence? What if contradiction and ambiguity persist for long periods of time?

Recognizing that irresolution for long periods of time is possible is important. It provides an antidote to unsophisticated thinking about orderly ends. In generating scenarios, typical story genres with fixed outcomes may be invoked, but with caution, for episode may follow episode without clear ending. Trends establish what is happening, but the purpose of scenarios is not to consider the past, which is embodied in trends, but what is likely to take place next. Often, people's natural tendency is to believe that the future will be roughly the same as today. This tendency provides for comfort and most of the time is borne out by experience, but the past is not always a good predictor of the future. Trends can slow down, level-off, and speed up, with many outcomes being possible.

The risk for scenario writers is to focus on just a few ends, fixing them at a single point of time and not revising and reconsidering them as additional evidence becomes available. Indeed, it must be recognized that the range of uncertainties is great. Stories have plot lines that have a logic that shows how things evolve—how they get from here to there. Scenario writers have to be careful that the plot lines they choose are both plausible and surprising. Of course, they will be tempted to create plot lines that are Pollyanna-like in nature and show infinite potential (romances) or Cassandra-like in nature and show infinite catastrophe (tragedies), but as has been argued greater intricacy than such extremes should be considered. Events do not necessarily move progressively toward such positive or negative ends.[5] Equally powerful and opposing forces can survive simultaneously for long periods of time. As has been pointed out, the world contains "multiple contradictory forces, all of great strength and relevance,"[6] each exerting itself at the same time. It may be far better to think of what can happen in terms of "both/and" rather than "either/or."[7]

Multiple, confusing, contradictory forces are not likely to go away. Thus, the future can consist of both the secular and the sacred, of power and vulnerability, and so on. These can exist simultaneously with not one prevailing at the expense of the others. Some parts of the world can be prosperous, while others are in dire poverty. For some period of time, things will look very bleak, and then there will be return to normalcy and even buoyant optimism, but in the end, no epic struggles with clear victors. Dynamic tension may prevail for long periods of time. Things can go backward as well as advance. The future may be more circular than a straight line. As a circle, it swings back and forth between extremes with no definitive direction. The tensions, which the stories pose, are *not* necessarily resolved. If resolved, perhaps there are winners and losers in a fixed battle where one group prevails, or perhaps, there is confrontation among a number of contending parties that leads to each getting something of what it wants, not complete victory but enough to satisfy the opposing groups for the time being, an unsteady equilibrium at best. On the other hand, there might be an out-and-out tragedy, with all the relevant parties experiencing great losses. Surprises always can take place; consider the fall of the Soviet Union and the rise of a semi-capitalist China as examples. "Heroes" may emerge who bring temporary coherence or impose harmony in unexpected ways. The heroes do not necessarily have to be individuals. They can be groups of persons, social movements, technologies, or even ideas.

Motors of Change

Van de Ven tries to create an order among possible futures by pointing to "motors of change" as a way to address how things might evolve.[8] For Van de Ven, there are four main "motors of change":

1. *Teleology*—rational actors guiding the future toward some desired or predetermined end;
2. *Life-cycles*—underlying logics that create a future by means of predetermined stages;
3. *Dialectics*—a future carved out of the conflict between forces locked in a struggle for dominance or control; and
4. *Evolution*—a future that emanates from a natural process of variation, selection, and retention.

These motors of change may be operating simultaneously, greatly complicating efforts to see through to the outcomes. Simultaneity, according to Van de Ven, is not just a function of time (one event follows another) but also of space (different motors in different contexts). Thus, the teleology of planning systems may exist simultaneously in different degrees in different parts of the world with marketplace forces that are evolutionary. They may be locked in dialectical struggles which proceed in a series of life-cycle stages.

"No Regrets" Strategy—Wal-Mart

Given that the evolution of future outcomes is so complicated, what can a company do? To hedge its bets, it can take a robust approach (see chapter 1). A robust or "no regrets" strategy that a company may decide to pursue means placing bets on many possibilities. The company essentially covers the waterfront. No matter what happens, it will be ok, or at least it hopes so. Though it may also make sense for some small companies just getting started, this strategy typically can best be pursued by a large company with lots of resources like Wal-Mart. Large companies like Wal-Mart are generally better positioned to carry out "no regrets" strategies than small firms. If the uncertainty is great and a business is as large and resourceful as Wal-Mart, it can move it in a number of directions at once.

Wal-Mart needs $3/4 billion more in sales in the next 12 or 50 years to reach its growth goals (see chapter 3). It must decide to whom it will make its sales, what products it will offer, and if it can sustain a profitable business model against serious competitors like Costco, Kmart, Carrefor, and Target. Wal-Mart needs a point of view about the future. Which social trends should it exploit? Which groups in the population should it target? Because of its sheer size, it has the potential to go for a broad swath of the market. How should it divide the market into different segments? Three broad groups have potential as targets for Wal-Mart's attention. Wal-Mart can attach such names to them (see chapter 3) as: (1) Old and Feeble, (2) Moving and Seeking, and (3) Young and Militant. Then, it can try for a robust, no regrets strategy that appeals to each of these groups.

Old and Feeble

The growing concentration of wealth among the elderly, who as a group always have been comparatively well-off in the United States, creates a huge market for Wal-Mart. Global demand for products and services aimed at the elderly are likely to grow very quickly. If the population of the developed world continues to live longer and remains healthier, then Wal-Mart has a large opportunity, but it must have the right set of products and services at the right price points that will attract the elderly. This means redesigning stores to make it easier for the elderly to navigate. It means providing transportation services to get the elderly from their homes to the stores.

A major reason for increased longevity is the development of new pharmaceuticals and medical technologies, which make it possible to prevent or cure diseases that would have been fatal to earlier generations. If Wal-Mart not only becomes the dispenser of these new therapies but a trusted adviser to the elderly about their health, it can get a leg up on the competition.

Government health programs fund many of the therapies and make the treatments available. Thus, Wal-Mart also must become expert at negotiating deals for the elderly with government providers. Because of cost concerns, governments will be pushing the availability of low-cost generics that Wal-Mart can feature. Its fetish with low prices can be useful if it can figure out how to keep medical costs down and make health more affordable for the poor.

If life expectancy grows particularly fast, this bet on the elderly made by a company like Wal-Mart can pay off big. But Wal-Mart has to be at the forefront of advances that slow the process of aging and in making these advances available to a growing elderly population that will need and want them. Wal-Mart is in a position where it can serve aging baby boomers who not only live far longer but whose have healthier lives involving fewer incidences of debilitating diseases. Taking part in the prevention of such diseases as cancer, heart disease, arthritis, and Alzheimer's could be a central part of the company's mission (See the following boxed insert, Growth of the Elderly in the World).

Growth of the Elderly in the World

- Worldwide, the elderly (age 65 and older) numbered 440 million and were 6 percent of the population in 2002. They were projected to nearly double by 2020 (to more than 9 percent of total population) and more than triple by 2050 (to nearly 17 percent), according to the U.S. Census Bureau's International Data Base.
- In the developed world, those older than 65 made up 15 percent of the population in 2000 and will become 27 percent in the next half century.
- Throughout the developed world, population growth was fastest among the elderly. In Europe, the United States, and Japan, the aged also are the wealthiest element in society.
- In Germany, the retirement-age population will increase from less than 16 percent of the population in 2000 to nearly 19 percent in 2010 and 31 percent in 2050.
- By 2050, one-third of the Italian population will be older than 65, nearly double the number today.
- Japan's over-65 population, 17 percent of the total in 2000, was projected to climb to 22 percent in 2010 and approximately 37 percent in 2050.

Adapted from the *Futurist Magazine,* March–April 2005, p. 33.

Moving and Seeking

The second group Wal-Mart could serve are movers and seekers. Mass migration is redistributing the world's inhabitants. Immigration, for instance, is rapidly altering the ethnic composition of the U.S. population. In 2000, Latinos accounted for 12.6 percent of the U.S. population, but by 2050, they will account to 24.5 percent. Asians, who were 3.8 percent of the U.S. population in 2005, will constitute approximately 8 percent of the population in 2050.

Higher fertility among Latinos will speed up this trend. As of 2002, women in the United States had about two children during their lives, which is about enough to maintain a stable population, but Hispanic women were averaging more than 2.7 births per woman and among Mexican immigrants the fertility rate was nearly 2.9. Within the United States, Wal-Mart has an opportunity to serve such immigrant groups. As Wal-Mart expands abroad, it has the potential to serve these groups in other parts of the world. In Western Europe, immigrants came mostly from North Africa, the Middle East, the Indian subcontinent, and central and Eastern Europe. Around one-half million legal immigrants have come to Western Europe from central Europe. Another 3 to 4 million are expected to join them in the next 25 years. If Wal-Mart is going to thrive in Europe, where so far it has not been successful, it might appeal to these groups. Despite xenophobic reactions to immigrants, cultural diversity is expected to rise subject to some reversals and interruptions.

Migration not only has been a factor in the United States and Europe but also in Asia where there has been a massive movement of people from the countryside and rural areas to large cities. In China, up to 100 million people have made this journey in recent years. Wal-Mart has expanded successfully into China and can capitalize on this trend as well.

Young and Militant

In addition to the "old and feeble" and the movers and seekers, Wal-Mart must consider what the impact of the "young and militant" will be on its operations. This group may be the hardest for it to appeal. A Department of Defense report has predicted that by 2020 a majority of the world's 25 or so most important Muslim countries might be in the hands of extremist religious governments like Iran. Mass consumer goods, however, still will be needed by the people in these countries. People everywhere still will have a need for the necessities that a firm like Wal-Mart can provide. For instance, there may be great potential for Wal-Mart in prosperous new cities of the Middle East like Dubai that has become the financial center for the Muslim world.

Large companies like Wal-Mart must be attentive to this type of demographic change. Competitive advantage means capturing specific market niches with roots in various demographic segments. Companies that do well must find and target these population niches.[9] Best Buy, for instance, is an example of a company that carefully targets such niches in the population (see the following boxed insert, Wal-Mart and Best Buy—A Comparison). Wal-Mart will have to do the same if it expects to continue its growth. As much as it tries to reach everyone, the way to grow is to have specific groups in mind. The dilemma is that Wal-Mart must appeal to a large mass of people while still appealing to specific segments. A "no regrets" strategy on Wal-Mart's part has to be narrow and targeted on specific population segments as well as broad and capable of reaching all consumers.

The key point is that even for a firm with the resources, stretch, and ambition of Wal-Mart, it will have to micro-segment its customers into smaller and smaller categories. To maintain its growth, it will have to follow carefully trends in population, values, and lifestyles. It needs plausible stories about what is happening and how it can capitalize on what is taking place. What commitments should it make now with the hope that there will be big payoffs in the future when the world will be a different place than it is today?

Wal-Mart and Best Buy—A Comparison

Wal-Mart may be compared to Best Buy. In the 1990s, Best Buy could raise revenues and profits simply by building new stores as quickly as possible. However, by 2007, it faced the problem of falling margins at the same time that it had few additional markets in the United States to enter. Best Buy's strategy was to continue to expand broadly and widely but to do so by meeting customers' individual needs through a program it called "customer centricity." Customer centricity was aimed at five distinct population groups, with each Best Buy store adapting to serve one or more of these segments:

- *Affluent professionals* who want the best in technology and entertainment and who demand excellent service.
- *Active, young males* who seek the latest technology and equipment.

- *Practical family men* who want technologies that improve their lives.
- *Busy suburban moms* who desire to enrich their children's lives.
- *Small business owners* who aim to use technology to enhance the productivity of their businesses.

Tests of the concept showed sales gains in comparison to similar stores. However, the sales gains came at a price of gross profits not increasing. Initially costs went up but as Best Buy learned how to implement the model better it was able to reduce them. The purpose was to engage more deeply with customers by recognizing them as individuals with specific and separate identities and needs.

Understanding Youth Violence

Young and militant people pose an especially strong challenge to multinationals like Wal-Mart. Many countries in the world today are overcrowded and poor, which is true of virtually all the Muslim nations, except for the oil-rich states of the Middle East. They have large populations of young men, many of whom are unemployed, and who may be attracted to extremist movements and violence. Despite having educational attainment, many of the young men in these countries find it hard to get a job. Even if there is economic growth, they feel as if their own status does not advance. The situation is especially irksome to them because they can see prosperity around them. Religious extremists dedicated to overturning "corrupt" regimes and societies can attract these young men. Companies operating in the global economy have to identify and adapt to these circumstances. Violent conflict and instability is a liability that can prevent them from successfully doing business. There is little doubt that it has serious effects on the strategies they pursue. Violent conflict has a human toll. It decimates economically active population and diminishes human and social capital. It destroys physical infrastructure—roads, power and communication systems, transport links, public and private buildings, and other essential physical assets. It raises the cost of doing business. Corporations often must spend heavily to provide for the security to protect their personnel and physical property.

Violence can damage corporate reputations if the corporations are implicated. It destabilizes governments. Their capacity to fight corruption falls. They are less able to guarantee contracts, may be prone to impose exorbitant taxes, and can be overthrown and replaced by regimes that threaten to renegotiate the terms under which multinationals operate, if not actual expropriation.

Though violent conflict adds to the dangers of doing business abroad and raises the likelihood that revenue streams will be curtailed or entirely eliminated, corporations have not desisted from increasing their activities in violent prone nations, such as Colombia, Sri Lanka, Algeria, Indonesia, Pakistan, and the Philippines. For firms in extractive natural resource-based industries, such as mining, oil and gas, hydroelectrical engineering, and forestry the benefits appear to outweigh the costs. Firms, facing maturity in their domestic markets, also are attracted to violence-prone nations because fewer companies invest in these nations. In these countries they may have the chance to earn monopoly or near-monopoly rents.

How can violence be better understood? The scenario writer must use such tools as historical analogies ("backcasting"), current indicators, empirical evidence, and theory.

Historical Analogies

Historical analogies are useful in constructing scenarios but care must be taken to highlight the similarities and differences between the past and the present. Though many analogies come to mind how to interpret them is not simple. Each analogy has its own lessons. For instance, was the end of World War I a victory for the United Kingdom and its allies, or just the beginning of another ominous cycle that led the onset of the even more appalling events of World War II? Another question would be—what is the best historical analogy for the situation the United States faces in Iraq? If the analogy is 1938 (Munich) then the lesson is not to appease, if the analogy is 1942 (World War II) then the lesson is to fight-on regardless, if the analogy is 1948 (the start of the cold war) then the lesson is to deter, if the analogy is 1972 (Vietnam) then the lesson is to withdraw, and if the analogy is 1914 (World War I) then the lesson is that the system is out of control. There is a need to regain control.

The favorite historical analogy among foreign policy realists is Chamberlain's 1938 capitulation to the Nazis that failed to bring peace. For foreign policy idealists, the favorite analogy is the imposition of harsh terms on the Germans following World War I. Both the realists and idealists may be right since it was wrong to impose such harsh terms on Germany, but once imposed it was equally wrong to appease the Nazis. Scenarios consciously draw on historical analogies. Much can be learned from an understanding of the past, but history does not necessarily repeat itself exactly.

For example, an element in the debate about the factors that lead to violent conflict is the controversial one that young people have been the "protagonists of protest, instability, reform, and revolution."[10] They provided the "recruits to fascist movements in the 1920s" and "demonstrations and protests in the 1960s" and are a main determinant of the violence that threatens business and the world in the twenty-first century.[11] The connection between young people and violence is an old one that has been investigated in prior studies of generational conflict and careful dissections of the role of population dynamics in such conflicts as Algeria, Biafra, and El Salvador.[12] An overabundance of young people is claimed not only to be a main culprit in international violence, but also in criminal activity where young people play a disproportionate role.[13]

Violent conflict is nothing new in history. The twentieth century has had but too many examples.[14] Young people are supposed to play a particularly large role in this violence because they are susceptible to strong leaders who cynically take advantage of their need for meaning and sense of belonging and try to instill in them the belief that their lives can be made infinitely better if they devote themselves to all-encompassing causes.[15] Neither today nor in the past have young people been distributed evenly in the world. Post–World War I turbulence in Europe was the breeding ground for Nazism, which preyed on disappointed youth who felt that they had fought in vain and had no place in the postwar economy.[16] In societies beset by instability, where the opportunities for a normal life are diminished, a rational weighing of the alternatives may lead young people to conclude that a violent path is logical. When the rule of law breaks down and strong ideologies support this decision, little stands in the way.

A wealth of historical analogies indicate that cycles of violence have coincided with periods when young people comprised unusually large proportions of the population. Recent examples include the following:

- Turkey's Kurdish population, which instigated an aggressive insurgency movement against the Turkish government, emerged from a 1995 youth bulge.
- The Sri Lankan Sinhalese national insurgency and the Tamil rebellion reached their peak levels when more than 20 percent of the population was 15–24 years old. The Sri Lankan government eventually moved 14,000 rebellious youth into "rehabilitation centers" to help alleviate the problem.
- Terror and civil strife in Algeria also coincided with a youth bulge. Extreme conflict diminished in that nation only after female fertility went down.
- By the mid 1970s, half of Iran's population was under the age of 16 and two-thirds was under the age of 30; this youth bulge contributed to the street politics of 1977–1979, the fall of the Shah, the rise

of a government hostile to the United States, and the bloody Iran-Iraq war.

• Youth-laden populations in such conflict-torn regions as the Balkans, Central, and Southeastern Asia also have prone to commit acts of violence. Violent street protests, for instance, continue to be a regular occurrence in Bangladesh, a country that from 1997 to 2005 had one of the highest youth bulges in the world.

• The populations of the Gaza Strip and Iraq are remarkably similar, both being youth heavy populations in striking contrast to the more age-balanced populations of Israel and the United States.[17]

Indicators

Credible indicators are needed to follow the evolution of a problem like youth violence. As the troublesome violence of the post–cold war period derives mainly from terror, the National Memorial Institute for the Prevention of Terror (NMIPT) provides a publicly available source of data on terror that people in companies can access. NMIPT takes its data from the Rand Corporation, which gets the information mainly from public sources such as newspapers. In comparison to government sources on terrorism such as U.S. State Department Country Reports, the Rand data are supposed to be more conservative.[18]

Terrorism can be measured in terms of the number of incidents and how lethal they are—that is, the number of deaths and injuries they cause. It also can be measured in terms of the type of attack—for instance, whether a suicide bombing or not; and it can be measured in terms of where the incident takes place and who are the perpetrators. Once such data are gathered, a baseline indicator must be established.[19]

The problem with such indicators is that they label the bulk of Middle East acts as terror and inflate the Middle East results while many civil wars and disruption in Africa are underreported. An alternative to reliance on them is to use the Conflict Barometer data of the *Heidelberg Institute for International Conflict Research (HIIK)*. The HIIK is a nonprofit organization that is a part of the Political Science Department at the University of Heidelberg, Germany. HIIK data are more subtle in incorporating various gradations and levels of violence. Since 1992, HIIK has published *Conflict Barometer*—an annual report that describes all of the conflicts in the world in the previous year. This report classifies conflicts into five categories based on their severity, the five categories being: latent, manifest, crisis, severe, and outright war.[20] In 2005, for example, India, Sri Lanka, and Iraq were the top three countries in terms of this index, whereas there were 45 countries with a conflict index of zero.

Empirical Evidence

After indicators have been found and trends established, there is a need for empirical evidence. For example, in a scrupulously executed empirical analysis Urdal looked at the proposition that "youth bulges—extraordinary large youth cohorts relative to the adult population" have been casually linked to armed conflict.[21] His findings provide strong support for the hypothesis that youth bulges increased the risk of armed conflict. Countries experiencing youth bulges had a 35 percent greater chance of conflict. Urdal also tested for whether all youth bulges resulted in violence. He found that objective grievances were needed for groups to carry out violent acts. When educated youth arrive on the job market and face widespread unemployment and/or autocratic governments that block their avenues for advancement, they were more prone to violence.

What happens when youth bulges diminish, however? What happens when the surges quiet and are followed by busts?[22] Today population growth is starting to slow down to historically low levels and in some cases shrinking. This is part of a larger pattern of demographic transition where population has moved from high fertility and mortality in traditional societies to low fertility and mortality in advanced societies.[23] Indeed, demographers once predicted more than 10 billion people in the world by 2050, but now are estimating that the world's population will not exceed 9 billion in the middle of the twenty-first century.[24] Middle East fertility rates have dropped significantly (see table 4.3). As population pressures begin to ease, will 15–24 year olds be less prone to violence? Empirical analysis continues to find that youth bulges are positively and significantly related to conflict as expected, but youth busts are not related to less conflict.[25] Control variables representing human and economic development, social solidarity, and government capacity are statistically significant, which suggests that youth bulges are likely to increase the tendency toward violent conflict but busts are not likely to decrease it.

Theory

Better scenarios rest on historical analogies, good indicators, and empirical evidence, but they also require theory. Scenario writers must have a theory to interpret empirical studies. A theory would be that violence

Table 4.3 Declining fertility rates in Middle East nations

Country	Total fertility rate in 1970	Total fertility rate in 2006	Percentage decrease	Percentage lower than replacement level
Algeria	7.38	1.89	−74.39	−10.00
Bahrain	6.97	2.60	−62.70	23.81
Egypt	6.56	2.83	−56.86	34.76
Iran	6.8	1.80	−73.53	−14.29
Iraq	7.18	4.18	−41.78	99.05
Israel	3.79	2.41	−36.41	14.76
Jordan	8.00	2.63	−67.13	25.24
Kuwait	7.41	2.91	−60.73	38.57
Lebanon	6.05	1.90	−68.60	−9.52
Libya	7.48	3.28	−56.15	56.19
Saudi Arabia	7.26	4.00	−44.90	90.48
Sudan	6.67	4.72	−29.24	124.76
Syria	7.60	3.40	−55.26	61.90
United Arab Emirates	6.77	2.88	−57.46	37.14
West Bank/Gaza*	*	4.28	*	*
Yemen	8.3	6.58	−20.72	213.33
Total	5.84	2.82	−48.42	34.35

*Historical Fertility Numbers were not available.

Source: 1970 numbers are from Globalis International Website at http://www.globalis.com/ and 2006 numbers are from the CIA Web site at https://www.cia.gov/library/publications/the-world-factbook/index.html

is not just a function of how many young people there are in a population. There must be motivation, rationalization, and opportunity for violence. Motivation comes from rising expectations—growing welfare and higher levels of prosperity (signified by high and/or rising levels of GDP or GDP per capita). Rationalization comes from festering grievances whether of a religious or ethnic nature. The opportunity to act out comes from a breakdown in the rule of law. Theory for why a bust that follows a bulge does not yield less violence is the burden and responsibility of the very young (0–14 year old) on those in the 15–24 year old category. With a surging baby boom generation, the current cohort of youth is forced to engage in the constructive and socially acceptable behavior of not only looking out for itself but caring for the generation that comes after it.

Thus, empirical results do not stand by themselves. They require theory to make sense of them. In the rest of this chapter, a theory of violent events is sketched out. What drives these events forward? The starting point is a *population's composition*—the proportion of young males plus such factors as lack of employment and opportunity in economically advancing societies where there is breakdown in authority, a high level of lawlessness, and absence of state control.

The next set of factors center on the *motivation* to commit lethal acts. Lethal events occur in fairly clearly defined waves around particular themes that spread from country to country and region to region. These themes differ from one historical period to another. Today, the theme that has gained prominence is religion. In history, religion often has provided a rationale for violence, with another theme that has gained prominence being victimization.

Thus, theory starts with objective social and political conditions and moves to the ideas surrounding the conditions. These factors—a population's composition and motivation—cannot fully explain what happens, however, for they do not delve into the momentum of lethal acts, the dynamic by which one violent deed leads to another in vicious cycles. So next in theory come the *lethal actions themselves*. Their commission has significance in that they change the rules of the game. They create a momentum of their own. The deeds speak for themselves and constitute a powerful way for those who carry them out to communicate, if murder and mayhem can be accepted as a way of communication. The deeds rearrange reality, a rearrangement that the groups that carry out the events consider to be in their interests. Thus, groups that carry out violence have almost always shown themselves to be addicted to the deed—their motto is to act first and talk second. Action originates in the heroic, instinctual deed, which scuttles the need for careful thinking or plotting. This romantic notion is behind some of the most lethal acts committed by disaffected youth. For the young person such deeds have a fatal attraction. There is a contagious effect as violent acts are spontaneously imitated by amateurs inspired by the fearlessness of earlier perpetrators. Nowadays, Internet amateurs who are inspired by others to engage in lethal activities obtain information and easy access to know-how concerning bombs and weaponry and find it relatively easy to plot by themselves and carry out their activities in a relatively unsupervised fashion. The replication of other's deeds is hard to restrain because what the copy cats do is largely decoupled from state sponsorship and known organizations that are watched by police and security services.

Ideological as well as religious justifications then build on these deeds. The audacity of the lethal events yields martyrs for a cause. The martyrs are idealized, worshiped, and inspire additional fervor that leads to enhanced devotion to the cause and a will and desire for additional bloodshed. Even the most callous person cannot murder unless provided with some rationale. Acting in the memory of a fallen comrade is a very powerful reason to kill. Because of the lust for revenge, lethal deeds build on lethal deeds in a spiral of violence that creates a mythology of heroism and sacrifice. However flimsy and fabricated are these justifications, the deeds themselves create passion and enthusiasm for a cause.

A more complex theory also must consider the *opposition* to this cruelty, an opposition that starts with the victims. The relative effectiveness of the opposition is an important factor in how widespread the lethality is going to be and how deep it becomes. Violent events do not go unopposed, but how good are the efforts of opponents likely to be? How effective? Those who perpetrate lethal acts may be defeated, but it is a complex, lengthy, and difficult process. Efforts taken against the perpetrators often fail or do not entirely reach their goals. Not only do they often fail to reach their goals, but they can be counterproductive. Those opposing the perpetrators, for instance, are left with a quandary about the rules by which they should play. They can fall into the rules used by those they oppose. The typical rules of the game that prevail in wars of a more conventional sort have to be thrown aside. The standards applied to the opponents are high and if they slip, the perpetrators win propaganda victories. Strategic and tactical mistakes then exacerbate the violence.[26]

As prevailing rules, dominant logic, and shared practices shift in the direction of greater lethality, it starts to become *taken-for-granted*. High levels of violence, though they continue to be disturbing, start to be considered normal, accepted, and everyday. Once taken-for-granted, the question is how long this high level of lethality, the increase in the incidence and severity of events, will last, and can it ever be stopped—or if not entirely ended, then made less lethal.

To answer this question, it is necessary to examine the organizations, tactics, and leadership of the *movements that commit violent acts*. They do not stand still. They evolve in accord with new circumstances. They adapt, changing from form to form in response to internal pressures and exogenous triggers. This dynamism must be considered. Movements engaged in violence struggle not only against outside foes. In fact, these external battles may be relatively mild in comparison to the battles they have with each other. Factions within lethal movements compete for the right to represent causes they create and hold dear. Factions try to assert their authority against one another. They make claims to power based on the continued boldness of their acts against internal enemies and external foes. The internal battles bring some factions to the forefront, while others fall by the wayside. As these factions struggle for power against each other and against interests that are aligned against them, their tactics evolve. The people who commit violent acts may move from isolated attacks carried out by a few slightly armed individuals to guerilla wars involving well-armed units of troops. By contributing to a situation already in disarray or creating fresh bedlam and chaos, they gain additional notoriety, recognition, and legitimacy. They do not have to win against the conventional armies but simply beat expectations by not being overwhelmed and quickly succumbing. They then seek political and other concessions from established interests to enhance their legitimacy.

Movements dedicated to the commission of violence may take control and dominate entire states and regions, which allows them to create staging grounds to commit further lethal acts. If they actually seize power in some state or region, the violence they heap on their internal enemies may grow. Nonetheless, the hope always arises that these movements will mature. Those who have opposed the violence grow weary. They fervently wish that with the responsibility to govern the lethal movements will mellow; their militancy will recede and prove to be just rhetorical. Once ensconced, insurgent groups will be responsible caretakers for the populations they have subjected. However, this hope mostly has been in vain, dashed many times in history.

Once a spiral of violence has started and lethality has gained momentum, there tend to be no easy, short, or final victories. For neither side are culminations clear-cut, like in World War I or II; nor is there likely to be a rapid cooling of passions or a retreat to a prior equilibrium, when lethality no longer is assumed to be legitimate and high levels of violence no longer seen as normal. Lethal events may peter out only in the long run if the opponents stick it out, some type of stalemate ensues, and mutual exhaustion suppresses both sides' will to fight.

What Businesses Can Do?

For business, the issue of youth bulges, busts, and violence poses unusual challenges. The negative impacts of a potential rise in violent conflict are many. Entry into certain regions of the world will have to be delayed or deferred. Alliances and partnerships will not be sustained, trade not undertaken, marketing and new product development cut back, and the sourcing of raw materials and labor jeopardized. A potential rise in violence can mean higher energy prices which require the shifting of global supply chains and operations. Firms require a semblance of peace, order, and stability to thrive.

What can firms do to respond to the violence? It is not enough that they understand the roots of violent conflict and its likely persistence. It is insufficient for them to just have better early warning systems and better means for avoiding the dangers. Businesses should not be just narrowly focused on the financial aspects of their operations. They can make a difference if they can motivate and guide youth to productive activities. In this way, they may be able to prevent some of the violence that otherwise would occur.

A question, of course, is whether businesses have the required capabilities and experience to take on this task. Many examples do exist, however, of companies that have been at some level engaged in such efforts. For instance, in 2000, Nokia and the International Youth Foundation (IYF) launched a global youth development initiative to strengthen the life skills of young people and prepare them for the future. To date, Nokia has invested US$26 million in 24 countries and directly benefited more than 330,000 young people.

Businesses must help spread a message of confidence and hope rather than despair and pessimism. The combined message of skills, opportunity, and hope is well-displayed in the "bottom of the pyramid" advocacy of such writers as Prahalad and Hart.[27] More experiments of this nature must be tried. The question of why violent conflict has surged in the post–9/11 world, whether it will continue, and what can be done about is as important for businesses as it is for the rest of humanity.

Tools for Creating Scenarios

Scenarios cannot predict where violent conflict will lead. There is no certainty. Nonetheless, creating plausible stories about the future depends on more than guesswork. A number of devices for establishing foresight into what can happen have been reviewed in this chapter. They include looking for patterns, finding drivers, attaching vivid names to possible outcomes, appraising trends, recognizing weak signals and wildcards, dealing with possible irresolution, and considering such motors of change as evolution, life cycles, dialectics, and teleology. To dig deeper this chapter has shown that the scenario writer should rely on the tools of historical analogies ("backcasting"), establishing indicators, using empirical evidence, and creating theory. While this chapter has used many examples to make its points, the real takeaways are these tools that people in organizations can use to exercise foresight. These tools should be applied in an ongoing way to create better scenarios for influencing the future in the light of shifting conditions.

CHAPTER 5

Political and Economic Challenges

Political and economic spheres are the next topics taken up in this book. The connections between them and population and security have to be examined. These different realms cannot be considered in isolation. Each has an impact on the other. The aim of this chapter is to tie together the stories sketched in the last chapter about national security and society with stories about politics and the world economy. Another important realm, the ecosystem, will be treated in the next chapter and the final chapter of the book (the afterword) will examine technology.

Vivid names encapsulate what can happen in these different realms. The vivid names used to describe what can happen in the realm of national security that were introduced in the last chapter are (1) Davos, (2) Pax America, (3) New Caliphate, and (4) Cycle of Fear. The vivid names that capture what can take place in society are (1) Old and Feeble, (2) Young and Militant, and (3) Moving and Seeking.

There are connections between these realms. A major threat to national security is uneven population distribution in the world. The elderly are concentrated in the world's richest and most developed countries, while youth are concentrated in poor and developing nations. Moving and seeking on the part of youth mitigates this imbalance and eases the pressure. The extent to which population movement is smooth and orderly increases the likelihood of a long boom or Davos. The extent to which it is turbulent and chaotic increases the likelihood of a Cycle of Fear.

Davos requires the free movement of people, goods, money, and technology. If instability overtakes the world, the benefits of globalization become more difficult to realize. Thus, the developed nations of the world must make the effort to absorb the young, educate them, and harness their drive, energy, creativity, and ambition. Politics and economics play a major role in determining whether this can happen.

This chapter assigns vivid names to possible developments in politics and economics. The vivid names attached to the political realm are (1) Free to Choose, (2) Well-Regulated, and (3) Special Interests. Those attached to the economic realm are (1) Turmoil and Instability, (2) Progress and Crisis, and (3) Stable but Slower Growth (see table 5.1). This chapter develops what these names represent, filling in more completely what they connote and revealing how these social, political, and economic realms are connected.

The stories about the future that are discussed in this chapter are simply examples of what can be created. Each person in an organization should engage in such an exercise. Select a business problem that is an important concern and attach vivid names to developments in realms that have bearing on the problem. Reflect on how the stories in the different realms

Table 5.1   Industry structure and alternative futures

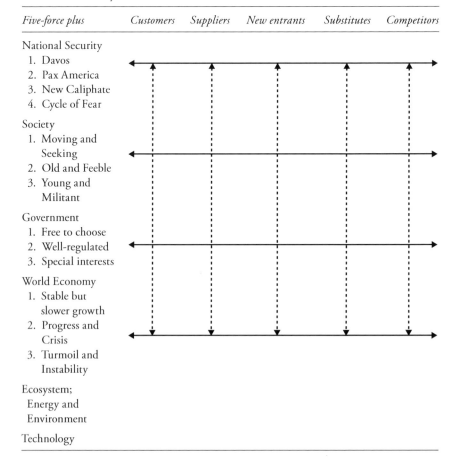

Five-force plus	Customers	Suppliers	New entrants	Substitutes	Competitors
National Security 1. Davos 2. Pax America 3. New Caliphate 4. Cycle of Fear					
Society 1. Moving and Seeking 2. Old and Feeble 3. Young and Militant					
Government 1. Free to choose 2. Well-regulated 3. Special interests					
World Economy 1. Stable but slower growth 2. Progress and Crisis 3. Turmoil and Instability					
Ecosystem; Energy and Environment					
Technology					

are connected and develop what the different stories signify. This chapter provides illustration and guidance on how to do this.

Reasons to Create Alternative Stories

Why create alternative stories about the future? The reasons for doing so must be in the forefront. Two main reasons exist for why people in business should create alternative stories of the future:

To Understand the Impacts on Industry Structure

On the one hand, the purpose is to understand the impact of alternative futures in the security, societal, political, and economic realms on industry structure.

- What effects will there be on customers, suppliers, entrants, substitutes, and competitors (see chapter 3 for additional discussion)? Are there, as a consequence, distinct opportunities and threats that an organization is likely to confront? Are there inflection points it should anticipate? What can it do about them?
  - Should it reposition products and services and change the value proposition for customers? Should it lower prices or add features to its products and services? Should it expand into or withdraw from global markets?
- Do the inflections change the set of opportunities and threats in an industry? Do they make the industry more or less attractive? To what extent does this mean fuller commitment to the industry? To what extent does it mean possible exit from the industry? Should the firm exit the industry, or at least take fallback positions outside it? Are the opportunities greater and the threats less outside or inside the industry?
- To what extent is there potential for creating entirely new industries by means of innovation? How much innovation is possible given the set of technologies, people, business alliances, and customers? How risky would it be?
  - Is there the chance of being a first or early mover? What advantages would this convey? And how sustainable would the advantages be?

Examining how alternative stories of the future in the security, societal, political, and economic realms affect industry structure is a springboard for action, a motivation for repositioning, changing global strategies, recommitting to an industry, altering it, or exiting from it to enter a new one. It is also a motivation for innovating that can lead to a reaffirmation of a company's existing strategies or to change.

To Examine the Potential Outcomes of the Moves a Company Can Make

The second reason for creating alternative stories about the futures in these realms is to examine the potential outcomes of the moves a company is considering making. How well or poorly will a company do if it takes these actions?

- Where will the moves that the company is proposing lead? What are the likely outcomes?
  - To what extent will the moves lead to increased revenue?
  - To what extent will they increase profits?
  - What is their likely impact on a firm's reputation?
  - How will they affect the firm's stock price?
- Can the moves the company is considering be made more robust, given that the future in these realms is uncertain and may evolve in different directions?
  - If outcomes in these realms take a turn for the worse, how much risk does the company face?
  - If they are more positive than expected, is the company well-positioned to achieve greater gain than anticipated?
  - How can the company modify its moves to lower the risk?
  - What can it do to put itself in a enhanced position to benefit should things turn out better than expected?

By examining the moves a company can make against possible future states in these realms its choices about what to do next become clearer. A company can adjust and fine-tune its strategies to different contingencies. The aim is not to accept what can occur, but to work for a better future, while avoiding worst-case possibilities. For example, Amazon has shown foresight by taking steps to deal with the possible decline of the bookselling industry, which it anticipates might occur. It unveiled Kindle, the first handheld book reader in 2007 as an alternative to the traditional book format. Kindle can hold approximately 200 books in a paperback-sized package and display them on pages that appear more like paper than a LCD screen. If the book industry continues to weaken, Amazon has a backup plan in place to help protect it.

A culture of foresight should come to the fore whenever challenges must be confronted, choices made, and the future is uncertain. As opposed to the gut-level approach that Gladwell advocates in his book *Blink*, the method proposed here attempts to structure the decision-making process.[1] Table 5.2 is a hypothetical example that aligns the options a company

Table 5.2 Testing options against future conditions

Future states of the world	Scenario 1 (Romance)	Scenario 2 (Romantic-Comedy)	Scenario 3 (Tragic-Comedy)	Scenario 4 (Tragedy)
Action plans				
1. Pick one	+++++	++	− − −	− − − − −
2. Pick all	+	+	−	−
3. Pick with backups	+++	++	+	− −
4. Delay	− − − −	− −	+	++++

might pursue against scenarios of what can come next. Pluses in the table connote the consensus view within the organization of positive results, while minuses connote the consensus view of negative results. People in the organization should try to determine how much consensus there is and where the disagreement lies. An analysis of this nature should be subject to internal debate and criticism. The debate should not be reserved for the top management team but should involve a broad range of employees who bring to bear different perspectives and points of view.

This is just a start—then comes the hard part—what to do once an understanding of this nature is achieved. Table 5.2 suggests that the company should avoid option four and should be wary of option two. The third option might be the best for it to pursue. The likely gains are greatest and the overall risks the lowest. The main downside is to be found in scenario four, but people in this company can choose differently based on their preferences for risk. If there is greater tolerance for risk, they might pick the first option over the third. Though the risks are greater, the chances of gain also are higher, which is especially true if the future evolves toward the first scenario.

People in the company cannot be certain about how the options they choose *actually* will play out in the light of different future conditions. All conclusions must be considered provisional and be subject to revision as events unfold and additional information becomes available. A high level of vigilance is needed. The company must regularly examine the upside potential and downside risk of various options under different conditions. It should not be stuck with premature conclusions. Preparation for this type of analysis is essential. It should be part of how each person in the company is trained to think. It should be ingrained into the company's culture. Consider more than one option. Do not assume that the world is headed in a single direction. Mull over different possible future states. Reflect on how options play out under different contingencies. Heed the uncertainties and revise plans as needed as the situation in different realms changes and more information becomes available. The company must hedge its bets to assure that backups are available should initial assumptions prove to be wrong.

To do this job well requires that the company have a deep understanding of the many trends and indicators that will affect it. There should be dialogue with people in the front lines of the company to determine what these trends and indicators are and how they should be interpreted. The judgment and opinions of people in the front lines should be respected since they are close to the action and may be able to see what is happening before it takes place.

The variables discussed in the last chapter are a good starting point. People in companies should take note of demographic and social changes, possible changes in population size, age structure, geographic distribution, and ethnic and religious mix. They also should pay attention to income levels, lifestyles, social values, growth and decline in household formation (a reason for the 2007 fall in housing prices), and attitudes toward work, education, consumption, and leisure. These indicators can provide insights about an industry and the strategies a company can pursue as the boxed insert about Amazon illustrates.

Strategic Change at Amazon

Trends in leisure have played a key role in Amazon's evaluation of the bookselling industry. They have affected its decision to become a shopping mart on the Web and facilitator of Web-based transactions and not just a purveyor of books.[2] Much of the reading that people do takes place during their leisure hours, with reading having many substitutes including a variety of types of entertainment. As opposed to reading a book, people can listen to Podcasts. They can go to a movie, the theater, or a concert. They can participate in voluntary activities like serving on the board of a charitable organization. They can be involved in sports—run a marathon, play golf, work out, or be a spectator at a sporting event. They can go to religious services, browse the Internet, or play a video game. They can play a board game, go bowling, or simply watch television. The substitutes to reading are limitless and they just keep growing. Activities from eating in restaurants to yard work to shopping compete with book reading. Besides reading a book, there are many ways to survey the world and gather information.

Amazon, therefore, realized that with its existing products it did not have a lock on its customers. These factors led it to the conclusion that it was likely to be in a better position if it situated itself as a leader in Internet commerce as opposed to just bookselling. In bookselling, the competition was intense, growth was sluggish, profit margins were slim, and the product sold—if a best seller—a low-priced commodity. Barnes and Noble was a powerful and dominant competitor and Borders was not far behind. New entrants in bookselling had great potential—both Web publishers who would be able to get their books directly to readers and independent stores that sold specialty fare. In light of this understanding, Amazon decided that channel innovation in Internet commerce had more potential than product innovation in a well-established and mature industry like bookselling, where growth in sales was slow, power over publishers and authors who supplied the books was weak, and substitutes were many.

Based on this understanding, Amazon changed from being a bookseller to a commerce platform, department store mall, and service provider on the Web. It developed kindle and the commitments it made to Internet commerce software, logistics, and warehousing took into account different contingencies. They provided Amazon with flexible options and the capacity to adjust to changing conditions.

Next up for Amazon was not how well it was going to do not against other booksellers but against search engines and portals like Google and Yahoo. Its moves were beginning to infringe on these companies' space but Amazon had prepared for this inevitability by accumulating logistics and warehousing capabilities that Google and Yahoo did not have.

From Society to Government

The reason to create stories of the future is to understand impacts of social, political, and economic trends on industry structure and examine potential outcomes of the strategic moves a company can take. Start with a concrete problem. People in a company should ask what commitments and investments must they make today to achieve higher levels of performance in the future given the risks. Examining trends in society will allow them to thrash out such questions as: Who are their customers? How many are there? Where will they be located? How much money will their customers have to spend? What will they want? How will they get what they want? How will the company distribute its goods and services?

A company must satisfy its customers in ways that its competitors are not able to do. Gaining a lock on a customer segment is a route to long-term competitive advantage. The social trends that inform the choice of customers do not happen in isolation, but are affected by politics and economics. People's ability and willingness to buy and pay for the goods and services they want and need are impacted by them.

People in a company therefore should be attuned to political and economic indicators. However, the quantitative data to follow political trends are not as easy to come by as the data to follow demographic and social change. To make sense of patterns that might emerge in the political realm, people in companies have to rely more on qualitative interpretations of what they read and hear. They must stay abreast of what influential people are writing and saying as the opinions of pundits, analysts, and experts have significant clout.

There are a number of potential indicators that people in companies can follow. One is *interest group activism*. It is connected to changes in the social realm; it often arises because of changes in lifestyles and values. Also, there is spillover from politically active interests to stakeholder groups that focus more on the firm than on politics. In light of increased stakeholder pressure on firms, firms have had to be active in managing stakeholder relations.

Another key indicator to follow is developments in *the regulatory milieu*. Regulatory laws and institutions govern the relationships between firms and stakeholders. In almost every instance, there is a corresponding government regulatory agency and a set of laws and regulatory requirements that preside over the relations between such key stakeholders as customers, employees, shareholders, and the firm. People in companies must be keenly aware of regulatory institutions and how they can affect the rules of the game, including industry structure, product features, and markets.

An additional indicator that people in companies must take note of is the intense *lobbying* efforts that businesses undertake to protect their interests in the political realm. This lobbying often is countered by that of public interest groups. People in companies should be familiar with the public interest groups, what they stand for, and what causes they are trying to advance. Of course, people in firms also must follow the money. Who is making large campaign contributions, and why? Who therefore has access to leading politicians and influential administrators, and how does this activity translate into power in Congress and in regulatory agencies?

The focus must not be just on U.S. policies. Firms operate globally and people in companies must keep abreast of developments throughout the world. There are many indicators of the *performance of governments* throughout the world of which people in companies should be aware. For example, World Bank researchers have summarized and aggregated indicators from 35 data sources provided by 32 different organizations into these dimensions:[2]

1. *Voice and Accountability*—the ability of citizens to participate in selecting their government, as well as freedom of expression, freedom of association, and a free media.

2. *Political Stability*—the likelihood a government will be destabilized or overthrown by unconstitutional or violent means, politically motivated violence, and terrorism.
3. *Government Effectiveness*—the quality of public services, the civil service and its degree of its independence from political pressures, and the credibility of the government's commitment to such policies.
4. *Regulatory Quality*—the ability of the government to formulate and implement sound policies and regulations that permit and promote private sector development.
5. *Rule of Law*—the extent to which people have confidence in and abide by the rules of society, in particular the quality of contract enforcement, property rights, the police, and the courts, as well as the likelihood of crime and violence.

A list of a number of other important political economic and social indicators can be found in Appendix B.

People in companies also must be critical of the conventional wisdom. Are patterns stipulated by experts likely to move in predicted directions? Connections among realms—the social, political, and economic—need to be explored because they reveal surprises. For instance, the conventional wisdom about population growth by the year 2050 is that convergence will take place in the fertility rates in developed and developing nations. The prediction that experts therefore make is that there will be fewer than 9 billion people in the world, down from prior estimates of more than 10 billion people, but government actions may not be supportive of this outcome.[3] For convergence in the world's population to happen, fertility in more developed countries has to rise, however, if the tide of immigration to the United States and Europe slows because of political opposition, will this happen? Fertility in less developed countries has to fall. However, what if many of these societies continue to be ruled by fundamentalist regimes? If the politics in these societies does not change, a bet on convergence would be wrong.[4] Another element in the thesis about convergence is that life expectancy will grow everywhere, including less developed countries, but this fails to seriously consider the possibility of wars, famines, and plagues brought about or exacerbated by government incompetence. In the United States and Europe, demand for new medical products and services is expected to increase but if people cannot afford them because government has not effectively contained the costs of medical care then companies will not benefit.

In sum, the number of people living in the year 2050, where they will live, their age distribution, what they want, and what they can afford to buy also depends on government actions. The political intrudes upon the social leading to changes in population composition and characteristics. Conventional wisdom will not hold if there is governmental insufficiency and breakdown.

The Centrality of Government

What takes place in the social realm, so critical to the success of business, is heavily dependent on what takes place in government. Positive social scenarios depend on governments being able to promote economic and social development and welfare. Governments have to be able to collect taxes and raise revenues and effectively run programs that create social solidarity and order and promote citizen welfare.[5] The programs governments must run effectively range from medical clinics and institutions for the elderly to defense, police, courts, and schools. The burden on governments is great and the consequences of failure high.

Today, governments least able to deal with sharp increases in population are the ones that have to deal most with this problem.[6] Population is rising most rapidly in such places as the Palestinian Territory (217 percent), Niger (205 percent), Yemen (168 percent), Angola (162 percent), Congo (161 percent), and Uganda (133 percent). In some of these countries, effective governments do not exist. How will these governments cope? Will they be able to meet the nutrition needs of their people, let alone their people's higher order needs for health, and welfare?

Less developed countries must have outlets for young people who might otherwise turn to violence.[7] More developed countries must accept immigrants from less developed countries.[8] However, if the migrants are impoverished, they strain social security, welfare, and educational systems. China faces this issue as well as it is in the process of absorbing more than 100 million people from rural areas into its cities. Large-scale population movement, whether from country to country or from rural to urban areas, makes it incumbent on governments to create the conditions where disparate people can coexist. Governments have to integrate the people who move from place to place. They must provide them with opportunities to meaningfully participate and contribute. How they cope is critical. Can governments peacefully and productively absorb migrants? Can they absorb them with a minimum of xenophobic reaction and growing acceptance of cultural diversity?[10]

To sustain prosperity, governments must assist in the absorption of immigrants, meet the needs of elderly, and fight youthful militancy, but are they up to these tasks? Throughout the world, governments are showing signs of weakness and fragility. Even developed nations have seen a loss of confidence in governments symbolized by the low-approval ratings of rulers in such nations as the United States, the United Kingdom, France, and Israel. In less developed nations, the problems are even greater—there is state failure and collapse in such places as Somalia, Lebanon, Liberia, Palestine, and Afghanistan.[11] In Iraq, as is well known, conditions have been near to anarchy, though they have been improving. Governments the world over are increasingly stressed.[12] The violence, disease, refugees, international crime, and drug trafficking that thrive in the world's weak and failing states have had spillover effects on other nations.

The nation-state as a governance system in the world is relatively recent. Sentiment in its favor reached its apex after World War II and the creation of the United Nations. The original 50 states that composed the United Nations have since grown into more than 190 states. This system of governance has largely taken over from the empires—British, Austro-Hungarian, Russian, Turkish, and French—that carved up much of the world in the nineteenth century. In that century, elements that form modern day Germany and Italy were small republics, tiny kingdoms, vassals of empires, principalities, or extended city states.[13] The conflict between empire and nation-state was an important backdrop to World Wars I and II. Out of the ruins of these wars, many nations achieved independence and new states were formed. Countless people's aspirations center on having a nation-state of their own but not all people have been satisfied, such as Kurds and Armenians. Unsatisfied longing for a nation-state creates considerable tension.

No one now doubts the centrality of the nation-state system that exists in the world, but as recently 100 years ago when it was still on the rise its legitimacy was far from universally accepted. A key aspect of this legitimacy is that states are supposed to be the sole legal means of force in domains they govern. Citizens, in fable if not fact, cede their right of self-preservation and self-protection to the state in exchange for the benefits of peace that the state can impose.[14] However, rather than creating peace, states often subject their citizens to war. They do not provide the protection which justifies their existence. The stability and order they promise come at the expense of persecution and tyranny.

The state's rise often is accompanied by the violence and civil wars it is supposed to suppress. Consider the United States where the Civil War was the most violent event in the nation's history, leading to more casualties than any other conflict in which the country has been engaged. Opposition to states comes about because they have not adequately delivered on their promise to create peace and stability. This opposition is both internal and external, with many competing institutions in conflict with the nation-state. Within nation-states, there are irredentist movements such as the Basque and Quebecois, which can cause states to collapse. Witness what happened to Yugoslavia. Outside the state, many institutions compete with it. Non-state and super-state actors abound. They range from al Qaeda to large multinational corporations. They include nongovernment institutions (NGOs) such as Greenpeace and the World Wildlife Found and supra-government organizations such as the Untied Nations, the World Bank, and the World Trade Organization. The global media giants such as Reuters, CNN, the BBC, SkyNews, and al Jazeera may be headquartered in a particular country but their allegiances are transnational in nature. People in organizations must keep track of these non-state actors. If states the world over are not up to checking violence and achieving peace and security, then the consequences for international commerce are great. States may not be the undisputed force in the world they were once thought to be. The state system has made the world more peaceful, but not without struggles that continue to this day.

With the growing legitimacy of states after World War II, there have been fewer and less violent wars than in the pre-War period. Since the end of World War II, the entire world has not been engulfed in a single all-encompassing conflict. An imperfect peace of sorts has existed that has stimulated commerce, but will the imperfect peace continue? Wedged between major realms—social, economic, and international security, governments have enormous responsibility for peace and prosperity and the welfare of society.

Government Scenarios

Three scenarios of the different directions in which the governments can go are sketched here—"Free to Choose," "Well-Regulated," and "Special Interests."[15] These three scenarios hinge on the connection between government and commerce. As is the case with all scenarios, these ideal types conceal great complexity. Actual state behavior may not easily fit the ideal types. Indeed the future may reveal unpleasant surprises, regression to authoritarian models and state planning that were once believed impossible after the fall of the Soviet Union.[16]

Free to Choose

The free to choose scenario is associated with classic liberal ideology which regards individual freedom as the highest value worthy of governmental protection.[17] It takes as its inspiration the Declaration of Independence that proclaims:

> All men are created equal and are endowed by the Creator with unalien-
> able rights among these being Life, Liberty, & the Pursuit of Happiness.
> To secure these rights, governments are instituted deriving their power
> from consent of Governed.

Because the market values and promotes individual freedom, the classic liberal places trust in the market. In the market, people barter and
exchange with one another. The offer to exchange valuable goods and
services does not depend on who is offering the goods or services, so long
as what is being offered is of high quality or low in price or has other desirable features. People barter and exchange not because of social status, but
because of self-interest.

The free-to-choose scenario accepts the need for government regulation
in some areas, however. In particular, there is the need for government to
preserve *civil order*, by means of having a police force for internal security
and armies for external defense. As well, the government has a role to play
as a *rule-maker and umpire*. When individuals have disputes, someone
has to resolve them. A judicial system, therefore, is needed. Governments
serve as arbiter when rights conflict. The government also has a responsibility to maintain the monetary system as part of the responsibility to be
a rule-maker and umpire, but it is unclear if it should be using monetary
policies for the purposes of stabilizing economic activity (see the discussion that comes later in this chapter).

The free-to-choose scenario acknowledges a proper regulatory role of
government in correcting or compensating for free market shortcomings.
There is a need for government antitrust regulation to counterbalance the
tendency of market systems toward monopoly. Another type of market
defect that warrants governmental action is *neighborhood effects*, the classic
example being pollution. The market is inefficient in dealing with external costs. The premise of a free market is that when two people voluntarily
make a deal, they both benefit. If society gives everyone the right to make
deals, society as a whole will benefit. Society becomes richer from the
aggregation of the many mutually beneficial deals that have been made.
However, in some instances in consummating a mutually beneficial deal,
there are negative or costly by-products to the transaction not accounted
for in the equation.[18] Government must correct for these negative or costly
by-products.

The market also presupposes that people are rational and capable of
caring for themselves. However, there is a need to acknowledges that

children, the mentally incompetent, and other vulnerable populations may not be capable of taking care of themselves. They lack the capacity for informed and voluntary decision making which is needed for proper participation in a free market. For this reason, governmental involvement is warranted to protect these groups.

Well-Regulated

The well-regulated scenario draws on contemporary liberal ideology. It also favors decentralized decision making and individual choice by consumers in the marketplace, but with more exceptions than classic liberals.[19] Rather than being inspired by the Declaration of Independence, this school of thought looks to the U.S. Constitution which proclaims that the purpose of the state is collectivist in nature. It is

> to form a more perfect Union, establish Justice, insure domestic Tranquility, provide for common defense, promote the general Welfare, and secure Blessings of Liberty to ourselves and our Posterity.

The justifications for governmental involvement stem from many of the same market imperfections identified in the free-to-choose scenario, including:

Uncompetitive factor and product markets: There must be no obstacles to free entry and full market knowledge. There has to be no barriers to the free exertion of market power on the part of producers and consumers. Government is needed to assure competition and to expand the knowledge of producers and consumers. Thus, it is not only appropriate for government to endeavor to prevent monopoly, but it is also appropriate for it to require that warning labels be attached to cigarettes and other products if citizens otherwise would not be aware of the full risks.

Public goods: It is also proper for the government to provide such public goods as national defense, education, roads and canals, and public space. The market alone would not provide these goods in adequate quantity. Why? Because, while use and enjoyment is shared by all, the costs of such goods would be borne by specific groups of providers.

The well-regulated approach differs from the free-to-choose approach because of inclusion of the following reasons for governmental activity:

Justice and equality: The free market system does not distribute equally. Oftentimes, it distributes unfairly as well. Thus, the state has a role in adjusting in these inequities by means of progressive tax structures, targeted tax policies, and similar devices.

Employment, price stability, and economic growth: The market system may not guarantee a high level of employment, price stability, and a socially desired rate of growth without government intervention. To correct for instability in the business cycle, the government should use a number of fiscal and monetary remedies. (These will be discussed later in the chapter.)

Though committed to a larger scope for government, the well-regulated approach acknowledges that governments, no less than private markets, can err and be inefficient in attempting to remedy market defects.

Special Interests

Both the free-to-choose and well-regulated scenarios recognize that government failures are possible. A main reason for these failures is special interest politics. Special interest groups consist of small numbers of people who are benefited very positively or negatively by public policies. They feel strongly because their interests are so much at stake. Because their interests are so much at stake, they tend to be very well-organized. The incentive for them to organize is high because what they can gain or lose is so great. Since their numbers tend to be small, their cost of organizing tends to be low.

Under this scenario, special interests dominate against poorly organized and diffused majority interests. Collectively, the impact of public policies on the majority may be greater than the impact on special interests, but the incentive for individuals in the majority to organize and make their voice felt is weaker. Each member of the majority is affected but only slightly by a proposed change in public policies. Each member of the majority may lose or gain $10, for instance, while the special interests may have many millions of dollars at stake. But when all the 10 dollars of the majority are summed up they add up to billions of dollars.

The problem is how to organize the disparate individuals in the majority. For a few dollars, is it worthwhile for these individuals to make the effort to be informed and to organize and to make their viewpoints felt among politicians and administrators? The costs of mobilizing individuals in the majority tend to be high which inhibits its activities and allows special interests to capture governments.[20]

Telecoms—An Example of Special Interests

Telecom public policy is an example of the influence of special interests. Free entry into this industry was first promoted in the Clinton administration by the passage of the 1996 Telecom Act, a law meant to spread the benefits of new telecommunications technologies. This intent ultimately was frustrated and defeated by the old Regional Bell Operating Companies (RBOCs). They fought back by means of a combination of lobbying and being in a strategic position in the industry value chain. Inasmuch as the RBOCs controlled final access to homes and business, they slowed down the introduction of high speed cable into the United States. In so doing they destroyed the business models of many Internet start-ups that depended on faster diffusion of high speed hook-ups.

The lobbying of the RBOCs, which was meant to preserve their monopoly-like hold on the delivery of telephone and telephone-like services, also hurt equipment suppliers like Lucent, Nortel, and Corning that bet on more rapid development of fiber-optic cable networks and systems. The equipment suppliers did not take into account the power of special interests and hedge their bets. They went out on a limb hoping that the intent of the Telecom Act would be realized.

The RBOCs did not have dominant influence nationally during the Clinton administration when the Telecom Act was passed. Rather they retained a dominant position at the state commissions' level. State commissions regulated the rates that the RBOCs charged both long distance operators like AT&T, MCI, and WorldCom and new entrants like Williams, McLeod, and Level3 which wished to access homes and businesses. By keeping these rates high and placing restrictions on it, the RBOCs effectively kept out long distance carriers and other new entrants. They acted in opposition to the spirit of the 1996 Telecom Act. Ultimately, almost all long distance carriers and new entrants failed and the RBOCs bought them at huge discounts. The most highly publicized example was AT&T's near bankruptcy and its acquisition by SBC, which then renamed itself the new AT&T.

On many fronts the government failed to control this special interest. It was an ineffective regulator of the analysts and investment banks that covered new entrants to the telecommunications business like WorldCom. Investment banks benefited from the series of mergers and acquisitions in which WorldCom and other new entrants engaged. Bernie Ebbers, CEO of WorldCom, made the statement that "Internet traffic was doubling every 100 days." This statement was false but nevertheless widely believed. His deception was not contradicted by government regulators. It had repercussions in the real economy, hurting equipment suppliers like Corning, which accepted the untruth and divested almost all its other businesses. Corning gambled nearly everything on telecom growth. It projected huge increases in carrier spending and telecom sales based on projections it made about the new environment of telecomm regulation that never came into being. Corning did not hedge its bets. To its detriment, it had a singular view of the future.

During the George W. Bush administration, the RBOCs gained unprecedented power. The president appointed Michael Powell as commissioner of the Federal Communications Commission (FCC). Powell supported the RBOC' special interest viewpoint that ample competition existed in the system, provided by such substitute technologies as Cable (Comcast and Time Warner), wireless (Cingular), and satellite (Echostar).[21] He therefore let the RBOCs destroy and gobble up new entrants and long distance carriers with whom they competed.

This caving into special interests had a large role to play; it did not just hurt suppliers to the industry like Corning but more broadly it stifled high tech prospects and contributed to the fading of the high tech boom of the 1990s. All suppliers to the industry, companies like Nortel and Alcatel as well as Corning, faced a capacity glut and took large losses. The broadband crisis meant that the anticipated information superhighway failed to materialize as quickly and in the form expected. Compared to other nations like Korea and Finland, broadband introduction in the United States was a sluggish and time-consuming process. The RBOCs, as representatives of their particular point of view, did not want to see rapid interconnection to homes of competing technologies. As late as 2002, the United States could boast only 2.7 percent installed capacity of high speed Internet access, which caused many Internet business plans to go up in smoke. The startups had no way to make money if most people had old-fashioned dial-up connections.

Is Monsanto discussed in the boxed insert that follows another instance of special interest politics slowing down technological progress?

Monsanto's Quest

Demand for grains and other food was expected to increase by 40 percent by the year 2020.[22] Since 1953, when James Watson and Frances Crick discovered the structure of the DNA that carries the information cells needed to build proteins, scientists had generated detailed maps of the genes of hundreds of organisms and the data-analyzing capabilities to understand and use them. In the late 1990s, Monsanto made a commitment to use this technology to bring genetically modified foods to the market. Technologies for genetically modified foods offered dramatic promise for meeting some of the twenty-first century's greatest challenges, but like all new technologies, they posed risks on which special interests seized to slow their development.

In 1995, when Robert Shapiro became CEO of Monsanto he decided to transform Monsanto into a biotechnology powerhouse. The path Shapiro set for the company was to remake itself as a "life sciences" enterprise, dedicated to improving the environment and human health by creating new food, drug, and combined food-drug (neutracitical) products. Monsanto left businesses with which it had long been associated like Nutrasweet and entered new businesses like genomics and seeds. From 1994 to 1997, the firm's stock nearly tripled in value.

Crop yield growth had started to decline in the world in the 1980s. Increasingly it was thought that genetic engineering would be needed to improve yields, but arguments about the importance of genetically modified crops for feeding the world's poor did not make a dent everywhere. Genetically modified crops had the potential to address such issues as hunger and disease, but in Europe people were neither hungry nor sick. Rather, they were fearful of new technologies that potentially tampered with the food supply. The Europeans wanted their produce fresh, but genes that extended ripening times meant little in developed countries where refrigeration was common and inexpensive and good roads to get produce to the market were everywhere. On the other hand, in developing countries almost 40 percent of the fruit and vegetables rotted in fields and never got to market. Genetically modified crops were a trade and diplomatic issue in Europe as the Europeans sought protection for domestic agriculture. The media in Europe therefore portrayed companies like Monsanto as evil manipulators of nature who were creating grotesque "frankenfoods." Because of European opposition, many companies exited the field of genetically modified food. The Swiss pharmaceutical company, Novartis, and the British pharmaceutical, AstraZeneca, for instance, combined their agricultural divisions and sold them. Under pressure, Novartis also stopped using genetically modified soy and corn in its Gerber baby food. In 1999, other large European companies—Unilever, Nestle, and Cadbury—announced they would no longer use genetically modified products. Deutsche Bank told its clients not to invest in companies that were involved in this industry. Had this special interest opposition to genetically modified food gone too far? In 2002, six African nations affected by drought refused U.S. food aid because the food had been genetically modified to resist pests.

Macroeconomic Scenarios

Governments have significant impacts on whether investments businesses make today will pay off in the future. The impacts extend from micro-issues facing leading sectors of the economy such as telecom and genetically modified foods to the prospects for the global economy as a whole. So far in this book, the methods which have been relied on to create scenarios are expert opinion (the national security scenarios found in chapter 4), assessment of trends (the social scenarios found in chapter 4), and reliance on political-economic theory (the government scenarios found in this chapter). These means of creating scenarios are powerful ones. With regard to the economy-as-a-whole, a different route has been chosen, with history being advanced as a way to construct scenarios. The macroeconomic scenarios presented here derive mainly from an appraisal of past economic conditions.[23] They are patterned after three periods in U.S. economic history that saw different degrees and levels of prosperity and fluctuations in the business cycle (see table 5.3).

People in companies must take business cycle fluctuations very seriously. They must be attuned to shifts in the growth of gross domestic product (GDP). The macroeconomic scenarios developed in this section are based on these shifts. They are called (1) Turmoil and Instability (1930–1955), (2) Progress and Crisis (1956–1980), and (3) Stable but Slower Growth (1981–2006). In each of these periods, the government played a different part in managing macroeconomic activity. Different economic theories and economists had leading roles in choosing policies government followed.

- The first period incorporates the Great Depression. It saw huge swings in economic activity, 10 years when economic growth was less than 1 percent, 12 years when it was more than 5.5 percent, and 4 years when it was between 1 and 5 percent.
- The second period incorporates the dramatic rise in oil prices in 1973 and 1979. It saw 5 years of economic growth less than 1 percent,

Table 5.3 Three patterns of past economic activity

Economic growth	Low <1%	High >5.5%	Growing stability 1–5%
1. 1930–1955	10	12	4
2. 1956–1980	5	8	13
3. 1981–2006	3	1	22

8 years of growth more than 5.5 percent, and 13 years of growth between 1 and 5 percent.
- The third period was one of relative calm. After a deep recession at the start of the 1980s, the economy enjoyed relative tranquility even after the events of 9/11. Growth tapered off some but cyclical variation slowed down.

To what extent can this latest pattern be sustained? Historical analogies can provide important insights about what will come next. With the current economic meltdown in place, fears are of another Great Depression. Which past will the future most resemble?

Turmoil and Instability (1930–1955)

Dogmas of a self-correcting economy where government should not intervene to manage the business cycle once held sway. At the start of the earliest period under consideration, the belief was that governments neither had the tools nor the capacity to play a role in smoothing this cycle. Governments were at the mercy of the downward movement of the economy during the Great Depression of the 1930s and the boom cycle that followed. Large upward and downward swings were not under government control. In this period, the theories of John Maynard Keynes (1883–1946) were not well-known or accepted. Forged in the midst of the turmoil of the Great Depression, these theories maintained that government deficits could provide a stimulus to aggregate demand and ignite a stagnant economy.[24]

To get an economy moving again when it is in recession, the government relies on deficit spending. It borrows freely and thereby stimulates aggregate demand. As governments in most developed states in the world typically encompass a high percentage of the total economic activity (in the United States approximately 20 percent at the national level), this borrowing injects money into the economy. The effect, indeed, is supposed to be multiplicative as the money injected into the economy moves from hand to hand, for example from wage earner to merchant to wage owner to another merchant. The effect of the government stimulus is magnified, but there is a limit to what government borrowing can do, for it ultimately raises interest rates and the higher interest rates cool an economy. In periods of inflation like those that prevailed in Germany during the 1920s, Keynes argued that government must create a budgetary surplus. It should reduce the size of the outstanding debt, thereby taking money from the economy and slowing down the rate of economic activity.

The means government should use to fight inflation are similar to the means it uses to fight recession. They are just used in the opposite way. To fight inflation, rather than reducing taxes and increasing spending, the government should create a surplus by raising taxes and lowering spending. How the government accomplishes these purposes does not matter. It does not matter if taxes go up or down or spending goes up or down so long as there is a deficit to fight a recession and a surplus to fight inflation. However, democratically elected politicians find it difficult to raise taxes or cut spending to suppress aggregate demand and cool off an overheated economy. They tend to lack the discipline to impose restrictive fiscal policy measures. Their bias is toward expansionary measures.

Built into the system, then, are automatic stabilizers, which accomplish this result regardless of what politicians do. No matter what politicians do entitlement benefits like unemployment compensation rise during a recession and no matter what they do corporate tax collections fall during a recession. The same phenomenon exists when the economy does well. No matter what politicians do entitlement benefits like unemployment fall during good economic times and no matter what they do corporate tax collections rise during good economic times. After the recession abates, the government can work its way out of the debt it has accumulated as entitlement benefits like unemployment fall and corporate tax collections rise.

During the Great Depression of the 1930s, governments did not understand these effects. Indeed, they acted against them, and did so foolishly. World War II forced the government to abandon this policy—there was no choice but to run a very large deficit—and as government did the economy surged and regained momentum. Each subsequent recession in United States has seen automatic stabilizers kick in to even out the flow of economic activity.

Progress and Crisis (1956–1980)

An early 1960s tax cut by the Kennedy administration, initiated by Walter Heller, President Kennedy's chief economist, produced a stimulus that helped to sustain economic growth in the 1960s. However, in the 1970s the biggest crisis the economy faced since the Great Depression took place, and it was very different than the Great Depression. The economy of the 1970s was overheated not depressed. The pre-eminent problem was inflation, not stagnation.

As well as GDP, inflation and unemployment are indicators that people in business must carefully follow. The inflation of the 1970s had a number of roots. One of them was spending on Great Society Programs and the Vietnam War. Another reason for the inflation was a weakening of the U.S. trade position. For the first time, the United States became a net importer of foreign oil. The postwar Bretton Woods agreement, in which nearly every currency in the world was pegged to the dollar, no longer could be upheld. It collapsed and the dollar was floated against other currencies. The dollar's value declined, which meant that Americans had to pay more for the foreign goods they imported. At the same time, oil-producing states organized to establish the Organization of Petroleum Exporting Countries (OPEC). Paid in petro-dollars, whose value declined along with that of the dollar, the OPEC nations seized on the opportunity of the 1973 Yom Kippur War to restrict the flow of oil, which had the effect of quadrupling oil prices almost over night.

This supply side shock to the economy was a major blow, bringing about unexpected inflation as so much of the economy was tied to oil prices.[25] A second supply side shock took place at the end of the 1970s as a result of the Iranian revolution and the Iran-Iraq War that followed. During the 1970s, inflation combined with high levels of unemployment to bring about a rise in the so-called "misery index." That is, a high level of inflation and unemployment plagued the economy throughout this period. The "misery index" was something that people in businesses started to carefully watch. Under these conditions, businesses were reluctant to invest, a reluctance that suppressed economic activity.

The experience of the 1970s, when a high level of inflation combined with a high level of unemployment, caught many economists by surprise. Many economists in the Keynesian tradition considered there to be a trade-off between unemployment and inflation. The basic economic problem had been solved by Keynes. It was just a matter of making this trade-off. What was less tolerable more inflation or unemployment? Governments had the power to balance this relationship according to their preferences. Liberal regimes would accept more inflation to keep unemployment in check. Conservative regimes would do the opposite.

Nobel-Prize winning economist, Milton Friedman, had been critical of this premise for a long time. He argued that high levels of inflation and high levels of unemployment could coexist. He believed that government policymakers could not so easily balance the two. His argument was that a fiscal policy stimulus could not be timed correctly. Rather than smooth the business cycle, its tendency would be to make economic activity more erratic. It would yield a more erratic business cycle because of the lag between *recognizing* that a recession might ensue, *introducing a fiscal stimulus* by means of a tax cut or increased budget spending, and the *actual impacts* of the stimulus on the economy. A fiscal stimulus must be introduced by Congress and the president working in concert. The likelihood of delay, therefore, is great. Rather than stabilizing the business cycle, Keynesian remedies would destabilize it, according to Friedman. When the Keynesian remedy was felt the economy already would have recovered and there would be too much stimulation.

Paul Volcker, head of the Federal Reserve in the late 1970s and early 1980s, used Friedman-like insights to defeat 1970s inflation. It remains unclear how intentional the actions he took were and the extent to which they were coordinated with the Reagan administration (Volcker had been appointed by President Carter) but they did work. Volcker relied on restrictive monetary policies, ones that were extremely tight, not fiscal policies, to tackle the inflation. The Federal Reserve is more independent of politics than Congress or the White House. It does not have to wait for either before it acts. The upshot was the recession of 1980–1982 which then took place. It was one of the deepest and longest in U.S. history. At the same time, President Reagan's supporters created a whole new economic doctrine, supply side theory, to justify a kind of Keynesian stimulus. Budget deficits were produced in two ways. There was a run up in defense spending to have a stronger posture with regard to the Soviet Union and lower-marginal tax rates for the wealthy, whom, according to supply side theory, would be more inclined to invest than to save or engage in leisure behavior.

Stable but Slower Growth (1981–2006)

A new period of stable, but slower economic growth then came into being. After the cold war ended in 1989, globalization gave an additional boost to the world economy. The scope of economic activity expanded worldwide without restrictions coming from super-power politics. Among economists, a consensus began to emerge about the limits of fiscal and monetary policies. What they could do was fine-tune an economy in disarray in the short run, but not much more. They could not raise overall production potential. The consensus that economists were starting to reach was that:

- Markets do not perfectly self-correct, but fiscal and monetary policies, because of issues like recognition and timing, also are not perfect. Thus, they are not able to perfectly correct business cycle fluctuations.
- An economy's maximum sustainable output is determined by its resources, technology, productivity, and the structure of its institutions, not by macroeconomic policies. The best formula for steady

growth is to keep a grip on inflation, lower taxes, and encourage
investment.

- Fiscal and monetary policies only modulate business cycles in the
  short run. To grow GDP in the long run, it is necessary to invest in
  productivity, physical capital, and human capital, skills, education,
  and technology.

Given this consensus among economists, what challenges remained?
They emanate from trade imbalances and currency fluctuations which
took on increasing importance after the Soviet Union fell. Indicators to
scrutinize carefully are trade deficits, foreign debt, and the value of the
dollar, as the dollar became unstable and weakened. Besides GDP, inflation, and unemployment, these are critical indicators people in the business community must examine.

The United States has had *a growing trade deficit* because though U.S.
merchandise exports increased rapidly after the fall of the Soviet Union,
they did not rise as rapidly as imports. Negative trade flows were primarily a result of U.S. consumers buying more autos, electronic goods, and
oil than the United States sold abroad. With regard to capital goods, U.S.
trade flows were more in balance. A rising U.S. trade deficit is not necessarily negative. The balance of payments has to even out. Current-account
transactions must equal capital-account transactions.[26] As long as the
U.S. economy offered attractive investment opportunities and generated
a large inflow of capital, a merchandise trade deficit is sustainable.

A problem is that United States *global debt* is held by relatively few
countries. What if they turn against the United States? The countries
that mainly bankroll the U.S. economy include China, Japan, Russia,
Taiwan, Kuwait, India, Brazil, Algeria, South Korea, Libya, Norway,
and Singapore.[27] For the most part, these nations are not enemies of the
United States. They also have not been engines of their own growth.
Rather they have provided U.S. consumers with money that U.S. consumers use to buy goods and services they produce. This bargain has been
how the world economy has functioned after the fall of the Soviet Union.
In particular, Asian production is heavily dependent on U.S. demand and
U.S. demand depends on Asian production to satisfy it. Asia, in effect,
is the world's workshop and the United States, its shopping center. The
Asian economies grow rapidly and U.S. consumers are by and large better
off. They have more goods to choose from, most of them offered at lower
prices than otherwise would be the case.

The negative consequences of this arrangement should be a weakening
in *the value of the dollar* in comparison to Asian currencies. If the dollar

declines, U.S. goods should become cheaper in world markets and Asian goods more expensive. Asian currencies should grow in value in comparison to the dollar, making it easier for U.S. businesses to export. However, governments in Asia have kept buying U.S. assets to avert appreciation of their currencies and prevent a slow down in their economic growth rates. Rather than invest in their own economies, they have supported U.S. consumption, stimulating demand in the United States, as opposed to demand in their own countries.

A key question has been how stable this arrangement is. Can it continue without major disruption? With sharp dollar depreciation, foreigners paid back in low-valued U.S. dollars will suffer large financial losses. Because of these losses they will demand higher interest rates to keep them invested in the United States. The Federal Reserve will be forced to hike United States' interest rates, and with these higher interest rates, the United States might fall into serious and prolonged recession, which will make the Asian producing nations poorer as well.

Intersecting Stories

Different stories in different realms—social, political, and economic—therefore intersect. People in business must examine these intersections—that is, how developments in one realm affect developments in another and how these developments affect their companies are grist for scenario writers' mill.

The world economy of the twenty-first century has been one of heightened interdependence. Consider the effects of global security on the economy after 9/11. After these horrific attacks, a drop off took place in consumer spending. Uncertainty and risk especially impacted such sectors as tourism, autos, and the airlines. A slowdown in business investment occurred, with GDP declining by an estimated 1 percent per year compared to what it otherwise would have been between 2001 and 2003. The relatively quick recovery that took place was built on government actions—loose monetary policies, tax cuts, increased military spending in the United States, and foreign investments, primarily from Asia, in the United States. After 9/11, all feet were on the accelerator. Policymakers used the tools they had at their disposal to prevent a rapid and severe decline. U.S. consumer spending was augmented by Bush tax cuts and by excess housing wealth, largely created by the Federal Reserve's low-interest rate policies. The fiscal deficit grew because of tax cuts and spending for the war in Iraq which brought about a greater need to sell U.S. assets, especially Treasury bonds, to pay for the deficit.

All of this worked pretty well for a while, but then a sense of gloom set in when the U.S. economy was punctured by a rupture in the housing market that spilled over into a worldwide banking and investment crisis. Energy prices temporarily soared as did the prices of commodities such as food. Unemployment and inflation rose and the stock market went into a tailspin. The over-stimulated post–9/11 economy was brought to its knees. The number of people forming new households was declined as baby boomers aged, which contributed to a housing slump that hacked away at household wealth and access to credit.[28] People in the financial system who assumed that housing prices would rise indefinitely were proven wrong. Businesses faltered and companies cut payrolls, taking huge amounts of purchasing power out of the economy. As always in tough economic times, African Americans and the young suffered disproportionately from job loss, but surprisingly a high percentage of the jobs lost were among men in the professional and business classes. Average wages did not kept up with skyrocketing energy and food prices.

How did the U.S. government respond? The Federal Reserve cut interest rates to encourage investment and spur economic activity and President Bush proposed a Keynesian stimulus that Congress passed. These stimuli were meant to encourage spending and generate jobs, but they were not sufficient as it took time for the money put into the economy to make its way through the system. The money never completely got there. A high percentage of the money was used by consumers to augment savings or pay off debt. A high percentage was used by banks to maintain their solvency. Money also leaked out of the country in the form of foreign purchases, helping to prop up foreign economies.

Central banks were between a rock and hard place. They could not raise interest rates to choke-off inflation from high energy prices and could not lower interest rates because of the drop-off in growth. Developing countries proved to be as vulnerable as developed nations. They too had to deal with inflation while trying to maintain economic growth. Inflation rates in Russia, China, and India soared and the central banks of these nations had the same problem. Monetary policy had reached its limits in terms of what it could do to stabilize the situation. As unemployment increased, inflation fell off and the economy slowed. In the United States an election campaign raged. Candidate McCain urged keeping taxes low, while candidate Obama held that tax breaks to big corporations and the wealthy should be eliminated. The Democrats in Congress wanted to extend unemployment insurance, while the White House maintained that benefits should not be extended because unemployment was relatively low by historical standards.

The Train Wreck

The bottom fell with a further collapse in the world's major financial institutions. A train wreck had taken place and there was a need to count casualties. Many people were being laid off and others would find it hard to keep their jobs, which would lower spending and stifle economic activity even more. Pessimism and uncertainty prevented a pickup in consumption. Maybe the belt tightening would help with productivity as individuals and corporations would learn to save and get by with less. Investment bank after investment bank failed. The U.S. government had to intervene in an unprecedented manner to inject solvency into the system. A $700 billion package to prop up the ailing banking system was proposed and passed by Congress. Meanwhile, additional bank failures, mortgages with deteriorating values, and scandals strangled the system. Governments throughout the world had no choice but to take steps that in effect nationalized aspects of banking. In the long run, it was hard to imagine seeing the Dow Jones Industrial Average as high as it had been. The typical investor was likely to be a permanent loser.

The best way to approach the future was to consider multiple possibilities and hedge through diversification, but this was complicated and put a great strain on individuals and institutions; people are reluctant to invest when fear outweighs greed. No safe havens exist; the municipal bond market, often thought of as a safe haven, also can collapse. There probably will be money to be made from the uncertainty but where and how are unclear. To go back and say that a train wreck had not happened was not possible. Governments had to flood the system with money to prevent additional collapse but their response was not without risks. Inflation at some point was possible and along with it currency depreciation. It all depended on how money put in the system was invested.

The incentives governments provided had to be sound, but governments probably were not up to the task of doing a good job in resetting incentives as they were overly dominated by special interests. Unfortunately, large parts of the economy were coming under government control. The United States and other bastions of capitalism were starting to look like China with a government dominated banking system and part-ownership of large and essential industries like autos.

The two illusions had been punctured. All the leverage (the collective Ponzi scheme) created an illusion of excess wealth. To which the real estate bubble added another illusion. No matter how sophisticated the economic and financial advice governments received they did not know exactly what to do. They would have to learn from mistakes made along the way because there would be plenty of them. Were governments, out of desperation and panic, trying to establish the conditions for another great bubble? An interesting question was if all bubbles were necessarily bad. Better a bubble than a global collapse? Was not the bubble of the 1990s better than the bubble of the 2000s in that the tech boom of the 1990s added much to productivity and prosperity while the housing and oil boom of the 2000s did not? Governments were pouring money into system, but would the money find productive uses? At best, under a Democratic agenda in the United States the money would not go into big cars, housing, and consumer debt. It would build human, physical, and technological capital that might boost productivity, but in the short run this proposition might just mean lots of churning to keep things afloat. Even with a more productive global economy, there would be aging populations and security challenges that would eat into the gains, were they to be made. The restoration of prosperity might take a long time indeed.

A generational transition might be underway. Had baby boomers peaked in terms of their life time wealth and assets? When they died, would most of them be poorer than they once had been? Like FDR, Obama might be able to maintain trust in the political system even without a full recovery, if the public was patient. The tide seemed to be permanently shifting against baby boomers. Of course, this vision of a long great slide might be entirely off. Things could turn around. Any vision of the future could be wrong.

Was this train wreck similar to the Great Depression? Though it could become the longest recession since the 1930s, as awful as things were conditions were not nearly as dreadful as they had been during the Great Depression. The steepest drop in output and employment occurred in the Great Depression's fourth year. From 1929 to 1933, GDP plunged close to 50 percent, unemployment peaked at 25 percent, roughly a third of all banks had failed, and stock prices fell by 90 percent. This collapse involved back-to-back severe recessions with the second one coming after the second Roosevelt election in 1936.

Were worse things in store for the economy in the twenty-first century? When would conditions hit bottom? Similarities to the Great Depression were a major expansion of consumer credit and a run up in home buying that preceded the downturn. Also similar were rising income inequalities, but most bank deposits now were insured, and such programs as Social Security, Medicare, and unemployment compensation put a lid on widespread destitution. A rigid gold standard was not in place which kept the money supply tight as was the case in the 1930s, and the governments of the world in the twenty-first century so far had not resorted to massive trade protectionism as they did during the Great Depression.

Nonetheless, it appeared as if a period when economic contractions were shorter and milder than any time in history was ending. Between 1945 and 2001, the average recession lasted just 10 months, while between 1854 and 1945 it had been 21 months. In the twenty-first century, the U.S. government had made a massive effort to fight the downturn. Despite the Federal Reserve allowing short-term interest rates to fall to near-zero and its putting more than $1 trillion of cash into the global economy, its moves had not resulted in a quick turnaround. In the future, the central bank might face the unpleasant dilemma of how to take money out of the system so as to dampen the effects of inflation it had caused.

Social, political, economic, and ecological (see the next chapter) systems are intricately interconnected. Complex and tightly coupled, they are hard to understand and move extremely fast. With consequences this vast and potentially devastating, the stakes are very high. The way this great economic crisis is handled has immense implications. Scenario writers have many ways to spin the future. To what extent will the future consist of a romance, a tragedy, or a comedy—and what kind of comedy will it be—tragic or romantic? How should people in businesses respond to these unparalleled circumstances? Never before has it been so important to ponder the future. For a generation used to stable but slow growth, business cycle fluctuations of this magnitude are hard to imagine. Are there any lessons to be learned from prior economic instability? (see the boxed insert "In and Out of Tune with the Business Cycle").

In and Out of Tune with the Business Cycle

Managing the business cycle can yield firms considerable advantage, but their timing must be perfect. Just being off by a little can mean the difference between outstanding and average results. Whether firms can consistently achieve perfect timing is an open question. It requires not only astute managers aware of the potential for benefits, but also the freedom to put aside other considerations and act primarily on the basis of business cycle opportunities and constraints.

The key for any firm is to have in place a number of scenarios of macroeconomic conditions and to act on the basis of what is known. Firms should fuel external growth via mergers and acquisitions in downturns and organic grow via R&D in upswings.

The best way to illustrate the opportunities and pitfalls of business cycle management is to delve into three examples of firms and their actions and performance during the 1997–1999 boom and 2000–2002 bust. These three firms are Danaher, which designs and manufactures instruments, tools, and components; Federal Mogul, which supplies vehicle parts and systems mainly to the automotive industry; and 3M, a diversified technology firm that operates in many segments including automotive. In the early and mid-1990s Danaher and Federal Mogul were in similar market niches, but by the late 1990s Danaher had moved away from its reliance on the automobile industry through mergers, acquisitions, and divestitures. 3M never has been that heavily dependent on one sector; its customers are spread out. Of the three firms, the best 1997–2002 stock market performance belonged to Danaher. 3M's was right in the middle, and Federal Mogul had a very rough ride.

Using the misery index that adds together unemployment and inflation and subtracts economic growth, the 1997–2002 boom and bust cycle can be divided into *early*, *middle*, and *late* phases. The early year of the boom was 1997 when the economy started to enter into good territory, staying there in 1998, the middle year in this cycle, but beginning to fade by 1999, the last year of this expansion. Similarly, the bust started in 2000, poor economic conditions continued in 2001, and a slight pick up was apparent by 2002. To take advantage of these shifts, management would have to anticipate the turning points, but a company also must have in place a sufficiently flexible culture and structure to move with the kind of alacrity that this situation requires.

With hindsight knowledge about economic conditions is perfect, but the capacity for foresight is difficult to have. In the period under consideration, Danaher made the right choices. The contrast with Federal Mogul is striking, as this company did everything wrong and paid dearly for its mistakes; Danaher understood that it no longer wanted to be a supplier of the automotive industry like Federal Mogul. Rather, it wanted to take advantage of its location near the capitol in Washington, D.C. and develop niche products. Being in the nation's capital provided Danaher with an advantage of keeping on top of regulatory changes.

What Danaher did in response to the economic downturn that Federal Mogul and 3M failed to do was that it masterfully managed the R&D and M&A trade-off. In the up cycle of the late 1990s, Danaher geared up for new product introductions by increasing R&D spending, while in the down cycle of the early twenty-first century it took advantage of bargains and purchased companies that were attractive on the cheap.

The contrast with Federal Mogul could not be greater. Just consider what Federal Mogul bought in the midst of the boom. The company made three massive acquisitions in 1998 all of which market watchers called "hasty." Federal Moguls' complete disregard for the lessons of sound business cycle management was manifest again as the boom died down and the recession set in. Again, Federal Mogul displayed perfectly bad timing. Rather than taking advantage of the reduced prices for companies, Federal Mogul essentially shut down its M&A activity in 2000, only starting it up again with improvement in the economy. In contrast, at the exact moment when its customers were most disinclined to buy, Federal Mogul kept up its R&D spending as a percentage of revenue.

How did 3M manage the timing issue? 3M shows that missing even by a little bit the right timing in business cycle management can mean that potential opportunities have been foregone. An organization's traditions and culture that represent long-standing commitments have to be overturned almost instantaneously to take advantage of the momentary opportunity offered by a business cycle shift. Not all firms have such loose commitments and unformed culture and traditions that they can make the fast alterations that are needed to respond to macroeconomic changes. 3M was one of these firms. Its strategic thrusts were more embedded in its past technological leadership and orientation and unlike a Danaher, dominated by finance people, 3M had a long history of being led and inspired by outstanding engineers and operations specialists. In 1992–1996 before the boom-bust cycle of 1997–2002, 3M's R&D spending as a percentage of sales dwarfed that of either Danaher or Federal Mogul. From 1992 to 1996, it did not stray much from this course regardless of business cycle shifts. In 1997, the company apparently anticipated the early stage of the expansion and sent the right signal of expected product improvement at the moment the market seemed ready for it. However, at the early stage of recession, the year 2000, the company mistakenly assumed continued expansion. In the middle and late stages of the bust, 3M trimmed its R&D spending, a reaction to necessity, not a proactive move carried out as a consequence of superior foresight. This midlevel performance of more or less doing what was called for at one point in time but not another was reflected in the midlevel of confidence investors placed in 3M's management.

This middle-of-the road performance also showed up in the handling of M&As. With the benefit of hindsight, management showed astuteness in 1997 when it cut back on M&A activity at the start of the boom. Acquisition values were about to soar and the value of engaging in the activity was in question. But the logic of restraining from engaging in M&As was too soon truncated. In the middle and particularly late stages of the boom, 3M's M&A activity accelerated despite the fact that bidding wars for overpriced acquisitions were a clear and present danger. 3M acted too early in increasing M&A activity in 1999 at the boom's end and before the recession's onset when the price of potential targets would be more of a bargain. On the other hand, that 3M maintained its M&A activity in 2000, 2001, and 2002 made some sense; there were opportunities galore and 3M was in the midst of the action. But the timing of the company's moves in boom and bust, its ability to be a first-mover and leader and discern economic changes before the pack and act based on this understanding was not as good as Danaher's.

Getting business cycle timing just right is not easy. The managerial implications are to create scenarios of the direction the economy may be going and to act decisively when anticipated changes take place. In a boom, step up R&D spending to signal to customers commitment to innovation and improvements in product selection and quality. Cut back on unnecessary M&A activity. Valuations of potential targets will soar. Do not get into bidding wars where you overpay for shoddy companies. In a bust, reverse course on both R&D spending and M&A activity. Cutback on the R&D spending because the signal to customers to send is a commitment to low prices. On the other hand, a recession provides an opportunity to flex a company's M&A muscles. Hopefully, it has the cash from astute management of the boom.

CHAPTER 6

Energy and Environmental Challenges

V ivid names have been used to describe possible states of the world in four realms—national security and society (chapter 4) and government and the world economy (chapter 5). The vivid names capture positive, negative, and in-between states—or as they have been referred to in chapter 2 romances, tragedies, comedies, and various sub-genres. Mixing and matching these different future states in different realms (for instance, new caliphate and free to choose, or young and militant and progress and crisis) yields nearly limitless possibilities that makes prediction about the future nearly impossible (see appendix A). Indeed, scenarios are not predictions about the future. Rather, they are descriptions of *possible* future states, as an easily described single deterministic future end does not exist and the world is not likely to move in a uniform or well-defined direction. The outcomes of human action are not simple. Rather from the vantage point of the here and now, almost an endless array of possibilities exists.[1]

To understand the possible outcomes that might come into existence starts with considering what is currently known and understood. In the area of energy and environment, nothing is particularly well-fixed.[2] What is relatively well-known are the fuel-types that can provide for future energy needs and thus the vivid names that are used to describe the possibilities that exist in this realm are (1) fossils, (2) renewables, (3) mixed, and (4) surprises. These possibilities rely on primary fuel type as opposed to expert opinion and assessment of trends, which were used for the national security and social scenarios found in chapter 4 and reliance on political-economic theory and history, which were used for the government and economic scenarios found in chapter 5. Indicators in this realm that are worth watching are energy prices, fuel mix, and national and local politics. Drivers of change are the demand for and supply of energy, war and global politics, and climate modifications induced by greenhouse gases. They are the main topic of this chapter.

An End to the Great Smoothing?

The full model developed in this book is found in table 6.1. In the 1970s, many of the factors in the full model converged to create an energy shock involving high oil prices, unexpected and significant inflation, reduced investment, and economic stagnation.

Will the future see a reemergence of these conditions (see table 6.2), a return to the 1970s or something entirely different because of the rise of China as a world power, its surging economy's need for oil, the wish by Iran to have nuclear weapons, the renewed aggressiveness of Russia, the global economic downturn, and/or other factors?[3] Will the face of things to come be L-shaped with lowered expectations for the foreseeable future or V-shaped with a big rebound in the offing (table 6.2)? To answer these questions, people in companies must keep abreast of the following indicators.

Energy Prices

The promise of a more bountiful future depends on world energy prices being held in check. Historically, as energy prices have risen, growth in the U.S. economy and in the world economy has gone down. Higher energy prices have meant less overall economic activity. With the exception of the early 1990s, and even then there was a threat of higher prices because of the Kuwait War, higher energy prices have been associated with reduced economic growth. However in the short run higher prices may be needed to stimulate the search for fossil fuel alternatives.[4] The rapid decline in fossil fuel prices that took place in the last quarter of 2008 has the potential to curtail the search for alternatives. The dilemma is that energy prices should not be so elevated as to stifle economic growth or so low as to remove the incentives for transition to new energy sources. However, the erratic way that energy markets bounce back and forth makes it hard to arrive at this balance. Booms and busts in energy markets assure that short-term thinking prevails over the long-term commitments that are needed. Governments, rightfully, have been reluctant to try to control these markets. Yet taxation and subsidies do alter them, providing signals that distorts overall fuel mix in both the short and long term.

Table 6.1 The full model

Five force plus	Customers	Suppliers	New entrants	Substitutes	Competitors
National Security 1. Davos 2. Pax America 3. New Caliphate 4. Cycle of Fear					
Society 1. Moving and Seeking 2. Old and Feeble 3. Young and Militant					
Government 1. Free to choose 2. Well-regulated 3. Special interests					
World Economy 1. Stable but slower growth 2. Progress and crisis 3. Turmoil and instability					
Energy and Environment 1. Renewables 2. Mixed 3. Surprises 4. Fossils					
Technology • Genetic Engineering • Telecom and Computers • Advanced Materials • Alternative Energy • Robotics • Artificial Intelligence • And the like					

Table 6.2   A return to misery?

Year	Combined inflation and unemployment rate	President
1989	10.09	Bush, G. H. W.
1990	11.01	
1991	11.10	
1992	10.52	
1993	9.87	Clinton, W. J.
1994	8.71	
1995	8.40	
1996	8.34	
1997	7.28	
1998	6.05	
1999	6.41	
2000	7.35	
2001	7.59	Bush, G. W.
2002	7.37	
2003	8.26	
2004	8.21	
2005	8.48	
2006	7.87	
2007	7.46	

Fuel Mix

The 2006 fuel mix in the U.S. was 39 percent petroleum, 22 percent natural gas, 22 percent coal, 9 percent renewables, and 8 percent nuclear. The future might consist of continued reliance on fossil fuels—petroleum, natural gas, and coal, large-scale introduction of renewable energy, or a mixed result in which fossils and renewable energy both play a large role. Surprises might come about because of technological developments that are not fully understood at the moment. The scenario of a long boom, the story of Davos described in chapter 4, was predicated on such positive developments. It included both accelerated discovery of oil and natural gas and the greater use of clean burning coal and a growth in the efficient use of energy, declining energy use per dollar of GDP, and increased production of renewable energy. Negative surprises are equally likely. Environmental catastrophe brought on by climate change would force rapid cutback in dependence on fossil fuels. Political instability in the Mid East and elsewhere may keep supplies of fossil fuels from moving to markets in Asia, Europe, and North America, where most consumption takes place.

Energy Politics

The political sphere is critical.[5] People in companies therefore have to keep an eye on what politicians will do. Politicians create the rules of the game under which new energy sources will be developed and old ones' lives extended. By 2050, dependence on fossil fuels may fall from more than 80 percent to less than 50 percent or less depending on the investments politicians make in new technologies and how regulatory and research programs are administered. How will the Obama administration spend the billions it is committed to spending on energy programs? What will be the return on this investment?

- Will the United States ratify the Kyoto Protocol?
- Will it further tighten fuel efficiency standards?
- What kind of funding will it give to clean coal and gas, hydrogen and electric vehicles, wind, solar, hydro, geothermal, nuclear, and other energy sources?
- Will the United States introduce a national cap and trade system?
- Will it tighten efficiency standards for buildings and appliances?

Politics at the local level can be as important as politics globally or nationally (see the boxed insert, "Overcoming Institutional Constraints in Minnesota"). Will politicians have the wisdom to create good rules and policies? Will these rules mobilize diverse people to work for the common good, or will special interest politics reduce the chances of unleashing technologies that have great promise?

Overcoming Institutional Constraints in Minnesota

In the February of 2007, the state of Minnesota adopted one of the most proactive and demanding goals in the United States.[6] Aimed at reducing the state's carbon dioxide emissions, the Minnesota Renewable Energy Standard (RES) required that Northern States Power (NSP), a division of Xcel Energy (Xcel), the largest utility in state, generate 30 percent of its power from renewable sources by 2020.[7] This was by far the most far-reaching law of its kind in the United States; it was well above the demands set by other states and beyond the 10–15 percent goals that had been debated as a national target in Washington.[8] The potential for wind power generation in Minnesota and adjacent states was large.[9]

Utilities were looking for ways to add capacity to their generating systems, as other alternatives, such as coal and nuclear, were blocked for environmental or political reasons. The costs of generating electricity from wind were dropping and wind was understood to be connected to jobs and economic development. In 2000, NSP merged with New Century Energies utility of Colorado and changed its name from NSP to Xcel. It integrated various fuel and technology types into its generation mix and had new leadership at the top, a CEO, who was sympathetic to alternative sources of power generation. NSP's management took seriously the prospect of operating in a "carbon constrained economy, the 'backdrop' of which would be an 'aging infrastructure and rapidly escalating prices for raw materials.' "[10]

From 1994 to 1998, more wind power was put in place in Minnesota than in any other state.[11] Nine percent of NSP's total generating capacity in 2007 was wind.[12] Under the state's energy plan, however, NSP would have to almost triple this amount in 12 years, a daunting challenge that would not only involve finding new sources of power, but developing the transmission lines to move the power from outlying and mostly rural regions to large metropolitan areas. Furthermore, with wind as the preferred means of generation, NSP would need technologies to store the wind. The wind in Minnesota and surrounding states was most plentiful in fall and spring, while the need for it was highest in summer. How could NSP simultaneously pursue environmental stewardship and maintain its financial integrity, when there were no guarantees that these goals would be mutually reinforcing?

NSP desired a process that provided predictability with respect to the construction of transmission lines, an issue that the state plan had not adequately considered. Under the state plan, small, mid-sized, and large developers fed renewable power into the NSP grid. These small, mid-sized, and large developers included farmers with windy fields, entrepreneurs that recognized a vast opportunity in major energy development, and corporations with the recognized know-how and experience in wind development. All of them had entered a queue for interconnection to the transmission network established by the Midwest Independent System Operators (MISO).[13] If all these projects were brought on line, Minnesota would have as much as four to five times the amount of renewable power it needed, and it would be a major exporter of this power to other regions. However, MISO could not expeditiously approve the projects because of inadequate transmission. Because of this issue, it had a backlog of projects that might take as much as 612 years to clear.[14]

In the winter of 2008, senior executives at NSP pondering a future that could be a romance, tragedy, or comedy, they drew up a plan to restructure the Minnesota energy market to better support the development of renewable energy. The blueprint, entitled the "Central Corridor Concept," was designed to better manage the movement of renewable energy from outlying regions of the state toward the metropolitan areas where it would be consumed.[15] The plan envisioned three energy development corridors with transmission lines that would better link the urban center of Minneapolis-St. Paul to the northwest, southwest, and southeast regions of the state, where most wind and other alternative energy sources were found.

However, political support for the proposed plan was critical and executives at NSP still were uncertain whether they could obtain this support. Potential bottlenecks for fully exploiting the large wind energy resources in the Midwest were large. The company's plan required a new level of coordination among different actors and institutions, and it was not clear whether this new level of coordination could be achieved. Even when landmark objectives were established, the institutional constraints posed a significant barrier. Would overcoming them become all the more difficult in an era of lower energy prices and reduced economic opportunity?

The Drivers of Change

People in business must keep abreast of the drivers of energy and environmental change. The main drivers to consider are demand for and supply of energy, war and global politics, and climate modifications that may be induced by greenhouse gases.

Demand for and Supply of Energy

With regard to demand for energy, there is great unevenness. Per capita consumption is much greater in some countries than others. North America leads the way in oil consumption per capita.[16] The good news is that the United States has become more efficient in its consumption of energy. Over time, the amount of energy needed to produce a dollar of GDP has declined.[17] In the world-as-a-whole, growth in energy use for transportation is likely to be dramatic, however, fueled by rising demand for private automobiles, not only in the United States, but in countries like China.[18] For instance, from 1978 to 2008, the number of private automobiles owned by Chinese consumers increased by more than

100 percent, from less than 500,000 in 1978 to more than 50 million in 2008. Approximately half of the estimated increase in demand for energy in the world in 2009 is expected to come from this country. Already in 2008, it had become the world's second-largest oil consumer, after the United States, and it was fast catching up. China subsidized the use of gasoline and electricity, keeping prices artificially low and thereby hiking demand as its concern for economic growth trumped its concern for energy conservation. Its rapid industrialization was a major reason for rising energy prices. Other Asian nations—such as India, Indonesia, and Malaysia also have subsidized their citizen's energy use.[19]

With respect to the supply of oil, there also were major imbalances. Saudi Arabia, the largest producer of oil, and other large producers such as Iran and Iraq, have gigantic reserves, while producers like the United States are quickly running out of oil. This situation does not bode well for the future as increasingly the world will be relying on nations with authoritarian governments hostile to the United States for its oil. In the decades after 1980, non-OPEC countries such as Russia, Norway, Canada, Mexico, and United Kingdom began to play a significant role in supplying the world. The North Sea oil discovery, while not large in comparison to the oil that lied buried in Saudi Arabia, played an important role in reducing the pressure on oil prices. Little increments added to the world energy market make a very big difference in prices. In the decades after 1980, OPEC's market share eroded because of an increasingly diverse supply base. The new supplies came into the market when U.S. production fell off. However, plentiful North Sea is starting to dry up.

U.S. exploration and production costs are high and the expected discovery rates low except in the state of Alaska. Russian growth in oil production is important because Russia may be able to take up the slack. Initially, Russian companies involved in oil production were closely allied with Western counterparts, but they have rapidly become independent of the West. They are operating as nationalized or semi-nationalized subsidiaries of the post-Communist regime. Attempts to increase the productivity of Russia's West Siberian field have been meeting with only partial success.

Canada has huge potential. Generally it is considered to have the world's second-largest reserves after Saudi Arabia but much of its production potential consists of nonconventional liquids such as oil sands and ultra-heavy oils. Until their costs are significantly cut and their environmental impacts go down, Canada will not be in a position to compete with the Saudis and other purveyors of cheap Middle Eastern oil. Caspian output in countries to the East and South of Russia also have limits. Exporting routes for this oil—whether pipeline or by sea—are not well-established.

OPEC's oil reserves remain significant, but the actual amounts are far from certain. The nations in the cartel have an incentive to over-report supply. On the basis of how much production potential they claim to have they are given the right to bring oil to the market. The cost advantage of average Persian Gulf oil is supposed to be substantial. Until now, countries in this region have not required high-investment to increase production capacity. The costs of OPEC producers outside the Persian Gulf to increase production has been only somewhat higher. Venezuela, for instance, appears to have the capacity to increase its supply at relatively low cost. It is estimated that it can increase production by 1 million barrels per day at a fraction of what it would cost to increase capacity by that amount in Canada. Other OPEC nations may be similarly well-endowed. Nigeria is believed to have substantial offshore oil production potential that can be tapped at a relatively low cost. Algeria and Libya as well may be able to find additional offshore oil and exploit it. However, the biggest potential for increased production lies in Iraq. Under a U.N. Security Council, oil for food program that existed in 1999, Iraq had expanded production to 2.8 million barrels a day in 1999, but since the U.S. occupation, its oil production has not returned to these levels. Some experts consider Iraq capable of producing more than 6 million barrels per day if it was free from insurrection and terrorism.

The Mideast's highest proven reserves appear to belong to Saudi Arabia. Belief is that the Saudis have more than 250 billion barrels. Iran seems to have approximately half of that much. In contrast, the most optimistic forecasts for the U.S. Alaska National Wildlife Refuge are estimated to be about 10 billion barrels. Though Saudi Arabia is assumed to have more reserves than any country in the world, questions have been raised about its oil fields' viability. These decades' old reservoirs no longer flow that easily. The costs of extraction could be more expensive than previously believed. Mat Simmons in his book *Twilight in the Desert* argues that the Ghawar field, the Saudi's largest with more than 50 percent of its oil, already is more than 50 percent exhausted and as additional depletion takes place the costs of extraction will just move upward.[20]

Typically, when an oil field reaches a 50 percent exhaustion level, it is necessary to go from relatively inexpensive primary recovery to much more expensive secondary and tertiary recovery. The DOE's long-term estimates of oil prices in the $60 a barrel range assume that Saudi Arabia can produce 18 to 22 million barrels per day by 2020–2025. Simmons maintains that it is questionable whether the Saudis can ever produce more than 10–15 million barrels per day.[21] If Simmons is right, then demand for oil overtakes supply much sooner than the DOE has assumed, perhaps as early as 2010 rather than 2025.

Each year production declines by more than 4–5 million barrels per day. To replace what is lost and to provide for added growth, the world requires 6–8 million barrels per day of more oil. In 2003 major oil companies spent $8 billion a year on exploration but discovered only $4 billion of commercially useful oil. If replacement lags, as Simmons and other analysts maintain, then the price spikes of 2008, quelled by the economic downturn, inevitably will return. Prospects of the average costs of oil over the next 35 years being greater than $150 a barrel are very realistic.

The controversy about so-called peak oil and its meaning for energy supply and demand is old. Many economists hold that resource limits do not exist, that it all depends on price, and that oil in the ground never will be exhausted because whenever prices rise technology reduces extraction costs. Many geologists and petroleum engineers, on the other hand, maintain that once about a half the oil in the ground has been exhausted, extraction becomes so difficult and expensive that prices remain high. Peak production (greater than half the oil in the ground being exhausted) occurred in the United States around 1970. Since then, the United States. has been increasingly reliant on the import of foreign oil. Peak production in other nations upon which the United States depends is rapidly taking place. Peak production in the Mid East and in Russia, for instance, is likely around 2011 or 2012.

Given these trends, the likelihood of fossil fuels continuing to dominate the fuel mix hinges on technologies like enhanced oil recovery. The output of an existing field typically declines 5 percent per year. In most instances, large oil companies give up on a field after 30 to 40 years. The Saudi's biggest field, Ghawar, is greater than 50 years old. Pre-World War II, oil companies extracted just 10 percent of the oil from a typical field. Since then, they have learned to extract more than 30 percent with water, pressure, and chemicals. After obtaining approximately 40 percent of the output, they usually sell what is left in the fields to companies that specialize in secondary and tertiary recovery. These companies usually are able to get another 30 percent or so of oil out of a field using gas, carbon dioxide, engineered microbes, and chemicals that force the oil out. However, not all fields respond well to this treatment. Extraction costs in old fields can be twice or more the costs of extraction in new ones.

As indicated, OPEC nations have had an incentive to exaggerate how much oil they have since their cartel production quotas are based on the amounts they claim are in the ground. Transparency among these nations does not exist, their actual reserves have not been verified by independent experts. Department of Energy supply models have assumed that Saudi Arabia alone will be able to produce 20 to 30 million barrels per day by 2025–2030, but many analysts wonder whether the Saudis can ever exceed 12 million barrels a day. No matter how analysts assess the situation, the likelihood of serious supply and demand imbalances is high.

War and Global Politics

With regard to how this situation resolves itself, war and global politics are major wildcards. Their past impact on supply and price is well-known and was mentioned in chapter 4. Major events in this saga have been the Arab oil embargo associated with the Yom Kippur War, the fall of Iran to the fundamentalist regime of the Ayatollahs under President Carter, Saddam Hussein's war with Iran, and the United States restoring sovereignty to Kuwait after Iraq's attack on that nation. As previously mentioned, the Saudi regime, which controls the world's largest oil reserves, can go in many directions (see table 4.1). The regime can stay much as it is now, it can radicalize, there can be an al Qaeda-like or Iran-like revolution, or it can modernize. Whatever direction it moves, there will be impacts on oil prices that will have ripple effects in society, global security, politics, and economics. Some of the effects on the world economy were discussed in chapter 5.

Increasingly, leaders of the world's nations will have to engage in difficult negotiations with Saudi rulers about increasing production and easing oil price pressures. In June of 2008, for instance, they hastily attended a summit convened by the Saudi rulers to discuss what were then very high oil prices. The Saudis announced a production increase of 200,000 barrels a day and an expansion of output capacity, if need be, in coming years. The Saudis already had increased daily production by 300,000 barrels, or approximately 3 percent, to 9.45 million barrels, but this increase had little immediate impact. To alleviate fears over the future supply of oil, the Kingdom announced it would add more to its production capacity in coming years. It said it would be capable of adding an additional 2.5 million barrels a day to its output. That would increase its production capacity to 12.5 million barrels a day in an expansion plan that was scheduled to reach completion by 2009. The Saudis maintained that they could grow production to 15 million barrels a day in future years but refused to go beyond this number—15 million barrels a day appeared to be their limit, which was far short of the more than 25 million barrels a day on which the U.S. Department of Energy counted.[22]

Another political issue of great importance has been Iran's intention to pursue nuclear weapons. Should Israel or the United States decide to bomb the Iranian reactors, would the Iranians close the Strait of Hormuz and cause serious oil shortages? Would the Iranians attempt to threaten world oil supply routes? They would be major losers as 60 percent of the Iranian government's revenues comes from the sale of oil. Would the world then become engulfed in a major conflagration with Iran? Threats and counter-threats have gone back and forth. For instance, when the ex-Israeli Defense Minister Shaul Mofaz called for an Israeli air strike, it was said that his words jacked up oil prices by as much as 10 percent. Since the 1950s, there have been 10 major disruptions in the supply of oil. The prospects of additional disruptions remain very real.[23] The belligerent anti-Western declarations of Iranian President Mahmoud Ahmadinejad do not calm the situation. Israelis feel that they have to be prepared for the worst, that Ahmadinejad will build a bomb and use it.[24]

Against this backdrop of rising demand, declining supply, and growing global tensions, U.S. automakers have experienced huge losses. They were not prepared for a ratcheting-up of petroleum prices that occurred in the summer of 2008 (see the boxed insert, "Hope or Hype at General Motors"). Can they develop the capabilities to assist the world in moving to less-oil dependence?

Hope or Hype at General Motors

In August of 2008, General Motors (GM) came out with a report that showed a 26 percent decline in light-vehicle sales in the United States the prior month. SUVs and pickups showed the steepest declines. Ford, Toyota, Honda, and other auto manufacturers also had lower sales. The U.S. auto market's weakness arose mainly from high gasoline prices, but the credit crunch in housing and brewing recessionary like conditions in the United States also were playing a role. GM executive Ray Young was quoted as saying that the auto market was experiencing one of the greatest changes it had ever had in its history. GM and other automakers would have to adjust and adjust fast, but would they be capable of making such a rapid adjustment? After roughly two decades of predominantly stable and low petroleum prices that provided little incentive for alternative vehicles, the sharp price rises were unsettling. Oil prices over the next decade or so could be anywhere from $20 to more than $400 a barrel, meaning that U.S. consumers would pay anywhere from $1.00 to $15.00 or more for a gallon of gasoline. Would a new round of energy efficiency, production, and replacement efforts take the upward pressure off prices, or not? What was GM to do?

A *middle-of-the-road scenario* holds that OPEC producers in the Middle East still have most of the world's reserves though they are stretched thin and are pumping near capacity (Iraq is the exception). Rising oil prices would stimulate renewed exploration and production activity both within OPEC and among non-OPEC producers that will bring new supplies to the market. Canadian oil sands development already was resulting in roughly 1 million barrels per day of oil being produced in the summer of 2008 with much more expected by 2010. There would be large investments in unconventional sources of petroleum such as U.S. western shale oil as well. When these investments paid off for the oil producers, it would mean increased supplies of oil, and GM would be back in business, pretty much at status quo ante. The run up in prices, while serious, would have a time limit. In the meantime, automobiles would become more energy efficient because of consumer choice and government pressure. In the short term, consumers in the United States and the rest of the world might abandon a preference for large and powerful vehicles but in the long term they would come back. What happened in 2008 was a hiccup on the road. High prices would encourage the investments needed to bolster supplies and return the situation to just about what it always had been.

A *pessimistic scenario*, on the other hand, suggests that modern seismic techniques have made exploration efforts more reliable and efficient, yet no new oil reservoir bonanzas have been found. Even if successful, it would take years to bring new supplies to the market especially with many of the most promising places for adding to world petroleum reserves in politically unstable areas. New supplies of oil not only would have to accommodate an expected increased in demand on the order of 2 percent per year, but must replace declining production from aging oil fields of which there were many, most particularly among non-OPEC producers, but even now also in OPEC itself. If this pessimistic scenario was correct and the promise of new sources and enhanced recovery of old sources failed to meet expectations and the decline rates of old oil fields accelerated, prices would stay high for a long period to come. Then, the world truly had entered a new era and GM could not just wait this one out. In this instance, unless new technologies came to the rescue, a slowdown and flattening of production capacity were fairly definite over the coming investment horizon, and disruptively high oil prices would persist far beyond this time range into the future.

On the other hand, an *optimistic scenario* suggests that with high prices, new supplies would be introduced quickly. It is conceivable that a major technological innovation would take place that would change the entire situation. Even without such a breakthrough, a large amount of additional oil could be extracted from well-tread techniques like enhanced recovery in depleted wells, ultra deep off-shore fields, Canadian tar sands, heavy oil, shale oil, and natural gas liquids. New supplies already were beginning to enter the market and the rush to get new supplies into the market with prices high only would accelerate. The potential of tar sands, for instance, was very large and though the cost of extracting oil from them was high this cost could be justified with high prices.[25] So even if estimates of oil reserves in the Middle East were overstated and oil fields there and in other developing countries are neglected or poorly maintained thereby reducing their potential, the world supply of petroleum was not going to seriously go down any time soon. In fact, oil shortages in the twenty-first century would be seen as an aberration, in no way a long-term trend. On the optimistic side, the marketplace also could engender breakthroughs in energy technologies yielding vehicles and other energy consuming products that consumers would want and that would have dramatic fuel savings. Petroleum supplies actually could go down by 2040 as some analysts predict and the result for the automakers would be good because their investments in alternative technologies had paid off.

Clearly, several scenarios existed for the evolution of supply and demand for oil. The question is, given the uncertainty what should GM do? Some in GM were saying that what was ailing the company had more to do with the economy than the price of oil. Once the economy picked up GM would do just fine. For now, the main issue for the company was to stay afloat until the economy rebounded. The energy issues would sort themselves out.

In 1998, the automaker had unveiled a prototype hybrid vehicle and started to do serious research on fuel-cell powered cars. It announced that it would try to create a workable hybrid by 2001 and that its aim was to produce a fuel-cell prototype by 2004. However, in comparison to Toyota and Honda, its exploration of the alternative vehicle market had not been successful. Going forward, how should GM manage the transition from today's conventionally powered gasoline autos to autos that are hybrid powered and run on fuel cells? Hybrid vehicles had grown in popularity. The advantages of hybrids, such as longer driving ranges and automatically recharging batteries during driving, however, were not always known to all consumers. Some consumers still associated them with an electric car that had batteries with limited ranges. Hybrids also had been marketed with an emphasis on their environmental benefits which did not endear them to mainstream consumers.

No matter what happened, hybrids ultimately might serve a useful purpose. Their components—electric-drive, power-control, and battery systems—were key elements in fuel-cell technology, a technology to which GM was very committed. By 2013–2015, there was some likelihood that fuel-cell vehicles would replace conventional vehicles. The experience gained in using the components by GM and other auto companies would assist in the design of these vehicles. Since hybrids were not completely pollution-free, GM could move toward the more innovative approach of utilizing only fuel cells, electronics, and a hydrogen tank.

What were drawbacks of fuel cells? The potential safety hazards of hydrogen, it was claimed, were a drawback. The hydrogen could explode, unless great care was taken, but this risk had been greatly exaggerated. In addition, and certainly more important, the hydrogen had to be produced. It could originate from water or carbon-based fuels like natural gas but if the production was from water it would consume prodigious amounts of energy. The popularity of fuel-cell technology was growing and all of the major U.S. automakers were creating prototypes. The competition could be stiff. Though fuel-cell cars were promoted as the technology of the future due to their running entirely on renewable fuels and zero emissions, no company had been ready to sell the technology to the public. Fuel cells would be commercializable only by 2012, at the earliest. Moving forward, GM faced a number of interconnected challenges. It had to have a vision of alternative futures and a sound business plan to deal with them. How should it proceed, given its vast losses?

Climate Change

Another driver companies must consider is global climate change.[26] Al Gore proclaimed global warming was for real, but others have argued there were few bases to say that more carbon dioxide in the air was going to lead to global catastrophe. They held there was legitimate uncertainty in the science. If global warming is for real, then current dependency on fossil fuels might have to end. If it is for real, then all fossil fuels are in trouble—coal more than oil because it is a larger source of carbon emissions.

Many scientists hold that heat waves and other weather events from storms and hurricanes to droughts are caused by concentrations of carbons from fossil fuel burning and the burning of other gases and their release into the atmosphere. In the future, there could be melting of ice caps and sea levels increases as much as 20 feet. Proponents of this view point to an increased incidence of these extreme events. Burning fossil fuels put greenhouse gases into the atmosphere that trap heat and warm the globe. Opponents object that the risks are exaggerated and any attempt to limit or get rid of oil, gas, and coal that provide 90 percent of the world's energy will yield economic disaster, including job losses, recession, and high inflation.

People in the business community should consider a number of elements in this debate: science, efforts to curb carbon emissions, and technologies that can solve the problem.

The science of climate change is not all that controversial. Most scientists agree that something approaching a 5-degree warming brought on by the increasing concentration of global greenhouse gases (GHGs) will change the climate system radically. When will the consequences be felt, however? To what extent are the impacts long term? Will they only become serious 30 to 50 years from now so that taking action now means concrete sacrifices for indefinite gains in the future.

Scientists agree that a distinction must be made between natural fluctuations in the weather and more fundamental changes that affect climate over a long period. What is important is not how hot it will be on a particular summer day or how much snow there will be on a winter day but patterns that prevail in the long run. The case for global warming requires centuries long temperature increases. The evidence comes from long-term records. Since the Industrial Revolution, new and growing uses for fossil fuels like coal, oil, and natural gas have emerged. When these fuels are burned, they are the sources for carbon dioxide and other greenhouse gases. The carbon atoms combine with oxygen in the air to make carbon dioxide. Every time people turn on a light or drive a car, they add carbon dioxide to the atmosphere. At the end of World War II, approximately a billion metric tons of carbon was being emitted to the atmosphere. In 2008, this number had grown to more than 7 billion tons. With more greenhouse gases like carbon dioxide emitted, the average global temperature was likely to rise very significantly. Venus has an extremely high concentration of carbon dioxide in its atmosphere and is very hot, while Mars, has very little carbon dioxide and is very cold. The earth has a moderate temperature that allows human beings and other forms of life to thrive. A major reason is that its carbon dioxide levels are moderate.

How will an increase in carbon dioxide and other greenhouse gases affect the planet? This question is complicated because carbon dioxide and other greenhouse gases do not act in isolation. The build-up of carbon dioxide in the atmosphere and other greenhouse gases from human activities increases sulfate aerosols that affect cloud cover which may have a cooling effect. However, because the sulfate aerosols only persist in the atmosphere for short periods of time, the cooling effect is not of the same duration as the warming that is caused by greenhouse gases. Other influences complicate climate models. For example, there are volcanic eruptions, like Mount Pinatubo, which may cause severe cooling for two to three years. There also are interactions internal to the climate system. The climate's response depends on a complicated chain of feedbacks that amplify and diminish initial conditions. Carbon dioxide, for instance, causes warming that heats the oceans, increasing the amount of water evaporating from the oceans. The evaporation adds to cloud cover and causes additional warming. Warming causes snow and ice to melt, exposing a darker earth surface that absorbs more sunlight. Feedbacks are complex. For example, with low-level cloud cover, the sun is shielded from the earth; thus the effect is cooling. With high-level cover, the heat is trapped; thus the effect is warming.

The models scientists have built try to take into account the complications. The prediction of warming and its effects therefore has a wide range. Exactly what will happen is unknowable. Credible models vary from somewhat benign to very catastrophic results. If the scientists are uncertain about precise impacts of temperature changes, they know even less about specific timing. When might sea-level rises caused by melting glaciers really result in flooding in coastal areas?

Scientists also have trouble modeling the extent to which people will be able to adapt to climate change. If it comes slowly, they may adapt well, but if it comes in a rush, they may not be able to do so. Rich nations may be able to do more than poor nations. If warming is only mild, people may consider it positive. They will see more sunshine and greater agricultural yields in some places, but if the humans can adjust, trees, birds, and animals may not be able to do so. Many species will face extinction. Even modest warming can destabilize ocean currents like the Gulf Stream that carries warm water from the equator to the north Atlantic and moderates the temperature of Britain and the Scandinavian. While the rest of the world warms, these countries may cool. After decades of research, climate scientists imagine different futures because of the feedbacks and complex interactions.

Efforts to prevent climate change have not been successful. In December 1997, representatives from 160 countries met in Kyoto, Japan to deliberate about a treaty that would limit world's greenhouse gas emissions. The problem these states confronted was the deceptively difficult phrase "common but differentiated responsibilities" which the countries in the world had agreed to at the Rio conference of 1992. This phrase meant that industrialized countries had to act first. Sustainable development, not curbing global greenhouse emissions, is the highest priority for developing countries. For developing counties, economic growth takes precedence over climate protection. The United States and other industrialized countries are large consumers of energy that yield massive emissions of greenhouse gases. They are mainly responsible for the problem, and it is their responsibility to fix it; but in the future they will need the assistance of developing countries. The developing nations do not want their prospects for economic growth to be hindered by restrictions.

Energy use by industrialized nations is the main reason for existing carbon dioxide in the atmosphere (see the insert "U.S. Carbon Emissions"). However, the future of emissions will be determined by what happens in developing nations like Brazil, India, and China, where three quarters of the world's people live. The developing world has higher rates of population and economic growth, which means huge potential for growth in greenhouse emissions as they develop electric power and transportation systems. In India, each person is responsible for one-fortieth as much carbon dioxide as an American, but India's population is so large and its growth so rapid that it will soon surpass the United States in total greenhouse emissions.

U.S. Carbon Emissions

Close to 60 percent of all U.S. electricity comes from coal. A single 1,500-megawatt coal plant can supply the electrical power needs of 1.5 million people. For electricity, coal is supplemented with other carbon-emitting fossil fuels such as oil and natural gas. Thus, a typical home in the Southern part of the United States uses approximately 4,000 kilowatt hours for air conditioning. It emits 800 kilograms of carbon per year. Each pound of carbon entering the atmosphere combines with oxygen to form nearly four pounds of carbon dioxide. Lighting an average house for a year emits 2,000 pounds of carbon dioxide. Lighting a large office building produces 2.5 million pounds of carbon dioxide. Using a computer 40 hours a week produces 600 pounds of carbon dioxide. Approximately, one-third of greenhouse emissions come from automobiles. People drive approximately 12,000 miles per year, and a typical new car gets approximately 28 miles per gallon. The average car uses 430 gallons per year and emits roughly 2,200 pounds of carbon per year. An SUV, which gets 14 miles per gallon, emits twice as much carbon. It is like having two cars. Apart from the energy people use to live, enormous amounts of power are required to manufacture the goods people buy. Each American thus puts more than 20 tons of carbon dioxide into the air each year. Together this amounts to about one quarter of the world's total.

The Kyoto Protocol was signed by nearly every nation in the world except the United States in 1997, but it was not ratified until 2005. Industrialized countries are committed to reducing their average annual carbon dioxide emissions by 2008–2012 to 5 percent below 1990 levels. The EU is committed to reducing to 8 percent below 1990 levels. The U.S. commitment would have been to reduce to 7 percent below 1990 levels. All countries may buy emissions reduction credits from developing countries or from each other rather than reducing their own emissions.

However, by 2008, it was clear that Kyoto's ambitious goals were not being achieved by the signatories to the agreement. Since its ratification, the United States, which is not a treaty member, has done as good a job as the Europeans in keeping its emissions in check. Forces at work in society, economy, and technology are the reason. For instance, an increase in new drivers, cars, and miles traveled in European countries like Spain and Greece has been very hard to stop.

Even if the United States had signed Kyoto and all countries had lived up to their commitments, the world would reduce the rate of greenhouse gas buildup by the year 2100 to only about 700 parts per million, approximately twice as what it is today. Instead of doubling the amount of carbon dioxide, it might increase by 90 percent. To stop the rise in atmospheric concentrations of greenhouse gases means that people in the world must go well beyond Kyoto.

A revolution in technology is needed, but how will this happen? There are a range of potential solutions, but none of them is quite adequate. The first option is to use energy more efficiently. Using energy more efficiently makes its use go further. To do so does not mean deprivation and enduring discomfort but technological improvements that permit human beings to do what they are accustomed to doing without using as much energy. Simple measures can be taken such as making electrical devices like televisions and computers so that they do not leak as much energy as they do currently. Large amounts of energy escape from these devices even when they are not turned-on. This is a design flaw that must be fixed.

A problem with efficiency is that when engineers develop more efficient devices people just use them more. Net energy consumption does not go down. The phenomenon is called snap back, and it is similar to what happens when there is abundance of diet foods. People just eat more of them. Even with more efficient technology, it may not mean less energy consumption. People will just buy larger and heavier vehicles and live in more vast and expansive homes.

Other options are a range of energy sources including nuclear power. The nuclear plants built in the United States for energy production are not the same as nuclear bombs.[27] Nuclear power already supplies 20 percent of U.S. electricity and it is carbon-free, but it has major problems. Environmental groups are opposed. Their concerns center on radioactive waste disposal and their belief that there are cleaner alternatives. No new nuclear power plants have been built in the United States since the 1970s. Many of the nation's plants are slated to be decommissioned in a few more decades. A problem with nuclear is the availability of the fuel. Conventional nuclear reactors rely on Uranium 235. Current reserves will not last long if the world is totally dependent on this type of uranium for all its electricity. The closer to exhaustion the more expensive the Uranium will be.

Conventional reactors do not solve the problem of uranium exhaustion. Breeders do. They turn a more abundant form of uranium into plutonium, which can potentially extend nuclear powers lifespan as a fuel source for hundreds of years, but breeders are a complex and an extremely dangerous technology. They produce bomb grade material and raise serious issues about nuclear proliferation. Virtually no research is being done on them today. Research into nuclear power has been in decline, which will make it very difficult to find a nuclear option that can overcome current obstacles.

Electric production in the world is likely to quadruple in the next 100 years. These projections show how hard the problem will be to solve. The world will have to stabilize greenhouse gas emissions at the same time it experiences a huge jump in the use of energy. A massive transition away from fossil fuels will be needed but where will the world find the energy? Hydroelectric power is carbon free but there are limited new sources of hydropower and it too has come under attack from environmentalists who claim that it disrupts waterways and ecosystems. Wind power has great promise particularly in parts of Minnesota and South Dakota (see the earlier insert), but the wind blows only 25 percent of the time. It is the strongest in the spring and the fall, when demand for electricity is the lowest and therefore without storage it requires natural gas or some other backup.

Solar power remains in its infancy as a mass source of electricity. For instance, a solar plant with a field of mirrors that captures the energy of the sun and turns it into electricity only generates power when the sun shines, during the day, not at night when most people turn on their lights. Such a plant may generate only 30 or so megawatts of electricity, and it may cost four times more to generate the power than an equivalent coal fired plant. Solar power can play an important role in developing nations where the sun is plentiful and the demand for power is less than it is in the United States, but what role will it play in developed nations like the United States?[28] The energy density of solar, wind, biomass, and other renewable sources of power is very low. They require large areas of land to produce the power that modern industrial societies need. For instance, to supply today's electricity with biomass might require an area of the earth that is approximately equivalent to 10 percent of its total surface. Not enough room would be left for food production and biological diversity.

Replacing fossil fuels in power stations is not enough, because roughly a third of fossil emissions come from vehicles. Cars some day might run on hydrogen fuel cells (see the prior insert on GM). The main challenge is in obtaining the hydrogen. If it is made from natural gas, energy has to be expended to make it and some carbon dioxide is released in the process. If it is made by splitting water molecules, there would be a need for large electric power input and there would be emissions from electricity used in splitting the molecules. Renewable sources such as solar and wind would have to operate on a very large scale to provide for the world's energy needs, but are they up to this task? Unless there are substantial breakthroughs, they are likely to be just a useful supplement.

No known energy technology can deliver all the carbon-free energy that is needed to stabilize greenhouse gases in the atmosphere. The most commonly cited examples such as energy efficiency, nuclear, and renewable have not yet lived up to their promise, despite some breakthroughs. Therefore, energy expert, Marty Hoffert, has declared that something entirely new will be needed, something the likes of which is hard for humans to currently conceive:[29]

Try to imagine what the world was like in 1899 compared to today and what the technologies were that were being envisioned by even scientists and engineers and what actually happened. They missed the movies. They missed airplanes. They missed automobiles. They certainly missed space travel with nuclear power and radar and lasers. And so there's really an issue of sort of timidity in the way that we've been projecting the technologies that might mitigate the fossil fuel greenhouse effect.

Hoffert calls for serious research on the scale of Manhattan Project to find technologies to combat global warming. The question he poses is taken up in the concluding chapter—to what extent can technology come to the rescue? To find other energy sources will require a technological revolution of immense proportions. It also will require the political will to make this revolution happen. Is this possible?

Technology to the Rescue?

with Massoud Amin

To the difficult problems raised in previous chapters, technology may be the solution.[1] Businesses are technology's commercializers; their role is to bring critical know-how and ideas incorporated in technology to the market. Foresight is needed to identify the opportunities and bring the technologies to the market. Generic scenarios (see chapter 2)—romances, tragedies, and comedies—set aspiration levels (romances), establish worst cases (tragedies), and conceive of surprising transitions that must be managed (comedies). The purpose is not to forecast the future but to visualize many eventualities. It is not to accommodate necessity and submit to fate, but to influence the course of events. Rather than predicting the future, managers have to change it. They should take action to bring about the positive outcomes (romances), prevent the negative ones (tragedies), and manage the surprising ones (comedies).

With this conception in mind, people in companies should consider what the future may bring. The number and types of scenarios extend beyond the generic types. People in companies should imagine many possibilities (e.g., see appendix B).There are a whole spectrum of colors— not just white (romance), black (tragedy), and gray (comedy)—but shades and hues of red, blue, green, yellow, purple, magenta, orange, fuchsia, mauve, brown, and so on (see tables A.1 and A.2). People in companies can use such ideas about the future to identify the opportunities and test their strategies for commercializing technologies. Indeed, people in companies can set up scoring systems for these purposes. Consider a variety of technologies, up to six, for example (see table A.1) and rate them given different future conditions represented by the various colors in the

Table A.1 Option identification: Scenarios to identify technological opportunities

| | Technologies | | | | | | |
Scenarios	1	2	3	4	5	6	Total
Red	2	0	0	0	0	0	2
Blue	0	0	0	10	0	0	10
Green	0	2	0	0	0	0	2
Yellow	0	2	0	0	0	0	2
Purple	0	0	0	0	2	0	2
Magenta	0	0	0	0	0	0	0
Orange	0	0	0	0	0	2	2
Fuchsia	0	0	10	0	6	0	16
Mauve	0	0	10	0	0	0	10
White	0	10	0	2	0	2	14
Black	0	0	0	0	0	0	0
Gray	0	0	0	0	0	0	0
Brown	2	0	0	0	0	0	2
Total	4	14	20	12	8	4	

Note: High customer needs = 10; Medium customer needs = 6; Low customer needs = 2; and No-needs = 0.

Table A.2 Option feasibility: Scenarios for examining business strategies

| | Strategies | | | | | | |
Scenarios	1	2	3	4	5	6	Total
Red	6	6	0	0	0	0	12
Blue	0	10	0	0	0	2	12
Green	0	2	0	2	0	6	10
Yellow	0	0	0	0	10	0	10
Purple	2	0	2	6	0	0	10
Magenta	6	0	2	0	0	2	10
Orange	0	2	2	6	2	0	12
Fuchsia	0	10	2	0	2	2	16
Mauve	0	0	2	0	6	2	10
White	0	0	2	2	0	10	14
Black	6	2	2	2	0	0	12
Gray	2	0	0	2	0	6	10
Brown	2	2	6	2	0	0	12
Total	24	34	20	22	20	30	

Note: High strategic feasibility = 10; Medium strategic feasibility = 6; Low strategic feasibility = 2; and Nonfeasible = 0.

table. The highest needs of customers may be assigned a score of 10; the medium needs a score of 6, and the lowest needs a 2. This scoring system can be altered to meet a company's requirements. Employees in different positions and locations in the company should help do the scoring. The analysis should not be carried out by top management alone since it may not be fully knowledgeable of customer needs. The analysis should not be static. It should be evolving and changing. It should be regularly updated as new information becomes available. Different orientations and perspectives should be included.

In table A.1, the highest scoring technological option is number three (20 points) and the best scenario for the company is fuchsia, so the technology of choice would be number three and the company would want to influence the world in a fuchsia direction. A risk averse organization, however, would want to have backups. It would be concerned that the world might not move in a fuchsia direction. The best backups would be technology number two (14 points) and technology number four (12 points) that cover scenarios represented by the colors blue and white. If the world evolves in these directions, then the company would have the resilience to switch gears and recover. It has alternatives in place just in case.

Of course, such choices that people in a company make require much discussion. A quantitative scoring system of this nature necessitates qualitative as well as quantitative thinking. Laying out the options in this way is the start of serious debate. It should not be its end. Gathering intelligence of this nature and using it is not a one-time only process. Nothing is static, nothing automatic.

The second role scenarios can play is in examining strategies that can be used to pursue technological opportunities (see table A.2). These strategies should consist of some combination of the moves a company can make. They might involve a combination of (1) product and/or service repositioning, (2) mergers, acquisitions, divestitures, and alliances, (3) globalization, and (4) innovation (see chapter 3). The moves can be carried out in different sequences. The question for people in a company are how likely are the strategies to succeed under the different conditions that might prevail in the future (see chapter 5)—red, blue, and so on? How feasible are the strategies given different future states? Again, a scoring system might be put into place with the high feasibility strategies, those that are most likely to succeed, assigned a score of 10; the medium feasibility strategies assigned a score of 6, and the low feasibility ones given a score of 2. The scoring of the strategies again should involve many people in the company. The knowledge to carry out this exercise does not belong exclusively to top management. The scoring should not be static. As new information becomes available people should make changes, revising and re-thinking what they believe will work and how.

In the example given (see table A.2), the dominant strategy appears to be number two (34 points), but it does not have a large lead over the sixth strategy (30 points). Strategy two makes the most sense if the future is likely to be blue or fuchsia. Under these conditions, it is the most likely to succeed. Strategy six makes the most sense if the future is white, while strategy five makes the most sense if the future is yellow. When there is a fuchsia future, the need for technology three is highest and the strategic option most likely to succeed is two. The company overall does best in a fuchsia world when it pursues the second strategy. This suggests that the company should take actions to make the world a fuchsia one. It is a matter of self-interest. If the company wants to succeed in commercializing the technology it should not sit-by idly. It should try to create the conditions that will bring a fuchsia world into being. It should try to shape the future to the extent it can.

Technology two and strategy six work best in a white world. A white scenario therefore is a good backup. A backup is needed because the company cannot guarantee that no matter what it does it will have a world it wants. The company must have an option it can turn to just in case. The company must be prepared should events not evolve as it hopes. Thus, it also should work for the white world.

The best case for this company is fuchsia. The second best case is white. Other possibilities should be resisted. The gray world scores particularly low on both technological opportunities (0 points) and strategic options (4 points). It should be especially opposed. The company not only should try to create a world to its liking but it should attempt to prevent a world it does not want.

Relying on scenarios does not assure the company's success. It improves the chances. People in the company must update such analyses on a regular basis whether formally or informally. They must remain skeptical about their own analyses. Their ideas must be considered provisional and subject to regular revision and alteration. In accord with new evidence, people in the company must be ready to reconsider their conclusions.

These techniques are highly useful in organizing people's thoughts and systematizing them, but they are not a substitute for ongoing critical thinking. People in the company should be ready to question their assumptions. Scenarios can help the company succeed, help it avoid failure, and help it discover what lies around the corner (see table A.3) provided that scenarios are used judiciously and not in some routine or formulaic way.

Table A.3 Three roles for scenarios

Romance: Farsighted	Tragedy: Blind sighted	Comedy/Farce: External sensing
To succeed	To avoid failure	To discover what lies around the corner
• Foreshadowing weak signals	• Developing early warning systems	• Being sensitive to the multiplicity of possible outcomes
• Discovering new customers, technologies, channels	• Being prepared	• Showing curiosity about what exists on the periphery and the edges
• Staying ahead of curve	• Avoiding being blind sided	• Dealing with the uncertainty of unstructured problems where the odds are not known
• Seeing opportunity early	• Preventing error	• Mapping out the uncertainty
	• Showing vigilance against threats	• Testing strategies with flexible options
		• Monitoring and exploring, rather than *solving* well-defined problems with established analytical tools and good data
		• Dealing with open systems, chaos, and complexity, rather than closed systems that are well-worked out
		• Removing regret

Key Differentiators

For any company wishing to succeed, the technologies it chooses to pursue can be key differentiators. Technological change has been described to be like a "series of explosions" with innovations concentrating in specific sectors, so-called leading-edge industries that provide the momentum for further growth.[2] Without these leading sectors to propel an economy forward, further growth is not possible. People in companies, seeing the opportunities for profit, vigorously exploit the possibilities inherent in the leading-edge sectors. The pioneers typically are followed by a swarm of imitators. The combined activity of the pioneers and imitators generates boom conditions. Soon, however, there are so many followers that prices for the new products and services that have been introduced fall and a bust follows. Lagging sectors fall behind, their time passes, and they wither and die or are kept afloat by government subsidies and bailouts. To spur a revival, commercialization of more new technologies is needed. a process that has been called "creative destruction."[3]

Economic progress, then, takes place in waves, each of which may last upward of half a century.[4] Each wave will have periods of prosperity, recession, depression, and recovery. Since the Industrial Revolution, these waves have been connected to specific technological innovations.[5] The first wave (1782–1845) saw major innovations in steam power and textiles; the second (1845–1892), in railroads, iron, coal, and construction; and the third (1892–1948), in electrical power, automobiles, chemicals, and steel. The prosperity of the post–World War II period was built on innovations in semiconductors, consumer electronics, aerospace, pharmaceuticals, petrochemicals, and synthetic and composite materials.[6] A dynamic growth phase existed from 1945 to 1973, but from 1973 to the present, growth rates in advanced industrial nations have slowed. From where will the next wave of technological innovation come?

What are the technologies from which people in companies can pick to increase the chances that their firms will succeed? Today, particularly promising technological developments are occurring in such fields as genetic engineering, advanced computing, telecommunications, biomedical engineering, the material sciences, and energy. These revolutions in technology offer many opportunities for better managing resources and improving the quality of life, but which companies will best be able to seize on them for commercial gain has not yet been determined. Scenarios offer a way to help sort out this problem.

Here are some of the technological possibilities that people in companies might consider.

The New Genetics

The new genetics (genomics/molecular biology/designer life forms) including the Human Genome Project provides the foundation for medical advances and for agricultural biotechnology that offers the potential for feeding the world's population using less land. The genetic code of living organisms has been mapped in preparation for restructuring and remodeling of genes to enhance or eliminate various traits in humans and other life forms. This map may provide scientists with the ability to predict and correct genetic diseases. It may allow them to create drugs to better fight diseases such as cancer. It should give them the ability to create crops that are pest-resistant and drought-proof and have other useful properties (see the boxed insert in chapter 5 titled Monsanto's Quest). It has been estimated by some that in 2010, the cost of synthesizing bacteria genome-sized DNA sequence will be equivalent to the price of a car. The potential of the new genetics may be staggering.

Information Technology

The impact of the ongoing information revolution (communications/computing/sensors/electronics/machine intelligence) already has been great. It has included the following:[7]

- Telecommuting ("tele-everything")
- Shopping at home, web-based, robotic delivery
- Entertainment/leisure (at home, immersive 3-D, interactive/multi-sensory via VR/holography)
- Travel (3-D/interactive/multisensory tele-travel)
- Education (at home, low-cost, web-based on-demand asynchronous, immersive/virtual presence, life-long distance learning)
- Health (at home interactive tele-medicine)
- Politics (increased real-time virtual involvement of the body politic)
- Commerce (tele-commerce, already ubiquitous)
- Tele-socialization
- Tele-manufacturing

An ability to disseminate knowledge instantaneously around the globe has given rise to virtual communities and an expanding international economy. It has resulted from fiber optics, which carry many signals at once (such as, television, telephone, radio, and computer) that have greatly improved and expanded communications. Microwaves send wireless digital information to satellite dishes. Advanced satellites are used for pinpoint surveillance and mapping. Advanced computing will unlock additional vistas. Evolving chip technologies are opening up the promise of even faster and more powerful computers. Information from audio, video, and film is being digitized so that it can be retrieved more quickly and used more effectively. The use of memory systems such as optical disks, film, and bar-code readers has been expanded. Parallel processing permits the use of many computers simultaneously. It greatly enhances computer power and performance and thereby increases the complexity of the scientific and technical tasks that can be handled. Computer use is continuing to expand to areas where human intelligence has been applied. Computers are increasing their ability to carry out such activities as learning, adapting, recognizing, and self-correction. Related developments are likely to take place in quantum technologies such as crypto computing, sensors, optics, electronics, and in societal systems such as motivational asynchronous "distance learning," immersive/virtual presence, "tele-everything," "robotic everything," and digital earth/digital airspace. The impact of the ongoing information technology revolution on society has been immense, and its full promise is only starting to be tapped.

Materials Advances

Designer alloys, ceramics, polymers, nanotechnology, and biomimetics offer new capabilities in areas such as computer memory and speed, sensors, superconductivity, and super strength. Many new materials are already more widely available. Lighter, stronger, more resistant to heat, and able to conduct electricity, new polymers can be used in many products from garbage bags to tanks, ball bearings, batteries, and running shoes. New materials can be constructed molecule-by-molecule and atom-by-atom using supercomputers in their design. Tailor-made enzymes for industrial use are being developed. High-tech ceramics resistant to corrosion, wear, and high temperatures are being used in autos and elsewhere to create cleaner-running and more efficient engines. Lightweight and noncorrosive fiber-reinforced composites that are stronger than steel are being used in buildings, bridges, and aircraft.

Energetics

Many new energy technologies (solar/biomass/storage) exist or are coming into existence such as fuel cells, which use hydrogen as opposed to fossil fuels like oil (see boxed insert in chapter 6: Hope or Hype at General Motors). Solar energy cells already are being used in pocket calculators and remote power applications. Superconductors carry electricity with less loss of energy. They make possible cheaper and more advanced magnetic imaging machines possible for hospitals. They can also be used in TV antennas. Later in this chapter, there will be additional discussion of potential developments in this area.

Biomedical Engineering

Microwave scalpels equipped with lasers (light amplified by the stimulated emission of radiation) are replacing metal scalpels used in surgery. Through bioelectricity, damaged or malfunctioning nerves, muscles, and glands can be stimulated to promote their repair and restore their healthy functioning. This technique can be used in humans with severed bones or defective hearts or lungs. It speeds the healing rates of wounds.

Nanotechnology

Nanotechnology holds out huge promise for the advances it can bring about in many related areas such as coatings, barriers, computers, sensors, materials, and assemblers. There are a number of ways in which nanotechnologies can play roles, including applications for a special use, like microwave water heating; applications to multiple uses; combinations that enable a single use; and combinations that enable multiple uses. Nanotechnology opportunities spread very broadly into many other technological fields, such as:[8]

Aerospace and Defense
- structural materials, coatings, fuel, electro-mechanical systems, weapons, surveillance, smart uniforms, and life support.

Automotive and Transportation
- structural materials and coatings, sensors, displays, catalytic converters and filters, and power.

Information Technology and Telecommunication
- photolithography, electronics and opto-electronics, quantum computing, and telecommunications.

Energy Production and Distribution
- fuel cells, solar power, rechargeable batteries, power transmission, lighting, energy savings (plastic batteries may be possible with up to eight times their nominal capacity charged in less than a minute).

Medical and Pharmaceutical
- detection, analysis, and discovery; drug delivery; prosthetics; antimicrobial, antiviral, and antifungal agents.

Chemicals and Advanced Materials
- catalysts, membranes and filtration, coatings and paints, abrasives, and lubricants, composites, and structural.

Indeed, the bio-nano world may be the next important stage in the development of technology. Is it the next megatrend that will transform nearly everything? (see appendix c).

Empowered by People

The Nobel Prize winning economist Robert Solow claims that technology typically drives 60 percent of the growth in the GDP in an economy. Technology, however, must be powered by people. It requires human skills, discipline, and creativity to make it work. It relies on people to bring about the prosperity the planet needs. Again and again, this book has emphasized the importance of people.

Though projections are far from certain (see chapter 4), expectations are that by the year 2050 the distribution of people in the world will be quite different than it is today. The most significant differences are Europe where the population is expected to decline by approximately 9 percent and Africa where the population is expected to grow by 120 percent. This will make Africa the second most inhabited continent in the world. Of course, many assumptions go into these projections and therefore they may not be realized. Overall trends obscure more than they reveal, for within regions there are likely to be areas of great heterogeneity. Pockets within each region will be growing and declining. Within a particular region change is likely to be as large as between regions, though throughout the world, the movement from countryside to city is likely to continue. By 2020, there are expected to be more than 30 megacities, many of the new ones being in developing countries. By 2050, there are expected to be nearly 60 such cities.

If the past provides a guide to the future, the pace of change will continue to be very rapid. For example,

- Internet use grew 183 percent from 2000. There were 1 billion users in 2007. By 2011, there are likely to be 2 billion users.
- In 2006, 2 billion cell phones were in circulation. By 2009, there are likely to be 3 billion in circulation.
- Wireless "hotspots" were taking off. In 2008, there were 100,000 of them. By 2010, there were expected to be 200,000.
- The Internet carried 647 petabytes (billion million bytes) of data each day in 2007. By comparison, the Library of Congress holdings represented only 0.02 petabytes. This number was only likely to increase.

These changes, however, will not always be smooth. There will be glitches; and there will be anxiety associated with the changes as some groups will be advantaged and others disadvantaged (see chapter 4).

Prosperity has been spreading fast but perhaps not fast enough. The results of the uneven distribution of technology's benefits in developing nations are obvious. They include such social and economic ills as population dislocations, social upheavals, extreme poverty, and debt. In developed nations, the results have included such issues as crumbling infrastructures, environmental pollution, and unhealthy lifestyles that lead to obesity and heart disease. With approximately a quarter of the world's population living in abject poverty, and as many as 800,000 people malnourished, feeding the additional people on the planet will continue to be an immense challenge. The only way out of this dilemma may be to rely increasingly on technology.

Another question is whether the United States will continue to be a center of entrepreneurial dynamism and vigor. There are signs of U.S. decline in this domain. U.S. venture capital is becoming less plentiful and less patient. Early stage venture capital is not as readily available. Estimated investments by angel funders are going down. Fewer seem to be willing to take the risks needed to develop new technologies.

Meanwhile more R&D is moving outside the United States. There are many indicators of the global diffusion of technology. China and India accounted for 31 percent of global R&D employees by the end of 2007, up from 19 percent in 2004. Seventy seven percent of new R&D sites planned by 2010 will be built in China or India.

Prosperity has been closely linked to the amount of money nations have spent on R&D. The leaders in R&D spending per unit of GDP have been such nations as Sweden, Finland, Israel, Japan, the United States, and Singapore, but will these countries continue to remain the leaders? How long will it take countries such as Brazil, Russian, China, and India to catch up?

In Europe, technologies such as printing, gunpowder and compass, which led to the Industrial Revolution created dramatic economic changes. Similarly, technologies including semiconductors, computer technology, lasers, and automation helped to turnaround the Chinese economy. The turnaround began after the West's opening to China when Premier Deng Xiaoping established a new direction for his nation based on modernization and other improvements in agriculture, industry, the military, and science and technology. A key to the turnaround has been a 20 percent cumulative average growth in R&D expenditures from 1991 to 2002. Total Chinese R&D expenditure is just behind the United States and Japan. The Chinese economy is on a well-planned transition from raw materials, agricultural, and manufacturing to information and knowledge-based products and services.

Worldwide there has been a mushrooming of industrial technology alliances between foreign owned firms and U.S.-owned companies. Most of these alliances involve companies from the United States, Europe, and Japan and focus on biotechnology and information technology. Other technology areas that have been the subject of these alliances have included advanced materials, aerospace, defense, automotive, and chemicals. Increasingly, the alliances are bringing in China and other nations into greater contact with the developed world. China is part of the structure that has fueled the growth of U.S.-, European-, and Japan-based firms.

In the future, will the most profitable companies in the world continue to be headquartered in the United States? Very likely fewer of them will be U.S. companies. In 2004, for instance, eight of the world's most profitable companies (ExxonMobil, Citigroup, General Electric, Bank of America, Freddie Mac, Altria, Wal-Mart, and Microsoft) were headquartered in the United States. The only non-U.S. firms to break into the list were BP (English) and Total-France (French). However, in 2008, only four of the world's most profitable companies were headquartered in the United States (ExxonMobil, General Electric, Chevron, and Microsoft). The other companies on this list represent a broad diversity of countries, including Shell (Dutch/English), Gazprom (Russian), BP (English), Total (French), HSBC (English), and PetroChina (Chinese).

The Energy Gap

The developing world still suffers from a huge energy gap (see chapter 6). Half the world's population subsists at agrarian or lower levels of energy access and their population density exceeds the environment's carrying capacity. Energy is critical for the basic food, water, shelter, and minimal health services that people require to survive. It is needed to increase quality of life through higher levels of literacy, life expectancy, improved sanitation, physical security, and social security, and lower levels of infant mortality. Amenities such as recreation only become more widespread when people have sufficient energy.

If energy is to become more amply available, there is a need for more international cooperation, greater R&D, investment, and technological diffusion. GDP and the quality of life, for instance, are highly tied to electrical consumption. The vast network of electrification that currently exists in the world was one of the twentieth-century's greatest achievements. However, the increase in greenhouse gas emissions that has been caused by this electrification is very troubling (see chapter 6). The greenhouse gases are concentrated in some of the world's most important manufacturing areas. Will they continue to grow rapidly in the face of this threat?

As countries get richer, their greenhouse gas emissions tend to go down as a proportion of GDP. The United States, France, and Japan are approximately at half the carbon intensities levels of China and India. Per unit of economic activity, they are creating less greenhouse gas emissions. In developed countries, huge advances, however, still are possible in increasing energy efficiency and lowering energy demand. The U.S. electrical system, for instance, loses 55.9 quads of energy for every 35.0 useful quads of energy it creates. For a carbon constrained world, a number technologies will have to grow in importance (see chapter 6): end-use efficiency, nuclear, renewables, biomass, and hybrids. For instance, gasoline engines are considered to be 13 to 18 percent efficient, while hybrid vehicle efficiency is considered to be in the 62 to 77 percent range.

Many new technologies must be tried by the people of the world. There have to be fundamental breakthroughs that cannot be easily imagined today (see chapter 6). For instance, smart grids will create a network of technologies and services that will not just provide illumination. Every node in the grid will be responsive, adaptive, price-smart, ecosensitive, real-time, flexible, and interconnected.[9]

The Problem for Companies

The problem for companies is that as these changes take place not all of them will be outright winners; there will be both losers and undecided contests. Many theories exist about how to win the competitive battles that must be fought to commercialize new technologies. These theories range from Andy Grove who argues that companies should anticipate what is to come next and concentrate on what they do best, ceding the rest to their competitors, to Michael Porter who maintains that they should dominate industry forces and be unique. Other theories are those of C. K. Prahalad who holds that companies should develop hard to imitate competencies that make them stand out from their competitors to Michael Eisner who argues for the importance of diffusing innovation through multiple distribution channels for creative content. Gary Hamel preaches that firms have to regularly make revolutions in their business models and strategies.[10] Business model and strategy revolution trumps technological innovation as a way to succeed.

Companies have many moves open to them (see chapter 3). After examining the external environment and investigating what are their critical internal capabilities and competencies, they can reposition the products and services they sell by lowering prices and thereby undercutting competitors and gaining market share. On the other hand, they can increase profitability by means of advertising, promotion, sales, and distribution to differentiate their products. These moves enhance customer loyalty and achieve higher margins companies may be seeking. Companies also can redefine the businesses in which they compete. This redefinition emerges as a consequence of mergers, acquisitions, and divestitures they may make and the alliances they may fashion. Companies can compete, as Hamel maintains, in the realm of strategic business models creating in the process whole new industries that do not currently exit. The moves that companies make cannot be one-time thrusts.

Often times, bigness is a liability that reduces flexibility and prevents companies from acting. It just adds to the bureaucracy. Large firms often have trouble competing against smaller and more nimble ones. The smaller firms may engage in a type of judo-strategy in which they use movement to avoid direct confrontation with the larger concerns. The small companies bend but do not break when they are subject to retaliation from the larger firms. They rely on leverage, using the weight and strength of their large opponents against them.

Winning is rare but being a small moving target often allows small firms to fly under the radar of large firms and to defeat them. In a study of 1000 companies from 1992 to 2002, only 32 firms were able to sustain competitive advantage for the entire period based on their stock performance, 64 did the exact opposite, and in 37 of 78 industry, there were no winners.[11] In this sample of companies, it was smaller companies that beat the larger ones. The 32 winners averaged $3.5 billion in revenues and 14,500 employees, while the 64 losers averaged $10.7 billion in revenues and 48,000 employees. Winners were less well known than losers. They included such companies as Alliant Tech, Amphenol, Ball, Brown & Brown, Forest Labs, SPX, Cabot, Donaldson, as well as Southwest Airlines, Johnson Controls, Harley Davidson, and Best Buy. In contrast, the losers included such well-known names as Goodrich, Delta Airlines, Disney, Conagra, ADM, Merck, Readers Digest, Kodak, McDonalds, Nordstrom, Halliburton, Kmart, Mattell, Honeywell, Pharmacia, and Saks as well as Snap On, Parametric, and LSI Logic.

To be a winner, a company has to have a number of important attributes, including:

1. Being in a *sweet spot* or a relatively uncontested market niche.
2. Having the *agility* to get into this niche.
3. Having the *discipline* to protect it.
4. And having the *focus* to fully exploit it.

Losers tend to have the opposite characteristics. They are in sour spots, rigid, inept, and diffuse and unable to fully exploit the market niches they occupy. The implications are that to succeed in the long run, companies must learn to manage the tensions that exist between growth and profits, reinvention and operational excellence, exploration and exploitation, and so on (see table A.4). The capacity for companies to manage these tensions are difficult to acquire.

Table A.4   Managing the tensions

A Sweet spot	Agility (move)	Discipline (protect)	Focus (extend)
Goal	Achieve growth Innovation Reinvention	Enhance profits Efficiency Operational excellence	Profits and growth Reform and refinement Fine-tuning
Actions	Explore Prospect	Exploit Defend	Explore and exploit Analyze
Strategies	Vision	Mission	Mission-vision
Conditions	Disequilibrium	Equilibrium	Equilibrium-disequilibrium
Technologies	Disruptive	Sustaining	Sustaining-disruptive
Industries	Dynamic	Static	Dynamic-static
Image of the future	Unpredictable	Like today	Gradually evolving
People	Revolutionaries *Break rules*	Controllers *Enforce rules*	Improvers *Fix rules*

Innovation versus Management

The paradox that companies must manage is that to succeed in the long run innovation means risk, while good management typically is based on an effort to minimize risk. Most people in business as in life have powerful reasons for keeping risk to a minimum.

Accounting and financial tools generally do not fully capture the value of risk-taking. In deliberating about whether to undertake a particular project, people in business become conservative. It is realistic for them to dwell on the technical and commercial feasibility. They have to estimate the following:

- Probable development, production, and marketing costs.
- Approximate timing of these costs.
- Future income streams.
- The time at which the income streams are likely to develop.

All of these calculations are fraught with uncertainty. The only way to reduce the uncertainty is to undertake projects that are as safe as possible. Thus, people in business tend to concentrate on innovations where the success appears to be easy. The bias is toward simple, well-tread areas, since fundamental research and invention involve greater uncertainty (see chapter 1).

People in business typically establish new generations of existing products, introduce new models, and differentiate a product further rather than creating different products and new product lines. They reduce uncertainty by licensing others' inventions, imitating others' product introductions, modifying existing processes, and making minor technical improvements. An automobile with a new type of body and engine, for instance, is less likely to be introduced than an auto which involves modifications of existing bodies and engines.

For a new product to be launched, people in business must have a bias toward optimism. Engineers, for instance, may make optimistic estimates of development costs even when they have strong incentives to be more objective in their appraisals, since without the optimistic estimates they would not be given the right to carry out the projects.

As hard as it is to estimate technical success, it is difficult to predict market success. Market launch and growth in sales are more distant in time, and conditions in the future are likely to vary. The reactions of competitors to the threat of new products cannot be known in advance. Also to achieve an advance understanding of the benefits, given changing circumstances in the future, is difficult. How long a product will be on the market and how dominant it will be given the threat of technical obsolescence is hard to predict.

Even after prototype testing, pilot plant work, trial production, and test marketing, technical uncertainty is likely to exist in the early stages of innovation and development. The question typically is not whether a product will or will not work; rather, the issues at this stage are what standards of performance the product will achieve under different operating conditions and what the costs will be of improving performance under these conditions. Unexpected problems can arise before a product reaches the market, in the early stages of a promising commercial launch, and after product introduction. It is not only technical uncertainty that affects new products. General business uncertainty also is a factor, and new products also can be hurt by inconsistent government support.

For technological innovation to take place, the great English economist Keynes believed that "animal spirits" were necessary. He proclaimed that innovation of this nature, where the full consequence of what is to take place can be known only very much in advance, requires a spontaneous urge to action rather than excessive rationality. If an individual is to do a quantitative analysis of the benefits multiplied by an analysis of the risks he or she is likely to conclude that it is better to go back to sleep than to proceed. If animal spirits are dimmed and spontaneous optimism falls, innovation is set back. Keynes therefore argued for supplementing reasonable calculation with animal spirits.

Systems Theory

Keynes does not argue for the elimination of reasonable calculation, just its supplementation. This book has been based on the argument that reasonable calculation can assist people in organizations when they take risks like introducing new technologies. Underlying this rational calculation is system's theory.[12] Foresight requires that individuals think in system's terms.[13] They must take into account the big picture, that is the entire realm of factors that may affect the success of their endeavors. To be long-term winners, they increasingly have to rely on an understanding of all elements in the external environment. Understanding the full impacts of decision pathways requires an integrated comprehension of the many dimensions of the external environment.

Changes in one factor (energy prices, terror, etc.) induce changes in another which in turn bring about changes in a third, and so on (see table A.5). These changes link together in chains of cause and effect. Identifying the discrete contributions of each factor to the end result is difficult because the factors are intermingled in causal webs that are hard to disassemble. The factors themselves are not coherent entities; each consists of conflicting tendencies. With an aggregation as broadly conceived as the global economy, there are countless driving forces. Examining system level propositions against actors' motivations and interactions (see chapter 2) may be useful in that it can help in understanding the logic by which systems cohere and/or disintegrate.

Systems generally display great resiliency. They can be in equilibrium for long periods of time, but countervailing forces do exist and they can migrate quickly in surprising directions. They throw systems off-course. The only way to understand the financial meltdown of the end of the first decade of the twenty-first century is in terms of the system's very rapid disintegration. Risks are corelated. Systems can plunge swiftly from high degrees of organization and stability to low degrees. What provides for ongoing coherence and prevents rapid disintegration? Is it the linkages among elements and feedback loops that freeze elements into fixed cycles? Or does the opposite take place—some elements in the systems experience strains, fall apart, and cause others to collapse? The questions to ask are when does linear change terminate and nonlinear transition take over and at what speed do these processes happen?

Table A.5   System-level propositions

High energy prices

- Population pressure increases energy prices.
- A robust economy increases energy prices.
- High energy prices negatively affect the global economy.
- High energy prices can stimulate new technologies.
- Technology can raise (or lower) energy prices.
- Government can raise (or lower) energy prices.
- High energy prices can inhibit climate change.
- Technology can accelerate (or reduce) climate change.
- Governments can accelerate or reduce climate change.

Terror

- Strong governments can prevent terror.
- High energy prices can increase terror.
- Youth bulges can bring about terror.
- A robust economy can mitigate terror.
- Terror raises energy prices.
- Terror negatively affects the global economy.
- Terror weakens government.
- Terror retards the diffusion of most technologies.
- Terror inhibits the free flow of people.

The global economy

- A robust economy can strengthen government.
- A robust economy can strengthen technology.
- A robust economy can increase population pressure.
- A robust economy can accelerate climate change.
- Population pressure increases climate change.
- Population pressure can have a negative effect on the global economy.
- Climate change can have a negative effect on the global economy.
- Government can affect population pressure.
- Technology can have a positive impact on the global economy.
- Government can affect technological development.
- Government can have a positive impact on the global economy.
- The interaction of government and technology can moderate the effects of terror, energy prices, population, and climate change on the global economy.

A comprehensive checklist of propositions may sensitize people to an array of different possibilities. To provide some examples, global insecurity, affects population movement and composition. It then can inhibit commerce by slowing down the smooth flow of technologies, goods, services, and money. Though terror raises energy prices, its impacts may be moderated by the extent to which national and international governance systems remain free, open, and strong in the face of these threats. Oil prices can skyrocket because of global prosperity and rising demand, thereby increasing global climate change, while scarcity may induce governments to raise energy taxes or take other steps to get people to conserve. Higher energy prices can limit economic growth unless there are technological breakthroughs in energy saving devices and fuels. These breakthroughs can be speeded up or retarded by the policies of governments and the kinds of investments they make or fail to make in research and development. All of these factors affect the degree to which economic conditions are stable or vibrant in various time horizons. The more stable and predictable that economic conditions are, the better the climate will be for investment. A better climate for investment creates a positive feedback loop that induces more investment and better economic results. The key is to understand these connections and be mindful of how system-level propositions affect and are affected by actors' motivations and behavior (see chapter 2).

Technology is a major hinge, forcing critical junctures to take place which speed change, but technology also can be a pinch point which inhibits forward progress. The goal is to target resources to maximize the benefits, and minimize the unintended consequences. In a systems model, there are blockers, accelerators, feedback loops, and temporary and permanent resting points. The tools for systems thinking are to focus on trends over time. This means standing back far enough to get a holistic view, or a view that deliberately blurs discrete events into patterns and structures that reveal broader patterns. Start with the certainties—the trends over time, but do not end there. What are the important variables that affect these trends? Historical data often is needed for evidence only lies in what already has happened, but this evidence is inherently limited because the future rarely repeats the past in a precise way that is useful (see chapter 4). Preferred outcomes like romances must be compared to distasteful ones like tragedies and the analyst must search for the surprises that lie between.

Causal mapping is a powerful tool. People in companies should attempt to determine *why* an increase in factor A makes factor B higher and *why* an increase in factor C makes factor D lower, holding all other conditions constant (see chapter 4). Feedback loops affect outcomes (see chapter 6). Reinforcing loops accelerate the action and destabilize systems. Balancing loops hold back the action, counteract it, and stabilize the system. Systems theory, thus, underlies foresight. In this book, five systems have been examined (see table 6.1)—national security, society, government, the world economy, and energy and the environment. Possible endpoints in each of these systems have been identified and the interactions among the endpoints explored. Analytical tools have been introduced for understanding the impacts on companies and suggestions have been made for how people in business should use these tools to not only understand the future, but to shape it, with the aim being to bring into existence the romances, prevent the tragedies, and manage the surprises.

APPENDIX A

Intersecting Stories of the Future

Surprises are possible because stories intersect. People in organizations must take into account the intersections of many stories. Imagine four realms, with different types of stories in each of them. These four realms are (1) global security/terrorism; (2) society—the distribution and movement of populations; (3) governance systems—the status of domestic laws and regulations; and (4) energy prices and the environment. The stories in each of these realms have vivid names to telegraph their logic. For example, the stories in the social realm are "old and feeble," "young and militant," and "moving and seeking," the stories in the government realm are "free to choose," "well-regulated," and "preferential treatment," and so on. In this exercise, the purpose is to gauge the impacts on technology. Do the stories stimulate innovation in a broad array of technologies such as genetic engineering, alternative energy, and so on?

In examining intersecting stories, the number of combinations is very high. On the one hand, preferred and nonpreferred outcomes may clump together. This clustering makes sense; various feedbacks and spillovers create consistency. Events might not unfold in a unified fashion. But clustering may not take place and there may be many in-between outcomes; these are essentially comedies in the language of this book and are to be distinguished from the romances and tragedies of straight clustering. Not every logical possibility with respect to the so-called comedies can be developed, but, it may be revealing to take a look at a number of them.

Young and Militant Davos: Davos combines with a young and militant population that lives in well-regulated societies. These societies endure economic turmoil. But they emerge in better shape. The economy has rugged times, but strong growth and other indicators of economic vigor are restored. All of this takes place while the Saudi regime has an Iranian style revolution and energy prices soar. Well-ordered governance moderates this turbulence and helps to restore prosperity after some rough patches. The climate for technological innovation is fairly good. Indeed, technology contributes to a relatively benign outcome.

Lack of Integration: There is a cycle of fear that does not go away because populations on the move are not well-integrated into the countries to which they migrate. Their outsider status causes all kinds of friction. Domestic legal systems in many nations where the immigrants come are controlled by special interests, there is vast corruption, and the newcomers have no way to break in. At the same time, the Saudi regime radicalizes to ward off external Islamic pressure, oil wells are in disrepair, and the Saudis restrict output. The climate for technological innovation is poor.

The Costs of Imposing Order: The U.S. government actually succeeds in imposing order, of course not without serious cost to itself and its few allies. To impose this order, it has to overcome the resistance of young militants in its midst and in the midst of its main allies. Domestic governance deteriorates under the stress and inhibits economic growth. Economic progress is slow and uneven, but because the Saudi regime hangs on and keeps finding and delivering oil, energy prices remain fairly stable. The Saudis themselves become richer and invest more in the West so they help prop it up despite the extremist challenges they face. Nonetheless, the climate for innovation is strained, though not stunted entirely. Some types of technologies, for example, those favored by the security branches of the government, do particularly well.

Good Governance: A new Islamic organization led by a successor movement to al Qaeda imposes a Caliphate on most of the Muslim world. Non-Muslim populations age rapidly, putting pressure on health and welfare systems. Good governance avoids the worst of outcomes, however. Social security does not collapse in such countries as the United States, Japan, Germany, China, the United Kingdom, and Russia that have aging populations. The elderly are saved from mass impoverishment, but the world economy languishes. It does not swing wildly back and forth, however, because central bank fine-tuning staves off crises. The Saudi regime, now a linchpin of the New Caliphate, continues to deliver energy at a reasonable price to help finance ambitious projects. Unfortunately, the climate for technological innovation is weak.

Well Integrated: The United States takes charge. It puts a tight reign on insurrectionist movements and eliminates most terrorist threats. Large numbers of militants leave their countries of origin and migrate to societies with free and open economies where they have the right to express their opinions in peaceful and democratic ways. They successfully take advantage of the economic opportunities, which gives them a stake in the system's stability. The world economy does not grow spectacularly fast because of the costs of fighting a successful war against terror, but it shows steady improvement. The Saudi regime, having exhausted most of its oil reserves (the pessimists in this instance are right), modernizes. Indeed, it may decide to invest heavily in alternative energy. Its investments may even make it a center for research on climate change. Technological innovation under these conditions is much in demand. Its success helps usher in better conditions.

One could go on in this vein. The point is that intersecting stories might unfold in unanticipated ways, hopeful and otherwise.

APPENDIX B

Social, Political, and Economic Indicators: Web Resources

Resources on Global Attitudes and Opinions:

The Pew Global Attitudes Project
Report on recent changes in global public attitudes, plus more polls and surveys, from the Pew Research Center for the People and the Press
http://people-press.org

United States Government Resources:

U.S. State Department, Bureau of Economic and Business Affairs, Country Reports on Economic Policy and Trade Practices, by region, through 1999
http://www.state.gov/www/issues/economic/trade_reports/

U.S. State Department Country Commercial Guides
http://www.state.gov/www/about_state/business/com_guides/2001/index.html

U.S. State Department Background Notes, by country
http://www.state.gov/r/pa/bgn/

U.S. State Department Policies
http://www.state.gov/www/policy.html

U.S. State Department information about regions of the world
http://www.state.gov/www/regions/wha/index.html

U.S. Library of Congress Country Studies
http://lcweb2.loc.gov/frd/cs/

The CIA World Factbook
http://www.cia.gov/cia/publications/factbook/

U.S. Embassies around the world and their host countries
http://usembassy.state.gov/

The U.S. Treasury Department's Bureau of the Public Debt
http://www.publicdebt.treas.gov/

The U.S. Treasury Department's Debt to the Penny
http://www.publicdebt.treas.gov/opd/opdpenny.ht

The U.S. Energy Information Administration's Office of Energy Markets and
End Use—includes Country Analysis Briefs and International Energy Statistics
http://www.eia.doe.gov/emeu/

International Economic Development Organizations:

The World Bank
http://www.worldbank.org/

The World Bank: World Development Indicators
Information on "global links" plus an index of globalization with trends and
country data.
http://www.worldbank.org/data/wdi2001/index.htm
http://www.worldbank.org/data/wdi2001/pdfs/globallinks.pdf
http://www.worldbank.org/data/wdi2001/pdfs/tab6_1.pdf

The International Monetary Fund
http://www.imf.org/

International Monetary Fund (IMF) activities, by country
http://www.imf.org/external/country/index.htm

Research at the International Monetary Fund
http://www.imf.org/external/pubs/res/index.htm

Commercial Web Sites:

The A. T. Kearney/Foreign Policy Magazine Globalization Index, which ranks
countries based on their levels of economic, social, technological, and political
integration with the rest of the world.
http://www.atkearney.com/main.taf?site=1&a=5&b=4&c=1&d=42

SmartMoney.com—Up-to-the-minute market news, information, and maps
http://www.smartmoney.com/
(See especially the dynamic market maps.)
http://www.smartmoney.com/maps/

Academic Web Sites:

International Economics Links—A portal to online resources related to international economics from the International Economics program at The Chinese
University of Hong Kong.
http://intl.econ.cuhk.edu.hk/links/

Economagic—economic time series
http://www.economagic.com/

APPENDIX C

Additional Technological Opportunities*

Advances in nanomaterials are expected to be especially valuable in energy and power system applications, from super strong metal alloys for rotating machinery to tough composites that resist corrosion attack, less-brittle ceramics for power line insulators, and slick coatings that will reduce biofouling in cooling water intakes. Nanoscale research on lattice structures and electron pairing are expected to improve our understanding of superconductivity, leading to new alloy formulations, novel fabrication techniques, and, it is hoped, a material that will superconduct at room temperature. Other research is looking into using nanotechnology in the remediation of environmental problems, in the development of "green" processing technologies, and for nuclear waste management systems.

Hydrogen is the ideal feedstock for fuel cells, but cost has meant that hydrocarbons must be used as fuel for the near term. While progress in the development of catalysts for internally converting methane to hydrogen has reduced operating temperatures for some fuel cells to the 300–400°C range, advanced nanostructural catalysts may allow hydrocarbon reforming at very low temperatures (below 100°C). Successful development of such catalysts would help substantially in making fuel cells that can operate at ambient temperatures.

Applications in advanced power generation technologies are also foreseen. The catalysts mentioned should improve the performance of fuel cells, which are pushing for commercial viability. Hybrid photovoltaic solar cells based on conducting polymers and semiconductor nanorods also hold special promise; by combining the excellent electronic properties of inorganic semiconductors with the process flexibility of organic polymers, researchers are honing in on PV devices with good efficiencies that are easier and much less expensive to

---

*Based on the Electricity Technology Roadmap, Difficult challenge, and Enabling Technologies meetings, discussions, and reports with colleagues at the Electric Power Research Institute (EPRI).

manufacture than conventional solar cells. Early prototypes have demonstrated power conversion efficiencies approaching 8 percent in the laboratory, about the same as today's commercially manufactured amorphous silicon thin-film PV modules. Researchers expect efficiencies to be improved significantly through engineering refinement and new material formulations.

Brand new generation options may also become feasible with the advent of new nanomaterials. Magnetohydrodynamic (MHD) generators, which produce electricity by passing a very hot, ionized gas through a magnetic field, have been stymied in the development stage by the insufficient durability of system components—especially the electrodes, which tend to corrode badly under high temperature. Tougher materials specially engineered for this application may reopen the investigation of MHD, which could be used in a combined-cycle configuration with a conventional steam turbine.

Biotechnology has already proved extremely valuable in agricultural applications, with genetic optimization of food strains boosting crop yields considerably. Work on environmental biotechnology, such as the development of microbes that can process and destroy toxic chemicals, has also proved valuable. The results of industrial bioengineering research, ranging from corrosion-preventing biofilms to ethanol-based petroleum substitutes to biodegradable plastics, also hold great promise. Biomimetic materials—man-made substances that imitate the characteristics of natural substances or systems—are the subject of much research, as these materials often promise superior properties, functionality, and adaptability. Biomimetic materials may be used as direct substitutes for existing technologies, enabling technologies for which existing materials are inadequate, or as the basis for new applications. It is hoped that biomimetic catalysis will provide an economic alternative to costly enzymes needed for conversion of biomass or other cellulosic materials to ethanol. New, protein-based adhesives modeled on those produced by mussels and barnacles may form stronger bonds with slick materials in wet industrial environments. Photovoltaic cells may be improved using light-gathering and self-assembly mechanisms suggested by plant photosynthesis. Hydrogen production and the desalinization of seawater are possibilities for a biomimetic process based on light-induced decomposition of water. Miming the ability of some biological systems to pump protons across cellular membranes may allow the development of advanced fuel cells that operate at room temperature. Realization of these biomimetic applications will generally require a better understanding of the natural processes being copied and substantial research on how similar functions can be engineered in a man-made system.

Recent experiments with wild and mutant algae in the chlamydomonas family suggest that the maximum thermodynamic conversion efficiency for converting light energy into chemical energy can potentially be doubled from approximately 10 to 20 percent when the potential difference between water oxidation (oxygen evolution) and proton reduction (hydrogen evolution) can be spanned by a single photon instead of the conventional two. Further investigation of this approach, especially to discover a biomimetic model for the synthesis process, may result in substantial improvements.

If a technique can indeed be developed for splitting water at industrially significant rates, novel process cycles may improve overall economics and provide additional benefits. For example, desalination of seawater—currently accomplished by high-temperature evaporation and condensation or by high-pressure reverse osmosis—could be integrated into the photo-induced decomposition process. The hydrogen split out of seawater could be combusted in a boiler or fed into a fuel cell to produce electricity. The water vapor resulting from combustion (or electrochemical reaction) could then be condensed and purified by conventional water-treatment technology to provide potable water. Such a cycle would, of course need to be economically competitive with the conventional desalination approaches.

Fuel cells appear to be a power generation technology tailor-made for a sustainable future. Producing electricity electrochemically rather than through fuel combustion, they have no moving parts and generate no noise or pollutant emissions. Still, the fuel cells now under development must operate at medium to high temperatures—some as high as 900°C. An ambient-temperature fuel cell would represent an important advance of technology. Biomimetic research into ion transport in plants at the macromolecular level may make such a device possible.

The electricity generation function of current fuel cells is dependent on catalytically stripping a hydrogen ion—a proton—from a hydrogen atom and inducing it to travel from the cell's anode, through an electrolyte, to its oxygen-bathed cathode. Electricity is generated when the electron remaining from each proton-stripped atom travels from the anode through an external circuit to reunite at the cathode. The process creates water and heat in addition to electricity. The ability of some biological systems to transport ions across cellular and intracellular membranes provides a model for a lower-temperature proton-pumping process. Specifically, bacteriorhodopsin (bR), a pigment in bacteria that grow in salt marshes, is a light-driven proton pump. In other words, bR uses the energy derived from light to pump protons across a membrane. It is postulated that a biomimetic (bR-like) proton-transmitting membrane could be the basis of an ambient temperature fuel cell. Recent research has aimed mainly at characterizing the structure and function of bR, but the emphasis is already shifting to investigation of how this phenomenon could be applied in a man-made system.

Despite substantial progress, the process of proton pumping is not yet fully understood on a molecular level, and a more complete understanding of the photochemistry involved is required. Still, if biomimetic proton pumping could be applied to develop a low-temperature fuel cell, it would carry with it real advantages in cost, weight, cycle life, and construction materials.

Notes

Introduction

1. Current writing about scenarios tends to focus on two questions: (1) how to create scenarios and (2) the content of various scenarios that have been written. For an excellent collection of papers and articles, see L. Fahey and R. Randall (eds.), *Learning from the Future* (New York: Wiley 1998). For examples of books that focus mainly on creating scenarios, see K. Van der Hejden, *Scenarios: The Art of Strategic Conversation* (New York: Wiley, 1996); G. Ringland, *Scenario Planning* (New York: Wiley, 1996); K. Van der Hejden, R. Bradfield, and G. Burt, G. Cairns, *The Sixth Sense: Accelerating Organizational Learning with Scenarios* (New York: Wiley, 2002); G. Ringland, *Scenarios in Business* (West Sussex, UK: Wiley, 1992); and M. Lindgren and H. Bandhold, *Scenario Planning* (New York: Palgrave Macmillan, 2003). For examples of books that focus mainly on scenarios that have been written, see P. Schwartz, *The Art of the Long View* (New York: Doubleday, 1996); P. Schwartz, *Inevitable Surprises* (New York: Penguin, 2003); P. Laudicina, *World Out of Balance* (New York: McGraw Hill, 2005); and E. Kelly, *Powerful Times* (Upper Saddle River, NJ: Wharton School, 2006). An older literature on scenarios also is worth noting. Important titles include H. Kahn and A. Weiner, *The Year 2000: A Framework for Speculation on the Next 33 Years* (New York: Macmillan, 1967); D. Meadows et al., *The Limits to Growth* (New York: Signet, 1973); D. Bell, *The Coming of Post-Industrial Society* (New York: Basic Books, 1976); and A. Toffler, *Future Shock* (New York: Bantam, 1984). Futurists' works include J. Coates and J. Jarratt, *What Futurists Believe* (Mt. Airy, MD: Lamond, 1989); J. Barker, *Paradigms: The Business of Discovering the Future* (New York: Harper Collins, 1993); and W. Bell, *Foundations of Future Studies: Volumes 1 and 2* (New Brunswick, NJ: Transaction, 1997 and 1998).
2. D. Loveridge, *Foresight* (New York: Routledge, 2009). Loveridge distinguishes between the informal and accidental and the formal and intentional uses of foresight. See p. 31.

3. That the pace of change has increased is by now a cliché, but the fast pace of change is really nothing new. Compare the last sixty years of world history with the prior sixty years that were even more turbulent. In 1936, Keynes wrote in his great book *The General Theory of Employment, Interest, and Money*: "The outstanding fact is the extreme precariousness of the basis of knowledge on which our estimates of prospective yield have to be made…We disguise this uncertainty from ourselves by assuming that the future will be like the past, that existing opinion correctly sums up future prospects, and by copying what everyone else is doing." But any view of the future based on "so flimsy a foundation" is liable to "sudden and violent changes."
4. F. Fukuyama *The End of History* (New York: Avon, 1992).
5. On p. 19, Loveridge writes, "situations are dynamic, occur in cascades and are never 'done with'…but simply change their context and content after every intervention."
6. M. Raynor, *The Strategy Paradox* (New York: Doubleday, 2007). An excellent book, but Raynor takes the opposite point of view. He maintains that only people at the top of the organization should be engaged in thinking about the future and exploring future outcomes. People at the bottom should be engaged in the orderly carrying out of everyday tasks in the most efficient way possible. In particular, see Chapter 6, pp. 106–138 of *The Strategy Paradox*.
7. The National Intelligence Council is an arm of the U.S. government affiliated with the Central Intelligence Agency (CIA). For the full report, see http://www.dni.gov/nic/NIC_globaltrend2020.html. For an update, see http://www.dni.gov/nic/NIC_2025_project.html.

1 Meeting the Challenges of the Future

1. See P. Ghemawat, *Commitment* (New York: Free Press, 1991).
2. See H. Courtney, *20/20. Foresight* (Boston: HBS Press, 2001) and M. Raynor, *The Strategy Paradox* (New York: Doubleday, 2007). The discussion that follows is indebted to their work.
3. On shaping the future, see G. Hamel and C. Prahalad, *Competing for the Future* (Boston: HBS Press, 1994).
4. D. Smith, R. Alexander, and D. Robinson, *Fumbling the Future* (New York: Morrow, 1988).
5. F. Knight, *Risk, Uncertainty, and Profit* (New York: Houghton Mifflin, 1921).
6. A past model may be deficient because of missing variables.
7. See P. Schoemaker, *Profiting from Uncertainty* (New York: Free Press, 2002).
8. N. Taleb, *The Black Swan* (New York: Random House, 2007).
9. D. Rigby and B. Bilodeau, "A Growing Focus on Preparedness," *Harvard Business Review*, July–August 2007.

2 Thinking about the Future

1. Michael Porter's classic *Competitive Advantage* (New York: Free Press, 1985) has an excellent discussion of how to create scenarios under conditions of uncertainty, see pp. 445–482.
2. In the management literature, a good discussion of narrative can be found in B. Pentland, "Building Process Theory with Narrative," *Academy of Management Review* 24, no. 4 (1999): pp. 711–724; there also are the works of A. Van de Ven, who tries to reconstruct management theory and practice in a narrative way. A summary of Van de Ven's thinking may be found in *Engaged Scholarship* (New York: Oxford University Press, 2007). In particular, see Chapter 7 "Designing Process Studies," pp. 194–233. In the popular management literature, a good book on the use of stories in management is S. Denning, *The Leader's Guide to Storytelling* (San Francisco: John Wiley, 2005). There also are many literary theories, which can be consulted, which are entirely outside the purview of management studies, including H. P. Abbott, *The Cambridge Introduction to Narrative* (Cambridge: Cambridge University Press, 2002); P. Cooley, *Narrative* (London: Routledge, 2001); G. Hughes, *Reading Novels* (Nashville: Vanderbilt University Press, 2002); S. Cohan and L. Shires, *Telling Stories* (London: Routledge, 1988); L. P. Wilbur, *The Seven Key Elements of Fiction* (London: Robert Hale, 2001); S. Keen, *Narrative Form* (London: Palgrave Macmillan, 2003); and S. Minot, *Reading Fiction* (Englewood Cliffs, NJ: Prentice-Hall, 1985).
3. A. Marcus, *Winning Moves* (Lombard, IL: Marsh Press: 2006), p. 206.
4. Ibid.
5. Any story that seems to provide certainty is suspect. "The brute fact is that it is very difficult to tell a compelling story about the future. No matter how thoughtfully you look ahead, the future is uncertain and inherently unknowable." Denning, *Leader's Guide to Storytelling,* p. 228.
6. See Wayne Booth, "The Empire of Irony," in *The Essential Wayne Booth* (Chicago: University of Chicago Press, 2006) edited by W. Jost, pp. 112–118.

3 The Challenges Businesses Face

1. A. Marcus, *Winning Moves* (Lombard, IL: Marsh Press, 2006).
2. Ibid.
3. This model is a modification of the framework proposed by M. Porter in "How Competitive Forces Shape Strategy," *Harvard Business Review,* March–April 1979. See L. Fahey and V. Narayanan, *Macroenvironmental Analysis* (St. Paul: West, 1986). Also see A. Marcus, *Management Strategy* (Burr Ridge, IL: McGraw-Hill/Irwin, 2005).
4. A. Grove, *Only the Paranoid Survive* (New York: Time Warner, 1999).
5. M. Gladwell, *The Tipping Point* (Boston: Little Brown, 2000).

6. For indicators to watch see such books as Worldwatch, *Vital Signs 2006* (New York: W.W. Norton, 2006) or M. Mazaar, *Global Trends 2005* (New York: St. Martins Press, 1999).
7. See A. Manu, *The Imagination Challenge: Strategic Foresight and Innovation in the Global Economy* (Berkeley, CA: New Riders, 2007).
8. This type of analysis is called morphological analysis. See M. Godet, *Creating Futures* (London: Economica, 2006). If all the in-between possibilities were listed there would be more than 200.
9. It is as if a short, middle-aged man decided that he wanted to be a basketball player because the opportunity was attractive, but he lacked the basic skills to pursue this option.
10. Table 2.2 is a more elaborate example.
11. E-mail from an executive of a large multinational.
12. G. Day, and P. Schoemaker, "Scanning the Periphery," *Harvard Business Review*, November, 2005.
13. P. Becker, *Corporate Foresight in Europe* (Brussels: European Commission (Scientific and Technological Foresight, 2002).

4 Population and Security Challenges

1. A. Marcus, *Big Winners and Big Losers: The 4 Secrets of Long-Term Business Success and Failure* (Upper Saddle River, NJ: Wharton School Press, 2005).
2. The National Intelligence Council (NIC) is a center of strategic thinking within the U.S. Government, reporting to the Director of National Intelligence (DNI) and providing the president and senior policymakers with analyses of foreign policy issues that have been reviewed and coordinated throughout the Intelligence Community.
3. Shell Oil. *Shell Global Scenarios to 2025* (Washington, DC: Institute for International Economics, 2005).
4. For example, see P. Schoemaker, "Multiple Scenario Development," *Strategic Management Journal* 14 (1993): pp. 193–213.
5. This was the view of the German philosopher Hegel. If scenario writers adopt a Hegelian worldview, they will imagine events moving toward positive ends. A transcendent point is reached that surmounts contradictory elements.
6. E. Kelly, *Powerful Times* (Upper Saddle River, NJ: Wharton School, 2006), p. 19.
7. Ibid.
8. A. Van de Ven, *Engaged Scholarship* (New York: Oxford University Press, 2007).
9. Some examples are Omnicare that has built its business around managing the prescription drug needs of elderly in nursing home, Thor that has built its business around the leisure time activities of the newly retired, Whole Foods that has built its business around the health consciousness of consumers, Dollar General that has built its business around providing for the needs

of poor and middle-class people, Fortune Brands that has built its business around the needs of the super-affluent, and Watsco that has built its business around the needs of people in the hot climates for air conditioning (see chapter 2).

10. S. Huntington, *The Clash of Civilizations and the Remaking of World Order* (New York: Touchstone, 1996), p. 117.

11. Ibid.

12. L. Feuer, *The Conflict of Generations* (New York: Basic Books, 1969); N. Choucri, *Population Dynamics and International Violence* (Lexington, MA: Lexington Books, 1974).

13. J. Wilson and R. Hernstein, *Crime and Human Nature* (New York: Free Press, 1998).

14. R. Rummel, *Death by Government* (New Brunswick, NJ: Transaction, 1997). Rummel estimates that there were 38 million direct deaths worldwide as a result of wars and revolutions and that if civilian casualties are included 169 million people perished in the world from 1900 to 1950.

15. The reign of terror during the French Revolution was mostly attributable to young persons, a pattern which has been repeated again and again in history.

16. In Europe today, the ratio of young to older men is low, but in the late nineteenth century and early twentieth century this pattern was different. Europe had large numbers of alienated young men ready to sacrifice themselves for the political movements of that time. The final passages in antiwar novel *All Quiet on the Western Front* graphically and poignantly illustrated the desperation of these young men returning home after battle.

17. L. Muraweic and D. Adamson, *Demography and Security: Population Matters* (Santa Monica, CA: Rand Corporation, 2000). It has been estimated that in the 1990s, countries in which young adults composed 40 percent or more of the population were more than twice as likely to experience an outbreak of violent conflict than those that were below this level. Why does such a high level of violence take place in societies with large proportions of young people? One is that people in this age group seek glory and the chance to show heroism. The typical inhibitions that block extreme behavior among other age brackets are not well developed. That the incentives for violence are greater than the patient pursuit of a narrow range of opportunities otherwise available in no way excuses this behavior. Though the attraction of violence for young people has been well established, not every young person decides to pursue this path.

18. The Rand Corporation defines terrorism "by the nature of the act," not by the identity of the cause. It holds that

> terrorism is violence, or the threat of violence, calculated to create an atmosphere of fear and alarm.... This violence...is generally directed against civilian targets...carried out in a way that will achieve maximum publicity...(and) intended to produce effects beyond...immediate physical damage..., having long-term psychological repercussions.

Relying on traditional just war arguments, terror may be defined as the targeting of innocent civilians in an attempt to instill fear and panic, not collateral damage. Terrorists aim to intimidate people and force them to relent and comply. The connection to the longing for some earthly utopia or paradise is strong. The ideology of the terrorist promises future perfection and ultimate meaning. Being on the side of nature and history in some glorious battle commands near total sacrifice and commitment. In comparison to the glory of a cause and its fundamental correctness, the existence of the individual and his victims is largely irrelevant. Rand Institute, *Long-Term Global Demographic Trends: Reshaping the Geopolitical Landscape* (Santa Monica, CA: Rand Corporation, 2001). Also see M. Walzer, *The Revolution of the Saints* (New York: Atheneum, 1968) and M. Walzer, "Five Questions about Terrorism," *Dissent* 49, no. 1 (2002): pp. 5–11. Walzer suggests that conventional war is defensive, fought at the command of legitimate authority, and pursued in limited ways without undue or excessive violence. It may be necessary and inevitable but it is not exalted. Terror, in contrast, has its roots in holy wars or crusades carried out by those who relish in violence and take it up with enthusiasm to purge the world of vice. For example, Robespierre, perhaps the first modern perpetrator of terror, wanted to create a "republic of virtue."

19. For instance, one can take the three years before 9/11 and compare them with three periods after it: (1) the year after the calamity, (2) the year after U.S. combat in Iraq ended, and (3) the year after the United States gave back sovereignty to an Iraqi government. In doing so, one would find that 9/11 started a cascading series of events where the number of incidents increased and their nature changed. Total incidents doubled and the number of injuries and fatalities increased four-to-five times. Another notable trend was that counter-terror efforts were not without effect, as Israeli counter-terror and the U.S. surge in Iraq became increasingly successful during this period.

20. The first two categories are nonviolent whereas the last three categories are based on the degree of violence that takes place. HIIK data can be used to develop a composite conflict index (*cflt_index*) based on the number and corresponding intensities of conflicts for 127 countries. Specifically, it is possible to calculate a weighted average conflict level on an annual basis for these countries.

21. H. Urdal, "A Clash of Generations? Youth Bulges and Political Violence," *International Studies Quarterly* 50, no. 3 (2006): pp. 607–630.

22. For more than 200 years, Malthus, whose views centered on the dangers of overpopulation, inspired most thinking about population. Malthus argued that the "power of population" was "indefinitely greater than the power in the earth to produce subsistence" and when unchecked, population "increases in a geometrical ratio,... (while) subsistence increases only in an arithmetical ratio" (Thomas Malthus, *Essay on the Principle of Population*, 1803). However, today population growth is neither exponential nor arithmetic.

23. This shift has occurred over a long period of time and in an unbalanced way. As economies grow and health conditions improve, mortality rates decline but only substantially later do fertility rates follow. Demographic transition takes place in stages with a pretransition stage (stage 1) characterized by a high birth rate, high infant and maternal mortality rates, and very short life spans. Population growth in this phase is stagnant. An early transition stage (stage 2) starts when infant mortality starts to fall off because of advances in GDP. With GDP growth, developments such as increased variety in the food supply, better housing, improved sanitation, and progress in preventative and curative medicine occur. Consequently, the death rate falls and youth populations surge creating bulges. The key driver in stage 2 is the delay between the declines in fertility and mortality. Demographic transition theory suggests that population growth is not unlimited, however. The next phase (stage 3) has a declining birth rate; population still grows, but mainly because the death rate continues to fall. The average age of the population starts to increase in stage 3. Late transition (stage 4) is characterized by a birth rate at or below the replacement level. It is substantially lower than at the start of the transition. This stage is marked by continuous advances in medicine and life-extending activities, which prolong life and lead to large increases in the number of elderly, a phenomenon now common in many advanced industrial countries. In stage 5, the birth rate is stable, but the death rate grows mainly because of aging, and thus the population starts to fall.

24. Busts follow bulges. The abundant 15–24 year old cohort sits a top of sparse 0–14 year old cohort as in Iran. Algeria, Jordan, and Lebanon have similar profiles. All these countries have seen declines of more than 65 percent in their birth rates, a fall off that is unprecedented in history outside of war, famine, and other unnatural disasters. However, fertility rates in the Middle East were so high in 1970 (on average 5.84) that even with a greater than 48 percent decline the rates in the region continue to be nearly 35 percent above the replacement level. And in some Middle East nations, population growth rates and fertility rates have not fallen. Several countries in the Middle East, notably Iraq, Yemen, Sudan, West Bank/Gaza, and Saudi Arabia have fertility rates more than 100 percent above the replacement level, while other countries are well below it. See H. Hakimain, From Demographic Transition to Fertility Boom and Bust: Iran in the 1980s and 1990s, *Development and Change* 37, no. 3 (2006): 571–597. This discussion of why there has been a drop off in the Iranian population is fascinating.

25. Two independent variables are used to test the proposition that youth bulge positively influences conflicts and bust has a negative influence. The baseline model uses the ratio of the population between age 15 to 24 to adult population (15 years and above). The analysis also uses an alternative variable to measure youth bulge. This variable is the ratio of the population of young people between age 15 to 24 to the total population in a country. The bust variable is defined as the ratio between the population within the 0–14 age

bracket to the population between the ages 15–24. The analysis relies on the *International Data Base of the U.S. Census Bureau* to calculate the bulge and bust variables. The analysis drops countries with population less than 250,000 in 2001 for two reasons. First, data for some of these countries is difficult to get. And second, some of these countries are tiny island nations such as the British Virgin Islands, Tuvalu and Solomon Islands that may not have the demographic characteristics of typical nation states. Controls are inserted for variables representing such factors as level of economic development, lawlessness, religion, and ethnicity. See A. Marcus, M. Islam, and J. Maloney, "Youth Bulges, Busts, and Doing Business in Violence-Prone Nations" *Business and Politics* 10, no. 3 (2008), Article 4, available at: http://www.bepress.com/bap/vol10/iss3/art4.

26. Pape for instance, argues that counter-insurgency often has the opposite effect—it has made situations worse. He points, for instance, to a common mistake of granting significant concessions to terror organizations that only inspire them to ask for more. R. Pape, "The Strategic Logic of Suicide Terrorism," *American Political Science Review* 97, no. 3 (2003): pp. 343–361.

27. C. K. Prahalad, *The Fortune at the Bottom of the Pyramid* (Upper Saddle River, NJ: Wharton University Press, 2006); and S. Hart, S. *Capitalism at the Crossroads* (Upper Saddle River, NJ: Wharton University Press, 2007).

5   Political and Economic Challenges

1. M. Gladwell, *Blink* (Boston: Little Brown, 2007).

2. See the case about Amazon and Barnes and Noble in A. Marcus, *Winning Moves* (Lombard, IL: Marsh Press, 2006).

3. http://info.worldbank.org/governance/wgi/index.asp.

4. See the Web sites of the U.S. Census Bureau and the United Nations. Convergence will take place because of urbanization, higher levels of education, and increased economic growth. Education alters attitudes and gender roles and leads women to have fewer babies.

5. Will there really be a continued rapid decline in fertility in Saudi Arabia, from 5.5 births per woman in 2000 to 3.5 births per woman in 2020? Even with greater oil wealth, Saudi family structure and the place of women in society may not change.

6. Governments must be able to draw on a vigorous private sector. There must be prosperity for governments to be effective.

7. R. Rotberg (ed.), *When States Fail* (Princeton, NJ: Princeton University Press, 2003). Also see J. Migdal, *Strong Societies and Weak States* (Princeton, NJ: Princeton University Press, 1988).

8. The more developed countries need to absorb a sufficient number of immigrants to support an aging population. Despite the difficulties and burdens of assimilating immigrants, immigration must go up dramatically in countries like the United States, Germany, Italy, Russia, and Japan, so that the

ratio working-age to retirees does not drop off significantly. The United States, for instance, not only needs more geriatric doctors. It also requires half a million more nurses by 2020.

9. In Japan and the EU, the workforce has been declining and will continue to do so at a rate of 1 percent per year until 2030 when the expected plunge is expected to be greater than 1.5 percent annually. In 1950, the percentage of people living in more developed countries was 23 percent, today it is approximately 13 percent, and by 2050 it is projected to be less than 10 percent.

10. The ugly specter of the Skinheads that have emerged in many countries has to be controlled. Prejudice against immigrants and a person of different racial and ethnic origin has to be prevented.

11. Rotberg, *When States Fail,* 2003.

12. Rulers of established nations have large and powerful armies but these armies are not been well-trained in social reconstruction. The armies are good at breaking states apart rather than building them. Problems in governance are not restricted to the less well-developed countries. Many countries have suffered from humanitarian crises. The incapacity to deal with Hurricane Katrina dealt a huge blow to the Bush administration.

13. The modern states of Germany and Italy only were forged toward the end of the nineteenth century. The German and Italian languages and their national identities took shape then.

14. The essence of the Hobbesian bargain is that life for most people would be "nasty, short, and brutish" were it not for the protection afforded by the state. In fact, in many parts of the world, life remains "nasty, short, and brutish" precisely because the state has not been successful in the task of nation building.

15. See A. Marcus and S. Kaiser, *Managing Beyond Compliance* (Cleveland, OH: North Coast, 2006).

16. D. North, *Institutions, Institutional Change and Economic Performance* (Cambridge: Cambridge University Press, 1990).

17. It goes back to Adam Smith, but the most celebrated proponent of this ideology in last fifty years or so was University of Chicago economist Milton Friedman. Friedman, *Capitalism and Freedom* (Chicago: University of Chicago Press, 1962).

18. Where neither benefited party has an obligation to pay the costs of this by-product effect, the costs fall on the society. The immediate parties to a transaction may be better off, but society-as-a-whole foots the bill. Friedman believes that to remedy this effect society must charge the individuals involved in the transaction the true costs. Whatever damage is generated should be internalized in the price of the transaction. By doing so, the market defect or inefficiency (the price of pollution which is not counted in the transaction) is corrected. Only with these costs internally accounted for will the market reflect the true "social costs" of the activity. Actual U.S. policy relies on regulations and fines instead of the market to discourage these adverse effects. But even a governmental approach that would tax polluters

and others using common resources is inadequate according to Friedman, since the extent of harm caused is often latent or long-term and the true diminution in value of the resource is often intangible and difficult to measure in monetary terms.

19. R. Musgrave and P. Musgrave, Public *Finance in Theory and Practice* (New York: McGraw Hill, 1989). Here and throughout this discussion of the well-regulated scenarios the Musgraves' views are featured.

20. Of course, this outcome does not always take place. Many factors influence the balance of power between special interests and the larger groups. Governments are large and complex. Their efforts to correct failures in one area create unanticipated consequences in other areas. Inequality of power and privilege exists among government officials. It may be troublesome as inequality in the marketplace. Governments have the right to command and coerce people. Abuses therefore can take place. Corruption may be rampant. In many areas, there is no choice but to give governments what amounts to monopoly power. Without adequate competition, it is hard for them to be efficient. They cannot easily define and measure their outputs. The programs they start lack the simple, well-understood bottom-line termination mechanisms that exist in the private sector. In a market, the costs of producing or sustaining an activity are linked to the prices that are charged. In government, revenues come from taxes, which are only indirectly related to the services provided. Taxpayers do not directly obtain what they want for tax dollars they give. Nearly everything governments do is bundled together. All citizens can do to express dissatisfaction is to vote out-of-office the politicians who support programs they oppose, but in voting these politicians out-of-office the citizens may put programs they support at risk. Hence governments to a greater extent than businesses tend to escape accountability for their actions. Simply because there are market imperfections that need to be corrected by governments does not guarantee that governments will effectively deal with these inadequacies. These views of government are skillfully summarized by the Rand Institute economist Charles Wolf, Jr. in *Markets or Governments: Choosing between Imperfect Alternatives* (Cambridge, MA: MIT Press, 1988).

21. A. Latour, "With His Latest Deal, SBC's Whitacre Is Telecom's Kingpin," *Wall Street Journal* (Feb. 1, 2005): p. B1. Michael Salisbury, MCI's former chief counsel, quoted in the *Wall Street Journal* as describing SBC's CEO Edward Whitacre, as being " 'a very tough-minded, focused executive with very clear idea of what he wanted to accomplish.' " Whitacre, Salisbury said, "created a regulatory environment in which... (the) Bells can succeed and competitors can't."

22. A. Marcus, *Winning Moves* (Lombard, IL: Marsh Press, 2006).

23. See F. Weaver, *Economic Literacy* (Lanham, MD: Rowman and Littlefield, 2007 edition). There are many other books like this that could be cited. A good introduction to macroeconomics that still has contemporary relevance is L. Silk, *Economics in Plain English* (New York: Simon and Schuster, 1978).

Another book in this vein is A. Sommers, *The U.S. Economy Demystified* (Lexington, MA: D.C. Heath, 1985). For a good book on economic forecasting, see J. Morris, *How to Forecast* (Burlington, VT: Gower, 2001).

24. The use of government deficits and surpluses to smooth the business cycle was Keynes great contribution to economics. Richard Nixon proclaimed in the early 1970s that "we are all Keynesians now."

25. The Great Depression of the 1930 was a demand side shock.

26. A current-account deficit must equal a capital-account surplus and a current-account surplus must equal a capital-account deficit. Current account transactions consist of merchandise trade (*import and export of goods*); service trade (*import and export of services*); and income from investments; and unilateral transfers (*gifts to and from foreigners*). Capital account transactions consist of direct investments by foreigners in the United States and by U.S. citizens abroad and loans to and from foreigners. The official reserve transactions of all governments have to equal zero.

27. These countries were the biggest holders of foreign exchange reserves in 2008.

28. The government pays nearly 50 percent of all health care expenditures through programs such as Medicare and Medicaid and more than 50 percent of all U.S. bankruptcies are due in part to medical expenses.

6 Energy and Environmental Challenges

1. D. Loveridge, *Foresight* (New York: Routledge, 2009).

2. What happens in the end is not likely to be "either/or" in character but rather "and/or/but/and/if" in nature. What happens in the end can involve extremes such as great wealth and poverty, radical belief and disbelief, democratic governance and authoritarianism, and so on (See chapter 4). People in organizations influence the course of events. The degree to which the risks can be mitigated depends on working across organizational boundaries, but this is not easy, see M. Gerencser, R. Van Lee, F. Napolitano, and C. Kelly, *Megacommunity* (New York: Palgrave Macmillan, 2008). The lack of definitiveness should motivate and inspire people in organizations to seize the opportunities. Seizing the opportunities promises big gains, but the risks too are very large. This is because a fluid and dynamic technological scene may quickly undermine any rigid ideas that start to coalesce. To what extent, for instance, is a fuel derived from corn-like ethanol likely to remain a significant part of the solution to energy and environmental challenges? Or to what extent must it be discarded because it raises food prices and contributes to hunger among the poorest of the world's population? People in organizations have to resist the desire for premature closure, but they also must overcome fear that may immobilize them when there is so much ambiguity. Fear immobilizes, when what is needed is action. The times call for probes, trials, and experiments of what can be done.

3. Will there be a combined misery index of greater than 10 percent indefinitely into the future as the economy spirals out of control because of seemingly intractable energy and environmental problems?

4. Government officials in the United States have not been very astute in predicting what future energy prices are likely to be. In 2004, the highest price possibility under U.S. Department of Energy's (DOE) projections was *less than* $35 a barrel in 2025. The DOE projected that future oil prices would be low by historical standards. Its estimates were upbeat, hopeful, and buoyant. The DOE's 2007 projections did not change that much. The federal department could imagine oil prices only approaching $100 a barrel by *2030*, when in May of 2008, the price per barrel already had jumped to more than $140.

5. In May of 2008, the U.S. Senate defeated a climate bill that had been thought very likely to pass. This bill would have cut U.S. greenhouse-gas emissions 66 percent by 2050 and introduced a cap and trade system somewhat similar to the one in place in the rest of the world under the Kyoto Treaty, but tailored exclusively for the United States. Some industries were against this bill, but many favored it. With a Democratic majority in the Senate, the failure to pass this bill was a surprise. But Democrats from oil and manufacturing states joined the Republicans in opposing it. The reason mainly was the weak economy and high energy and food prices. Instead of this bill, Democrats in Congress were trying to find ways to lower gasoline prices and to tax oil-company profits, while Republicans favored drilling in off-limit areas such as the Arctic National Wildlife Refuge.

6. Adam Fremeth assisted in researching and writing this case. See Minn. Stat. Ann. § 216B.1691 (2006) for a view of Minnesota's renewable energy legislation.

7. Besides NSP, there were 4 other utilities and 11 cooperatives and municipal agencies that were subject to RES legislation in Minnesota. They had a similarly demanding standard of 25 percent renewables by 2025.

8. A. Nogee, J. Deyette, and S. Clemmer, "The Projected Impacts of a National Renewable Portfolio Standard," *Electricity Journal* 20, no. 4 (May, 2007): pp. 33–47.

9. David Sparby, President and CEO of NSP-Minnesota, interview by author, Minneapolis, MN, February 6, 2008. Under a May 1994 agreement, the governor of Minnesota had allowed NSP to store spent nuclear fuel in aboveground dry casks in exchange for the creation of a fund, the purpose of which was to explore the potential for greater renewable energy power in the state and to build or purchase at least 825 megawatts (MW) of wind generation.

10. There also was a mandate to introduce power generated by biomass and requirements for greater demand side management.

11. Xcel Energy Renewable Energy Plan, December 10, 2007. All of this capacity was procured by purchase power agreements with small independent power producers. In 2007, NSP also had other renewable resources including

111 MW of biomass energy capacity, 277 MW of hydro, 15 MW of landfill gas, and 100 MW of refuse derived fuel.

12. MISO is the nonprofit organization that is responsible for managing the power grid and transmission of power in 15 states in the Midwest United States and Manitoba in Canada.

13. H. Cummins, "And the wind waits…and waits…," *Star Tribune*, January 27, 2008, p. 01.C.

14. A similar approach had been adopted in Colorado and Texas.

15. In 2006, the average person in North America consumed more than 3 tons equivalent of oil per person, according to British Petroleum estimates. Within the European Union, there was variation in the amount of oil consumed per capita per year, but it was almost universally below 3 tons per capita. In most of South America, Africa, and Southern Asia, consumption was below 0.75 tons per capita.

16. Most of these advances were made in the 1970s in response to higher energy prices, but not much additional progress has taken place since then.

17. Demand was rising for each of the major ways that energy was used, for residential, commercial, industrial, transportation, and electricity uses, but the biggest gains were likely to pace in the industrial and transportation sectors, where the most energy already was being used.

18. In June of 2008, there were long lines in China's gasoline stations. People rushed to buy the subsidized Chinese gasoline that producers were reluctant to supply at relatively low allowed prices. Power shortages also were spreading as Chinese electric utilities could not get their hands on enough fuel at government subsidized low prices. More production was needed to help prevent the possibility of blackouts during the summer Olympics. To alleviate these shortages, the Chinese government increased gasoline prices 17 percent and diesel prices 18 percent, but still energy prices in China were far below the levels found in most of countries of the world, including the United States. The equivalent Chinese price for a gallon of gasoline moved up to slightly to more than $3.00 a gallon, while the equivalent U.S. price was more than $4.00 a gallon in the summer of 2008. Other Asian nations—such as India, Indonesia, and Malaysia that also subsidized energy use reduced their price supports around the same time as the Chinese. All these governments faced mounting inflation and popular opposition if they did too much to raise energy prices. Yet they needed to provide producers with sufficient incentive to bring oil to the market.

19. M. Simmons, *Twilight in the Desert* (New York: Wiley, 2006).

20. Ibid.

21. The Saudis call for the June 2008 meeting showed that they were aware of growing frustration caused by surging prices in oil-importing countries, and they were concerned that price inflation was causing consumer nations to look seriously at energy alternatives, which would hurt oil prices. While the Kingdom was reaping record profits, it was increasingly concerned that high prices would reduce world economic growth and that this would lead to

lower demand. Already in the United States and other developed countries demand was going down in response to the high prices. High prices made alternative fuels more viable and threatened the long-term prospects of a worldwide petroleum-based economy. The Saudi summit meeting made it clear that additional options available to push prices down were limited. King Abdullah called for OPEC to pledge $1 billion to help developing nations deal with the effects of the soaring energy costs. This crisis was a central issue in the American presidential race, where arguments over who was to blame for high oil prices raged. President Bush supported calls by John McCain to allow for more drilling off the coast of the United States, while Barack Obama at first opposed more offshore drilling and then supported it. He called for a crackdown on speculators and on the oil companies. Senator Joseph Lieberman was going to hold hearings over the question of the extent to which speculators were influencing prices.

22. In June of 2008, more than 100 Israeli aircraft carried out an exercise over the eastern Mediterranean Sea and Greece as a trial run for a large-scale air strike against Iran. Israeli intelligence claimed it had changed its forecast and that the Iranians had passed a nuclear threshold. The Israelis captured the attention of oil traders but what they were doing may have been psychological warfare to demonstrate that they could carry out an attack against Iran if need be. What threshold would the Iranians have to pass before Israel might attack? Would it be that the Iranians produced sufficient fissionable material to build a bomb, that they had achieved a nuclear explosion under test conditions, or they had the capability to deliver the bomb? Was it specifications that were found on a computer owned by a Swiss businessman that A. Q. Khan, the former head of Pakistan's nuclear program, who sold nuclear technology to Libya, North Korea, and Iran? He had detailed design specifications for constructing a nuclear weapon small enough to be mounted on missiles available to the North Koreans and Iranians. No matter how dire the threat to Israel, no one was certain how close Iranians experts were to understanding these blueprints or being able to implement them. Did Iran have enough trained engineers and technicians to build a bomb and delivery system?

23. The most complex part of any operation in which the Israelis would have to engage to knock out the Iranian capability would be refueling the aircraft, which probably would require U.S. cooperation since the United States controls Iraqi airspace. For the United States, it would be easier to take out the Iran's facilities on its own than to rely on Israel. There were many Arab Sunni states that might formally protest against an Israeli or U.S. attack but quietly be pleased that the Iranian Shiite bomb had been defused. Israel and the United States might be engaged in a type of psychological warfare to scare Iran. The Iranians apparently were split between opponents of Ahmadinejad and supporters, and the prospect of an imminent attack might put the president's opponents in the driver's seat.

24. Unconventional sources of oil include heavy oils that are pumped just like regular except that they are thicker, more polluting, and require additional

refining. Approximately 30 countries have heavy oil, but the highest percentage of the estimated reserves are in Venezuela, which has as much as 1.2 trillion barrels, approximately a third of which is recoverable with existing technology. Tar sands are found in rocks that must be dug out and crushed, which takes significant amounts of energy and causes pollution. Because so much processing is required, including adding hydrogen to the product, oil from tar sands is very close to being a synthetic fuel. Alberta, Canada has estimated reserves of more than 1 trillion barrels although most of this is not recoverable with existing technology. The United States has large amounts of oil shale in Colorado, Wyoming and Utah. However, it would be hard to extract and process because it demands large amounts of hot water. Big oil companies have been investing money in improving the production method.

25. See the transcript of the PBS Nova Documentary "What's Up with the Weather?" which was posted on the Web at http://www.pbs.org/wgbh/warming/etc/script.html on August 15, 2008. The last part of this chapter is heavily indebted to this excellent piece of work.

26. Only if breeder technology were used would it be an issue.

27. There could be a huge breakthrough because so much venture capital money is going into solar and other similar alternatives.

28. Ibid.

Afterword   Technology to the Rescue?

1. The material in this afterword originally was presented in somewhat different form at the Nile University Strategic Management Breakfast Seminar in the Cairo, Marriott Hotel Zamalek, Aida Ballroom, July 13, 2008.

2. J. Schumpeter, *Business Cycles* (New York: McGraw-Hill, 1939).

3. Ibid.

4. N. Kondratiev, "The Major Economic Cycles," *Voprosy Konjunktury* 1 (1925): pp. 28–79; English translation reprinted in *Lloyd's Bank Review*, 1978, no. 129.

5. I. Kirzner, *Perception, Opportunity, and Profit* (Chicago: University of Chicago Press, 1979); J. Schumpeter, *Business Cycles* (New York: McGraw-Hill, 1939).

6. R. Rothwell and W. Zegveld, *Reindustrialization and Technology* (Armonk, NY: M.E. Sharpe, 1985).

7. Based on Massoud Amin's meetings and discussions with Dr. Dennis Bushnell, Chief Scientist, NASA Langley Research Center, June 2008.

8. D. Polla Environmental Areas identified from *The Nanotechnology Opportunity Report*, CMP/Cientifica, Vol. 1, March 2002.

9. The power delivery system of the future will have these characteristics. It will be

   • Intelligent: autonomous digital system identifies surges, outages
   • Predictive rather than reactive, to prevent emergencies

- Resilient: "self-healing" and adaptive-instantaneous damage control
- Reliable: dynamic load balancing
- Flexible: accommodates new off-grid alternative energy sources
- Interactive with consumers and markets
- Optimized to make best use of resources and equipment

Integrated, merging monitoring, control, protection, maintenance, EMS, DMS, marketing, and IT "The Energy Web," *Wired Magazine*, http://www.wired.com/wired/archive/9.07/juice.html, July 2001.

10. The books of these strategy gurus include M. Porter, *Competitive Advantage* (New York: Free Press, 1985); A. Grove, *Only the Paranoid Survive* (New York: Time Warner, 1999); G. Hamel and C. Prahalad, *Competing for the Future* (Boston: HBS Press, 1994); and D. Yoffie and M. Kwak, *Judo Strategy* (Boston: HBS Press, 2001); also see A. Slywotzky and D. Morrison, *Profit Patterns* (New York: Random House, 1999).

11. A. Marcus, *Big Winners and Big Losers: The 4 Secrets of Long-Term Business Success and Failure* (Upper Saddle River, NJ: Wharton School Press, 2005).

12. Overheads of public lecture at the Humphrey Institute by G. Richardson, Professor at Rockefeller College of Public Affairs, University at Albany, SUNY. Richardson points out that J. Sterman and T. Fiddeman are eminent systems theorists whose works should be carefully studied. Some of the classic books in systems theory are L. von Bertalanffy, *General Systems Theory* (New York: Braziller, 1968) and C. Churchman, *The Systems Approach* (New York: Delacorte, 1968).

13. D. Loveridge, *Foresight* (New York: Routledge, 2009). Loveridge has attempted to integrate systems theory and foresight. His book can be read as a useful companion to this volume.

Further Reading

Abadie, A. 2006. Poverty, political freedom, and the roots of terrorism. *American Economic Review*, 96(2): 50–56.

Arendt, H. 1954. Tradition and the modern age. *Partisan Review*, 11(1): 53–76.

————. 1958. *The origins of totalitarianism*. New York: Meridian Books.

Arndt, J., Greenberg, J., Schimel, J., Pyszczynski, T., and Solomon, S. 2002. To belong or not to belong, that is the question: Terror management and identification with gender and ethnicity. *Journal of Personality and Social Psychology*, 83(1): 26–43.

Barnett, M., Starbuck, W., and Pant, P. 2003. Which dreams come true? *Industrial and Corporate Change*, 12(4): 653–672.

Berman, P. 2003. *Terror and liberalism*. New York: Norton.

Bishop, P., Hines, A., and Collins, C. 2007. The current state of scenario development. *Foresight*, 9(1): 5–25.

Bruner, J. 2004. Life as narrative. *Social Research*, 71(3): 691–710.

Campbell, A. 2002. *Risk analysis and conflict impact assessment tools for multinational corporations*. Working Paper, Country Indicators for Foreign Policy, Carleton University.

Cetron, M., and Davies, O. 2005. Trends now shaping the future. *The Futurist*, March–April: 27–42.

Choucri, N. 1984. *Multidisciplinary perspectives on population and conflict*. Syracuse, NY: Syracuse University Press.

Clayton, A., and Radcliffe, N. 1996. *Sustainability: A systems approach*. London, UK: Westview.

Cornelius, P., Van de Putte, A., and Romani, M. 2005. Three decades of scenario planning in shell. *California Management Review*, 48(1): 92–109.

Crozier, M., and Friedberg, E. 1980. *Actors and systems*. Chicago: University of Chicago Press.

Day, G., and Schoemaker, P. 2000. Avoiding the pitfalls of emerging technologies. *California Management Review*, 42(2): 8–33.

Deffeyes, K. 2001. *Hubbert's peak: The impending world oil shortage*. Princeton, NJ: Princeton University Press.

Deffeyes, K. 2005. *Beyond oil: The view from Hubbert's peak.* New York: Hill and Wang.

Dixit, A., and Pindyck, R. 1994. *Investment under uncertainty.* Princeton, NJ: Princeton University Press.

Enders, W., and Sandler, T. 2006. Distribution of transnational terrorism among countries by income class and geography after 9/11. *International Studies Quarterly,* 50(2): 367–393.

Fallows, J. 2005. Countdown to a meltdown: America's coming economic crisis. *Atlantic Monthly,* July–August: 51–65.

Feldman, S. 2002. *Memory as a moral decision.* New Brunswick, NJ: Transaction.

Fink, A., Marr, B., Siebe, A., and Kuhle, J. 2005. The future scorecard: Combining external and internal scenarios to create strategic foresight. *Management Decision,* 43(3): 360–381.

Fort, T. L., and Schipani, C. 2004. *The role of business in fostering peaceful societies.* Cambridge: Cambridge University Press.

Frey, B., and Luechinger, S. 2002. How to fight terrorism: Alternatives to deterrence. *Defence and Peace Economics,* 14(4): 237–249.

Fukuyama, F. 2006. *America at the crossroads: Democracy, power, and the neoconservative legacy.* New Haven, CT: Yale University Press.

Garvin, D., and Levesque, L. 2005. A note on scenario planning. Boston: HBS case 9-306-003.

Ghemawat, P. 2003. Semi-globalization and international business strategy. *Journal of International Business Studies,* 34: 138–152.

Godet, M. 2006. *Creating futures.* London: Economica.

Goldstone, J. 2001. Demography, environment, and security. In P. Diehl and N. Gleditsch (Eds.), *Environmental Conflict,* 84–108. Boulder, CO: Westview.

Grant, R. 2003. Strategic planning in a turbulent environment: Evidence from the oil majors. *Strategic Management Journal,* 24: 491–517.

Hart, D., Atkins, R., and Youniss, J. 2005. Knowledge, youth bulges, and rebellion. *Psychological Science,* 16(8): 661–662.

Henisz, W. 2000. The institutional environment for multinational investment. *Journal of Law, Economics, and Organization,* 16(2): 334–364.

Higgins, M., and Klitgaard, T. 2004. Reserve accumulations: Implications for capital flows and global markets. *Federal Reserve Bank of New York,* 10(10): 1–8.

Hoffman, B. 1999. *Inside terrorism.* New York: Columbia University Press.

Hudson, R. 1999. *The sociology and psychology of terrorism: Who becomes a terrorist and why?* Federal Research Division, Library of Congress, Washington, DC.

Itzkoff, S. 2004. The future of the world 2000–2050. *Mankind,* Spring–Summer: 385–401.

Jacobson, R. 2000. *Leading for a change.* Boston: Butterworth Heinemann.

Kenan, G. 1951. *American diplomacy 1900–1950.* Chicago: University of Chicago Press.

Kobrin, S. J. 1979. Political risk: A review and reconsideration. *Journal of International Business Studies,* 10(1): 67–80.

Krueger, A. 2007. *What makes a terrorist: Economics and the roots of terrorism.* Princeton, NJ: Princeton University Press.

Longman, P. 2004. *The empty cradle: How falling birthrates threaten world prosperity and what to do about it.* Cambridge, MA: Basic Books.

Lutz, W., Sanderson, W., and Scherbov, S. 2005. *The end of world population growth in the 21st century.* London, UK: Earthscan.

Marcus, A. 1992. *Controversial issues in energy policy.* Newbury Park, CA: Sage.

Mayer, A. 2002. *The furies: Violence and terror in the French and Russian Revolutions.* Princeton, NJ: Princeton University Press.

McGrath, R., Ferrier, W., and Mendelow, A. 1997. Response: Real options as engines of choice and heterogeneity. *Academy of Management Review,* 29(1): 86–101.

Merari, A. 1993. Terrorism as a strategy of insurgency. *Terrorism and Political Violence,* 5(4): 213–251.

Miller, K., and Shapira, Z. 2004. An empirical test of heuristics and biases affecting real option valuation. *Strategic Management Journal,* 25(3): 269–284.

Miller, K., and Arikan, A. 2004. Technology search investments: Evolutionary, option reasoning, and option pricing approaches. *Strategic Management Journal,* 25(5): 473–485.

Milliken, F. 1982. Three types of perceived uncertainty about the environment. *Academy of Management Review,* 2: 130–140.

Mirvis, P.2000. Transformation at shell: Commerce and citizenship. *Business and Society Review,* 105(1): 63–85.

Narvarro, P. 2005. The well-timed strategy: Managing the business cycle. *California Management Review,* 48(1): 1–21.

Obstfeld, M., and Taylor, A. M. 1998. The great depression as a watershed: International capital mobility in the long run. In M. D. Bordo, C. D. Goldin, and E. N. White (Eds.), *The defining moment: The great depression and the American economy in the twentieth century.* Chicago: University of Chicago Press, pp. 353–403.

Palmer, R. 1970. *Twelve who ruled.* Princeton, NJ: Princeton University Press.

Ross, J. 1993. Structural causes of oppositional political terrorism: Toward a causal model. *Journal of Peace Research,* 30(3): 317–329.

Sandbrook, R., and Romano, D. 2004. Globalisation, extremism, and violence in poor countries. *Third World Quarterly,* 25(6): 1007–1030.

Starr, C., and Amin, M. 2003. Global transition dynamics. Palo Alto, CA: EPRI, April: 1–10.

Taylor, T. 1979. *Munich the price of peace: The definitive account of the fateful conference of 1938.* New York: Doubleday.

Witt, M. A., and Lewin, A. Y. 2007. Outward foreign direct investment as escape response to home country institutional constraints. *Journal of International Business Studies,* 38(4): 579–594.

World Economic Forum. 2008. *Global Risks 2008*. Geneva: World Economic Forum.

Yaniv, I. 2006. The benefit of additional options. Hebrew University of Jerusalem Center for the Study of Rationality, Discussion Paper # 422.

Zaheer, S. 1995. Overcoming the liability of foreignness. *Academy of Management Journal*, 38(2): 341–363.

Index

Note: Page numbers in *italics* refer to figures and tables, respectively.

Printed and bound by CPI Group (UK) Ltd, Croydon, CR0 4YY